# LET'S TALK ABOUT YOUR WALL

# LET'S TALK ABOUT YOUR WALL

## MEXICAN WRITERS RESPOND TO THE IMMIGRATION CRISIS

Edited by

CARMEN BOULLOSA AND
ALBERTO QUINTERO

NEW YORK
LONDON

Published in the United States by The New Press, New York, 2020
Distributed by Two Rivers Distribution

ISBN 978-1-62097-618-0 (hc)
ISBN 978-1-62097-619-7 (ebook)
CIP data is available

The New Press publishes books that promote and enrich public discussion and understanding of the issues vital to our democracy and to a more equitable world. These books are made possible by the enthusiasm of our readers; the support of a committed group of donors, large and small; the collaboration of our many partners in the independent media and the not-for-profit sector; booksellers, who often hand-sell New Press books; librarians; and above all by our authors.

www.thenewpress.com

*Book design and composition by Bookbright Media*
*This book was set in Minion Pro and Univers.*

Printed in the United States of America

10 9 8 7 6 5 4 3 2 1

# Contents

# LET'S TALK ABOUT YOUR WALL

# Introduction

I was born in 1954, the year in which Operation Wetback forcibly deported a million Mexicans and Mexican Americans from the United States. Though my family lived in Mexico City—roughly 1,500 miles from our (current) northern frontier—and though my family extended far back into Mexican history, the border and "el otro lado" (the other side) have been omnipresent and complicated factors in my life.

Even before attending kindergarten, "la chivera" (a smuggler of American commodities) was a familiar presence in my grandmother's home. We treasured the objects the chivera sold us. One of these was my uncle Gustavo's portable record player. At the time, there was a ban on the import of American electronics and other products, a legal measure to protect our national industries, but the chivera had supplied us with the newest model, together with some seven-inch acetates—rock-and-roll songs, the real thing, not the diluted Spanish versions that aired on Mexican radio. At preschool, I rejoiced in other chivera merchandise: lunch boxes, pencil cases, Barbies, socks, and some candies that only existed "del otro lado."

From time to time my father traveled to the United States, for work. A chemist, he undertook advanced studies in Minneapolis, where he lived with my mother when they were newlyweds. He had mixed feelings about the Americans: deep admiration, and also deep disgust. On the one hand, he took us (his two oldest daughters, not yet in primary school) to baseball games, and back in Mexico he enrolled us both, and my other sisters, in a bilingual school run by American nuns (Ursulines). On the other hand, he despised those Mexican lawyers who fronted for American companies in Mexico, pretending to be the owners, and literally cried each time a big Mexican company was bought by the Americans. But—a third hand?—he also helped build Bimbo, a 100 percent Mexican owned industrial bread company that, using American technology, outpaced its chief American competitor, Sunbeam.

The Mexico-U.S. frontier was thus a central fact of my life, as fixed and eternal as were Heaven, Hell, and the Devil in my Catholic girlhood years. It remains so, not least because I'm married to an American, and we routinely travel back and forth between Coyoacán and Brooklyn. But in the long sweep of Mexican history the frontier has been anything but fixed.

In the fourteenth century there was no northern frontier—certainly not at the Rio Bravo (or Rio Grande, like Americans call it), as there is now. The first major frontier came with the Aztecs (or the Mexicas, as they named themselves), who were based in Tenochtitlán, site of today's Mexico City and founded in 1324. Over the next century, the Mexicas forged a coalition with various city-states, eventually numbering fifty or sixty, collectively populated by roughly seven million people, and constituting itself as an empire—an expansionist empire. The Mexicas headed south and north, extending their sway, and exacting tribute through a combination of force, negotiation, and a ceremonial dramaturgy of terror (though they didn't impose their religion or language on their domains). Their northern borderland was roughly 300 miles from the capital and peopled by rebellious subjects who refused to pay tribute or be drawn into the imperial web.

In 1521 the Mexicas were themselves conquered by Hernán Cortés and a coalition of their enemies; their imperial domains were absorbed into the Viceroyalty of New Spain. Driven by their lust for land and gold, the Spaniards took up the northward thrust. By 1541 they had reached a point 500 miles from Tenochtitlán (and 1,000 miles south of the Rio Bravo). Their 15,000-man army was met and defeated in battle by a coalition of indigenous peoples. The Spanish struck back by burning their towns, destroying their fields and orchards, hanging their leaders, and feeding their aged to the dogs; those left alive were given away as slaves.

For two centuries more, the Spaniards ground northward, repeatedly overcoming resistance, consolidating every victory by building an imperial infrastructure of presidios (fortified garrisons), and constructing a network of churches and convents to house the priests and friars dispatched to convert the now pacified peoples and towns. The farther north they went, the more ferocious were the rebels, fighting for their lives and lands. Displaced denizens of the states of Durango, Coahuila, and Chihuahua looted and burned Spanish outposts. But the frontier kept moving farther north, reaching and surpassing the Rio Bravo, until New Spain included lands that today are occupied by California, Texas, New Mexico, Arizona, Utah, Nevada, and portions of Colorado, Georgia, South Carolina, and Florida. Spain's claim to this land was, however, contested by Navajos, Apaches, and Comanches. During 1754, a force of 2,000 Comanches attacked the mission of San Sabá, in Texas. In 1775, New Mexico's governor wrote that six New Mexicans were buried for each Comanche killed. Comanches were all over Texas, Oklahoma, Kansas, Colorado, and New Mexico. Santa Fe lived under the Comanche gun.

In the seventeenth and eighteenth centuries, the Spanish empire came up against a force even more formidable than indigenous warriors, that of the rival empires of the English, French, and Dutch. A series of wars and treaties assigned and reassigned various territories. These were reflected in maps that were as much wishful thinking as they were accurate representations of what was happening on the ground. By 1774, at least on paper, New Spain stretched from Patagonia to Alaska.

In truth, the empire's hold on its territory was tenuous at best. Not only were there constant assaults from indigenous peoples, but their immense territory was subject to repeated incursions from the

British, the French, and the Russians, for instance in the far north fur trade and the great plains. And the establishment of twenty-one missions along the California coast was unable to prevent challenges to Spanish authority from within the empire's borders.

In 1821, Mexico won independence from Spain and inherited a northern frontier that ran into the upper reaches of the North American continent. Recognizing the need to populate its de jure frontier, notably Texas, the new nation launched a drive to foster migration from lower Mexico and immigration from the United States and abroad—principally by offering grants of land. Germans, Russians, and other Europeans arrived, along with settlers from the slave states of the southern United States. In 1836, the territory of Texas declared its independence from Mexico and legalized slavery, which Mexico had outlawed in 1829. In 1845, the United States annexed the Lone Star state, and declared the Rio Bravo its southern border. Mexico refused to recognize the acquisition, and claimed the Nueces River, 150 miles to the north, was the boundary. The United States sent a deliberately provocative patrol into the disputed territory, which the Mexican military repelled, and in 1846 the United States launched the "Intervención Estadounidense en México."

After fierce fighting, the Americans conquered the entire country. An *All of Mexico* movement urged total annexation, which would eliminate the northern frontier altogether. In the end, the United States rejected the notion, on the racist grounds that absorbing millions of "mongrels" would imperil America's survival as a white republic. The northern boundary, accordingly, was established as the United States wished, running along the Rio Bravo, and extending west through desert and mountains to the Pacific coast. California itself was ceded to the United States, just in time to reap the benefits of the 1848 gold rush. So were all the sparsely settled states above the new boundary line. Apart from a minor adjustment (the Gadsden Purchase of 1854), the line drawn by the 1848 Treaty of

Guadalupe Hidalgo became the border's final resting place, separating an engorged America from a truncated Mexico.

But the border was porous, as it still is to this day. Commerce flows through (or over) it. So do culture and capital. So do illegal commodities, alcohol during prohibition, marijuana, cocaine, and heroin during the war on drugs. So did people migrating from south to north, for despite a series of racist laws—the Chinese Exclusion Act of 1882, the Immigration Act of 1917 barring immigrants from the Asia-Pacific region in 1917, and the Immigration Act of 1924, which imposed quotas that largely impacted Jews and Italians—immigration of Mexicans was not restricted until 1965. The Border Patrol, also created in 1924, was not established to deter Mexicans but to block immigrants from Asia and from southern and eastern Europe.

On the contrary, Mexicans were welcomed in the 1920s as pools of cheap labor that were vital for the developing U.S. agribusiness. The construction of a north-south rail network made migrating easier and led to greater numbers crossing the border. But when the economy crashed in 1929, a massive deportation campaign got underway, and in the early '30s, raids organized at the federal, state, and local levels rounded up between 400,000 and 1,000,000 "Mexicans" (an estimated 60 percent of whom were American citizens), put them on trucks, buses, or trains, and shipped them south to the border. Justification for these measures focused on mitigating unemployment—President Hoover's administration promoted "American Jobs for Real Americans"—though modern research has found that the economic impact of the deportations was negligible.

With the advent of World War II and the Japanese attack on Pearl Harbor, immigration policy changed course again. In 1942 the Bracero Program was established ("bracero" meaning manual laborer, "one who works using his arms"). In theory, a binational agreement governed wages and working conditions, but given the labor shortage in agriculture, many U.S. employers preferred to hire outside those parameters. The program outlasted the war years, until the early '50s, when opponents of the program had it reversed. Starting in 1954, Operation Wetback—"wetback" was a derogatory term for a Mexican—swept up those with or without papers, including naturalized citizens. Race, not legal status, was the issue. Mexicans were depicted as inherently lazy, dirty, and disease-bearing "greasers." The Border Patrol adopted brutal but effective methods of "repatriation," deporting over a million the first year, and eventually 2.8 million more.

More than seven decades later, President Donald Trump is proposing another purge, another constriction and fortification of our northern frontier. We've been here before. Yes, we should give the devil his due. His peculiar blend of racism and xenophobia, opportunism and cynicism, foolishness and cunning, cruelty and hypocrisy demands attention. But we must beware the glare of the spotlight with which he focuses attention on himself, and investigate the movement behind his presidency, its historical particularity. That is the task that has been tackled in this book by a constellation of activists, anthropologists, artists, classicists, critics, diplomats, entomologists, essayists, journalists, linguists, novelists, philosophers, translators—Mexican Voices All!

*Carmen Boullosa*

# SNOW AND BORDERS

YÁSNAYA ELENA AGUILAR GIL
TRANSLATED BY ELLEN JONES

A long time ago, a dear childhood friend of mine spent many days walking across a huge desert. Not long afterward, he called me from somewhere in the United States and explained that he could now help me finish paying for the degree that I was, at the time, struggling to complete in Mexico City. I was touched by the offer and relieved to know he was alright after a journey I'd tried many times to dissuade him from taking because so many of the stories I'd heard about crossing the northern border involved death and violence. Some years later, my friend was deported. The next time I saw him was in Ayutla, a Mixe town in the Sierra Norte, in Oaxaca, and as we sat drinking mezcal he told me that he had seen snow. I myself had never seen snow—the closest I had ever got was a thin layer of white frost covering the perishing plants at dawn. As teenagers we had dreamed of seeing the world, of visiting other places and experiencing the kind of snow we'd seen in the movies, or read about in the Russian novels we borrowed. He told me about the snow, about how they survived up there in winter, and about how our people's community spirit was being recreated in U.S. cities. I think it was the first time I'd heard of that—of communities recreated as a way of dealing with the daily challenges of living in a new place. In my friend's case, he joined a small community of Mixe speakers who, when he met them, were planning, among other things, the best way of paving a track in Ayutla, Oaxaca, starting on the outskirts of town and heading all the way into the center. When he returned to Mexico, he became actively involved in the project. In a certain sense, the community had traveled with him, and his own plans were sketched out against the backdrop of the whole community's wishes.

Some years later, the Indigenous Front of Binational Organizations (IFBO)—coordinated for the first time by a woman, the Zapotecan Odilia Romero—invited me to Los Angeles to a festival of indigenous language literatures organized there every year. It was there that I saw and heard for myself about the indigenous communities from here that have recreated themselves over there, and the structures that sustain them—the way communal institutions of the Sierra Norte of Oaxaca are giving new meaning to many indigenous peoples' understanding of community living. The struggle for linguistic rights with which I am involved is being developed over there too, through forms of direct action that include the training of Los Angeles police to identify, among other things, what linguistic needs migrants might have over and above the jump between Spanish and English. Watching and listening led me to question my own ideas about the importance of territoriality in the process of identity creation, and even my ideas about what a nation is. The history and very existence of a Romani traveler population has long had me questioning the idea of territory and its relationship to the concepts of nation and indigenous communities. The Romani people's relationship with the land, established over centuries, poses a radical challenge to one idea that modern nation-states have imposed on the world: that we must establish physical borders in order to then create processes of identity homogenization within them. Being Mexican, Argentine, or from the United States means belonging in a legal sense to a certain territory delimited by artificially established borders. The Romani, with their constant wandering, clearly challenge that understanding because they are not anchored to any particular land. From what I managed to glimpse in the interesting conversations I had with members of the IFBO, being Zapotec, Mixtec, or Mixe in Los Angeles challenges the existence of borders and the very idea of these indigenous nations' territoriality. A Zapotec community continues to exist as a Zapotec community in Los Angeles because it has community representatives elected in assembly, because it organizes community festivals, because reciprocal working patterns are constantly weaving and interweaving the fabric of the community. The pillars of "communality" that the Mixe anthropologist Floriberto Díaz and the Zapotec anthropologist Jaime Luna described in the 1980s have found expression many miles from the original communities from which those Zapotec migrants departed. The battles we fight in our communities in Oaxaca are rooted entirely in our conception of territory; however, in view of this new evidence, it seems to me we urgently need to broaden our definition of territory to cover the communities that have been created north of the border.

The establishment of a world divided into nation-states, known as countries, is very recent in the history of humanity. Nevertheless, the existence of these countries as naturally given entities has been so powerful that it has taken over our imaginations and our identity narratives, and even projected itself onto our past. The official narrative of Mexico as a country is rooted in a more than two-thousand-year-old "pre-Hispanic" world in which the concept of Mexico did not exist. It's as though all of human history only happened in order to give rise to the countries currently in existence—as though every country, every nation-state, was always predestined to exist in its current form. Humanity is organized into states and chooses the representatives of those states via a democratic system that narrates itself as the ultimate endpoint of a civilizing process, although the incredibly violent way in which today's borders are managed negates that idea entirely. According to data from the United Nations, the world has been divided into approximately two hundred entities. That's two hundred flags, two hundred nationalities imposed on thousands of different peoples. Generally speaking, each one of those entities has the same model of internal organization, with an executive, a legislature, and a judiciary. Representative democracy has been established as the ideal model under which these states should be governed. This diverse world, with its many nations, peoples, cultures, and languages, is divided into just two hundred entities. All the peoples, languages, and nations that have not constituted their own state remain enclosed within those two hundred legal entities known as countries: they are stateless nations, stateless peoples, stateless languages. Behind each state, there is a homogenizing ideology that tries to have us believe that all the people who share the legal status of Mexican or of U.S.-American have cultural, linguistic, or identity traits in common. But there is no single cultural trait shared by all of us who have the random legal status of Mexican. What is more, those in power who are involved in the formation of states have denied and contested other types of organization, other identities and territories, other languages not used in state administration. The state has consistently shown itself to be founded on the idea of exclusion. The idea that Mexico's northern border divides two cultures is imprecise: the border divides two states, each of which contains multiple languages, cultures, nations, and identities. A state is not a culture; it is a legal entity that administrates territorialities by means of a violent monopoly.

The first operation necessary for the creation of the modern state was the establishment of borders: its borders are where Mexico starts, whatever *Mexico* means. A border is, first and foremost, a violent intervention into a given territory on the basis of an ad hoc legal justification. Why were borders laid down in their current configurations? Before establishing physical barriers, nation-states claimed the right to establish boundaries, and this process took a considerable amount of time, which demonstrates the artificiality of the process itself. In Mexico it was the *criollos*, the whites, who established the state; in the United States, too, it was the dominant sector of society. Those in power determined who was to be considered a citizen, which gender should have the right to vote, and what color their skin should be. In Canada, in the first half of the twentieth century, First Nations people who wanted to vote in elections had to legally renounce their right to consider themselves indigenous. These fledgling democracies were designed for the convenience of the dominant sector of society. Likewise, it was those in power who oversaw the drawing of borders; arrangements were made between states and their representatives without ever taking into account the territorial dynamics of stateless nations. This explains, for example, how the Yumanos territory was divided in two—half in Mexico, half in the United States. Mexico's southern border, which cuts across the enormous Mayan territory, is further evidence of borders' violent imposition. These state borders were not established instantaneously, but, once they were, they colonized even our imagination. To almost anyone, the shape of a country's territory looks completely natural, but that image, that figure, symbolizes the enactment of multiple violences. A country's silhouette marks a boundary on the map of the world, but what it really signifies today is the separation of families, death, human trafficking, and torture.

I have read the news about the caravans of Central American migrants who have decided to cross the Guatemala–Mexico border without papers. It pains me to hear of the thousands of comments people in Mexico have made about them, comments so similar to those that anti-immigrant white people have made about Mexican migrants in the United States. Fear becomes hatred, and that hatred is given a legal justification, when in reality it's nothing more than an administrative offense: coming into Mexico without papers is not a crime. I have read about Mexicans who say that they would happily give their vote in elections to anyone who promised to seal the southern border, and as an attempt to subvert that terrible narrative I draw the map of a state—a country—that existed briefly during the nineteenth century and that included, in addition to what we today know to be Mexico, the countries of Central America, where Nahuatl is still widely spoken today. If the huge country I have drawn were to exist now, the current southern border wouldn't exist, nor would those terrible comments about the migrant caravans. The series of historical events that determined the current silhouette of Mexico also determined what we think of as "us," an artificial "us" that could well have included people born in El Salvador or Guatemala. Historic events shaped by the dynamics of power determined what the word *us* means and why others cannot pass freely through all the territories they would like to. The same can be said of the northern border, where the voices of stateless peoples and nations did not play a part in its establishment. "They have no reason to enter a country that is not theirs" is a phrase repeated tirelessly without anyone ever really questioning how that country came to be "theirs" or why it can no longer belong to someone born in Honduras.

Even as borders are legitimately and legally established, preventing free passage through the world, the ongoing dynamics of colonialism continue to exert their power. Most people have forgotten that it wasn't long ago that we could move around the world without passports or customs checkpoints. The historical, economic, and social flows that shaped the emergence of states and state borders also gave rise to mass migration. Colonialism, capitalism, and patriarchy—the macrosystems organizing our world—are administrated by the legal entities known as countries. It is a legal entity intervening in other states, creating unsustainably violent situations that force people to flee, people who are detained at a border established via a legal framework. It is a legal entity that grants mining companies access to indigenous peoples' territories, thereby impoverishing them until they are forced to migrate elsewhere and to face another legal entity.

The current president Donald Trump's announcement that he planned to construct a wall on the southern border of the United

States is the physical evidence of these dynamics. I see it as the discursive, almost natural evolution of the ideology that created a world divided into states, because the wall, as many have pointed out, already exists in a legal, figurative, and objective sense. The physical, totalizing materialization of borders is the most extreme evidence of the violence on which nation-states were built. Donald Trump's followers find the construction of an immense, impregnable, metal or concrete wall plausible because they already find the existence of national boundaries completely natural, given that those boundaries rest at the heart of nation-states. But they are an arbitrary concept to justify the existence of U.S. nationality and passports, creating an artificial distinction between "us" and "them" that legalizes fear and consequently hatred. The promised wall is the materialization of the violence on which the idea of the modern nation-state rests.

Within state borders, the powerful people that created them have systematically ignored other legitimate claims to territory from stateless nations. Indigenous peoples' campaigns have often centered on the struggle to prevent the state from violating their lands. These peoples in the United States and Mexico have had their lands plundered by the states that contain them. However, by migrating to the United States, the indigenous peoples of Mexico challenge the legitimacy of the border the state *does* recognize. States strengthen and build walls along the borders they have legally established, but ignore the boundaries of stateless, indigenous peoples' territories. The legitimization of Zapotec territory has not prevented it from being violated by extractivism; Mexico's northern state border, however, detains and violates the Zapotec population trying to migrate to the United States. From here in the southern Oaxacan mountains, as someone who has not walked through the desert or crossed the northern border, I see that paradox on which Trump's wall—both an ideological and a physical artifact—rests: the wall constitutes the reinforcing of a border that dreams of being impenetrable while at the same time penetrating into and violating the territories of the nations separated by it. Within its borders, the state undermines indigenous peoples' territories, plundering them, annexing them to its totalizing and homogenizing project while seeking to seal the borders it forcibly created.

The very existence of indigenous peoples, and their defense of their territories, calls into question the legitimacy of state borders. In the 1980s in Australia, various aboriginal peoples created their own "aboriginal passport"; it is not recognized by the Australian state but has symbolic power, calling attention to aboriginal peoples' legitimate claim to the land. Similarly, the North American Iroquois people, also known as the Haudenosaunee, have issued their own passports since 1923 as a way of claiming a sovereignty that the state, of course, does not recognize. Having constituted itself as the main administrator of the idea of the border, the state, at one radical extreme, hopes to give it material shape in the form of a wall, a supposedly impenetrable physical entity: a border taken to its own limit.

Donald Trump's wall—a wall that in reality already exists but that is made doubly threatening by his words and actions—is perhaps the evolution of nationalism in the extreme, the physical materialization of a border that began simply as a legal declaration. The wall as a physical intervention makes material the continual violence of the systems of oppression that order the world, makes material the idea on which states were created. Undocumented migration therefore seems to me to question the very idea of the state and its control of territoriality. I think about the remittances that nourish, year after year, the shared fabric of the Oaxacan communities from which migrants in the United States originally came. Mexico's indigenous migrants completely destabilize the impregnable border of Trump's dreams, and also strengthen, through their participation in the community and the remittances they send, the processes of collective resistance to the Mexican state, such as those we have experienced in my own community.

To return to my conversation with my childhood friend, he told me about the people he had met who had lost their lives attempting to cross the border. Stories that those of us who have never undertaken such a feat cannot even begin to comprehend. After that conversation, we often heard news stories about the violence on both the northern and the southern borders of the map we call Mexico, about families separated, cages, teargas, persecution. "I'd go back and do it again if I had the strength, just to be able to show you something," my friend said to me one day when we were talking about such things. The first time he saw snow in the United States he was reminded of our shared childhood and adolescence, and so he wrote my name in the snow and took a photograph. All those years later, he handed me the photo: "I would go back just to show you that there is no border, no wall in the world that can stop our desire to see something we have only ever imagined." I am very fond of that photo, which I keep safe. I am still here, and I have still never seen snow.

# CONVERSATIONS WITH THE WALL

RENÉ DELGADO
TRANSLATED BY SAMANTHA SCHNEE

It's often said that walls have ears, and if they can hear, then maybe they can speak too. Though it hasn't yet been built, Donald Trump's wall certainly rants and bellows. His apparent eagerness to erect a so-called security fence disguises a political gambit that has successfully yielded substantial electoral benefits, and as far as he is concerned, it doesn't matter if all this noise creates a deep wound along the U.S.-Mexico border that won't be easy to heal.

When a political amateur with no vocation or experience becomes obsessed with power and political ambition, they care nothing about solving shared problems together or damaging the relations of two unequal regions that happen to share a border. On the contrary, if profits can be made from the problem, the goal is not to lessen or solve it but rather to magnify and complicate it. There's nothing strange about that. Donald Trump has proven he is a savvy businessman. In politics, he's a vote trafficker gifted in the art of extortion.

Although segments of the wall have been built by other presidents without fanfare or threats, Donald Trump's wall is, so far, nothing but sheer braggadocio. Yet it has certainly paid off. His repeated declarations that he will build a wall both separate and isolate his neighbors, while uniting and inciting his fanatics at home. The biggest beneficiary of this ruse, this mixture of social and electoral issues, is obviously the blowhard, who strengthens his leadership. Nevertheless, this wall—made of saliva and words, not bricks and mortar—creates a problem: it doesn't build a barbed-wire fence to keep immigrants away but rather destroys understanding between Mexican and U.S. citizens. It embodies the corruption of politicians who profit from the desires of some and the fears of others and consolidate their power.

Even though it doesn't exist, this wall speaks. It speaks of the deterioration of diplomacy, the perversion of politics, and something even worse: the capitalization of the misfortune of those who are forced to leave their country in search of opportunity in another. It speaks too of the exploitation of primitive sentiments held by those who view these migrants as different, as foreigners, as the root of all ills, as interlopers worthy only of hate and rejection. Furthermore, Donald Trump's immigration politics—if we can call it such—is based on a fundamental misconception that views immigration as a problem that can be solved rather than as a phenomenon that must be managed. How can we learn otherwise?

Migration has been going on for centuries. It has never ceased, and it will continue into the future. If jungles and deserts, rivers and oceans, mountains and ranges have not stopped people from fleeing unbearable circumstances, a wall is hardly going to stop them. There will be more danger, but that won't deter them. History has witnessed this time and time again.

Despite the numerous submissions to a competition to determine its architectural design, the proposed wall isn't a high, thick, strong, long wall with deep foundations. No, it's a different shape. It resembles a ballot box and a funeral urn. (In Spanish, a ballot box is called an electoral urn and an urn for cremains is called a funeral urn.) The wall is an optical illusion, a mirage; it's actually an urn.

The illusionist in the White House has turned this wall into an urn, one in which he'd like to place the ashes of immigrants and in which he hopes to collect votes of his supporters, confining both "criminal migrants" and his unwitting compatriots in one urn. All this in service of a personal desire, sheer evil: the craving for power, without a vision. That's how Donald Trump understands diplomacy and politics, and how he understands the dreams and nightmares of others. Therefore, to him, the border doesn't just draw a line; it represents a horizon: the possibility of extending his stay in the White House, albeit to occupy it without living in it.

In Trump's eyes, the wall is beautiful (as he himself has said). For him, on both sides it hides the greatest prize in politics: the veto and the vote. The wall vetoes people who wish to cross the imaginary line, and it secures the votes of those who fear the invasion of their lands. This wizard, the author of *The Art of Negotiation*, has not created a wall, he has created a myth: it's enough just to speak about the wall over and over again without building it; for some, an obstacle to clear, for others a holy monument. That's successful politics. A small investment that pays big dividends. In the end, it doesn't matter if there is a wall, or if it has a moat filled with crocodiles and snakes. It's the wizardry of creating a something with a double meaning, making the word *wall* both insult and praise. It's the ability to arrest some (*apresar*) and to captivate the attention of others (*cautivar*). And here's another pitfall of language: in Spanish, *apresar* and *cautivar* are synonyms.

Incredibly, this wall is built out of lies and saliva, a mixture resistant to logic and empathy. The wall is meant to stop an ancient phenomenon, immigration, which is looked down upon and which the American head of state views as the relocation of hordes of barbarians and criminals from south of the border, intent upon invading an America that is no longer what it was, but which he will make great again. His solution? Evict those immigrants who have only contributed to the country's decline and prevent the entrance of the stupid immigrants hastening its demise. It's that simple. The cycles of the labor market, which require waves of laborers to come and go, laborers that are part of the American economy, are completely absent from this discussion. It's so poorly thought out, so lacking in common sense, so out of touch with reality.

If reality doesn't matter to those in power, then the conflict created by the mere idea of building a wall matters even less. Confrontation and polarization in the United States diminish both civility and political institutions. They have strained relations with the Democrats, whose sensible resistance neutralizes the initiatives of the government. Hostility and blackmail characterize U.S. relations with Mexico: the deterioration of respect for the human rights of immigrants and disdain for those who fight climate change, who are concerned the wall will adversely affect wildlife all along both sides of the border. Lawsuits about the budget halt or slow administrative activity within the United States.

Yet, according to current politics, the damage caused by these conflicts is nothing compared to the advantages to be gained at election time. In terms of time and resources, for Donald Trump, insisting upon building the wall comes at no cost, and so, in the issue of immigration, he has stumbled upon a motherlode. It matters little if, in the future, as the years pass, a wall is built along the border, or is damaged, destroyed, forgotten, or if it becomes a tourist attraction representing shame and stupidity. What matters is that it's paying off today. Trump doesn't care about the past or the future.

The most painful consequence of the diplomatic breakdown between Mexico and the United States represented by the wall is the normalization of extortion as a means to manage relations between the two countries. Of course, it's the United States' right to build a wall on their land, but not to make their neighbor pay for it, and certainly not to threaten the imposition of trade tariffs for failing to bring immigration to a halt. Elevating extortion to the level of diplomacy is an appalling choice, especially since Mexico and the United States have partnered—not without differences and difficulties—and cooperated on joint initiatives to bring them closer together in recent decades. Donald Trump has trashed these efforts because at the end of the day it won't be his job to repair the damage caused by his extortionary politics.

All the walls built throughout history, at different latitudes around the world, generally share three characteristics: they impose a border and erase the horizon; they separate instead of unite; and over time their original purpose changes. As useless as they are grand, these edifices serve a variety of purposes: they aim to inspire defense against invasion; they protect and secure territory; or they conjure the threat of an ideology different from the predominant one. Ironically, sometimes all they do is help you figure out where you are.

At the heart and soul of the proposed wall along the Mexican-American border is racism, hate, and xenophobia, prejudice expressed with vulgarity, hostility, and pugnacity, the province of small minds, whose intent is to capture and maintain power without any clear goals. It's impossible to have a conversation about all this with a man who mistakes cynicism for civility, extortion for diplomacy, the use of force for politics, and an urn for a wall. It's easier to have a conversation with a wall.

# AFTER THE WHITE NOISE

YURI HERRERA
TRANSLATED BY LISA DILLMAN

One day, a little over a month before the 2016 general election, a man came and sat beside me on the Route 88 bus, one of the two I take to get to work in New Orleans. He was a white man, over forty, maybe a construction worker. I was reading a book in Spanish; I don't remember the title. As he spoke, he kept glancing at me out of the corner of his eye, as though making sure I was still there.

"Used to be, you knew how to fight for a job," he suddenly declared. "Sometimes there was one and sometimes there wasn't, but you knew it was a fair fight, and if the other guy got there before you, good for him, you'd get there first the next time—but it's not like that anymore. Now, some Honduran gets there"—and at this he gestured toward me vaguely with one hand; while in other places they call all Latin American migrants "Mexicans" no matter what country they're from, in New Orleans the equivalent is "Hondurans"—"and says for the same price, he'll bring his kid and his nephew along too. And then what? Then it doesn't matter whether you're the first one there or you're good at your job, the guy who's paying is going to hire whoever charges the least. And no matter what you say, what the boss will say is: 'You willing to take less pay? No? Then the job goes to the Honduran.'"

He paused and then said, "And that's not right. They should give the job to the people who speak English. That's our right, the right of

---

This text was first published in Spanish in *Revista de la Universidad*.

the people who speak the language of this country. The language *of this country*. But now, these guys come, they can't even understand instructions, and they're the ones who get the jobs. That's not right. It's not right."

He fell silent. I didn't say anything. He hadn't asked me anything. Then he got to wherever he was going, stood up, and got off the bus without turning back to look at me. At no point did I feel threatened, by either his tone or his body language. He hadn't come over to insult me, but—maybe because of my book or the way I look—to tell me something people like me needed to hear, something that was obvious to him. Not the fact that some people are exploited by bosses who pay a far lower that just wage, but how wrong it is that some migrants' ability to get by on a miserable, paltry wage was valued more than the rights his language conferred upon him.

The idea of the United States as a country that is and always has been exclusively anglophone is not a fantasy that was invented by workers in precarious labor conditions to express their discontent; it's an idea long embedded in the U.S. conservative public sphere. However, in the last year it has become overt—in the form of physical assaults on migrants and xenophobic public policies.

The very same day the new administration took office, the Spanish version of the official White House website disappeared. This is no minor change, particularly when the president has chosen the internet as a means of firing public servants, enacting government decisions, and altering his foreign policy. It's the horrific paradox of a functional illiterate whose language holds tremendous power. That's why it is also no coincidence that in February 2018, the Office of Citizenship and Immigration Services struck from its mission statement a line defining the United States as a "nation of immigrants." It's part of the white nationalist narrative: "This land was destined for us; in practice, it's as if we'd always been here. The foreigners are the ones who came later."

Countries confect dramatic versions of their pasts, which become crystallized into official Histories often parroted by their citizens as truth. There are multiple theories explaining how to interpret the past, but I'm referring here to simple narratives, institutionalized or popularized and repeated as tantamount to national identity, used to help make sense of the present.[1]

For instance, the history of South Africa is not only one of segregation but also one detailing the way that resistance and, once apartheid was defeated, forgiveness made reconstruction possible. Russia is an empire that collapses every so often, only to succeed in finding a way to carry on as an empire: no matter how bankrupt the country might be, it has got to be an empire. In Mexico, the official history is recounted as a series of external aggressions that have left very deep wounds that can only be healed if we all erase our differences, become *mestizos*, and accept that the current administration is not to blame for the disaster; only then, at some vague point in the future, will things improve.

The United States conveys its own history as some heroic feat in which the country, the "most extraordinary country in the history of humankind" (and any politician neglecting to employ this premise as point of departure is not only a political loser but flirting with treason), has dedicated itself to liberating other, less fortunate countries and thus sent its army time and again to conquer their people and exploit their natural resources. But lately there's been a subplot accompanying that of liberator: the United States as a country under invasion that must liberate *itself.* This invasion is being carried out not by an army but by millions of people easily identified because they speak another language—one which, as the narrative goes, didn't used to be spoken there.

A few weeks ago, the *New York Times* published a story about a man who decided, after Trump was elected, that he didn't want to hear any more news, at all. To achieve this goal, he self-imposed a series of rules: don't read the paper or watch the news; get off social media; warn friends and family not to pass along any information;

and listen to white noise on headphones when going to a café so as to avoid accidentally overhearing anything about the country's state of affairs. This man lives off of his investments, administered by a financial advisor in San Francisco, and thus doesn't need to interact with anyone to earn a living; nobody upsets the comfortable routine he's settled into in a small town in Ohio. The man is bored as a result of all this but claims that's a good thing since he's in possession of his mental health. In his world, the president of the United States has not legitimized neo-Nazis, or equated Muslims with terrorists, or mulishly insisted on building a wall that would not impede migration but would make it more dangerous, or awarded a presidential pardon to Joe Arpaio (the sheriff who made a practice of arresting people for "looking" undocumented). This man sensed what was to come and decided to create a small island, safe from Trump's vulgarity and xenophobia. He's a "liberal," after all, a "progressive." But the way he has decided to narrate the world to himself—as a dreamlike place where the only thing for him to do is enjoy the slice of nature he purchased—is a narrative that's also perfectly suited to the other one, the one that anathematizes migrants.

Because millions of people haven't had the privilege of getting bored. Those who are afraid that that ICE—the anti-immigrant police, to state it plainly—will turn up looking for them at their place of work; those afraid to speak their first language in a restaurant because they run the risk of not being served, or who work at a restaurant and when they go to pick up a check discover that in place of a tip, the customer has left a message insulting them for looking like foreigners; those who have been arrested in hospitals or at schools for lack of papers; those who must live beside self-righteous neighbors who decided to pretend they didn't hear it when Trump called millions of Mexicans rapists and criminals.

It's true that there are journalists who have denounced the persecution migrants are suffering, mayors who have decided to protect undocumented workers residing in their cities, and activists who have provided legal aid, but the mainstream, both major parties and the big news corporations, have kept a complicit silence or, at most, raised their voices a bit, like someone carrying out an irksome chore and then turning the white noise back on.

It should come as no surprise that silence and selective hearing are prerequisites for the narrative of this Latin American invasion. Institutional xenophobia is nothing new. The Obama administration deported more migrants than all previous administrations combined. There are those who claim this was no reflection of xenophobia but simply a matter of following the law. But just how efficiently certain laws are followed reveals a government's priorities. While millions of undocumented individuals were treated like criminals, detained in inhuman conditions, transferred in chains, and shackled with electronic ankle monitors by the progressive Obama administration, not one—and this bears repeating—*not one* of the top executives who decimated the world economy while Obama was campaigning was sent to jail; on the contrary, they were allowed to cash in bonuses financed with public funds. Regardless of the fact that this cartel of CEOs acted as a sort of criminal enterprise, it was the others, the impoverished invaders, who were the dangerous ones.

The hunting of migrants and building of walls have brought and will bring more dangers to undocumented workers, will galvanize sadistic police and terrorists claiming to be patriots, but won't end migration or the flow of drugs that U.S. citizens claim as an inalienable right; and without a doubt, they will not reverse the fact—obvious to anyone who decides to take off their white-noise-filled headphones—that the United States has been a Spanish-speaking country for some time now. In multiple regions it always has been, even before the country existed as such, but now it's a wider reality, more visible, more audible, and more documented.[2]

Migration is among the several factors that have made New Orleans one of the most culturally dense cities in the world. After the Spanish and French migrations and the forced migration of African slaves came the migrations of Haitians and, to a lesser degree, Irish, Germans, and Hondurans. Although the flow of workers from Mexico has increased since Hurricane Katrina, Hondurans are the Latin American community that remains the most organized and influential in the region. There are Honduran restaurants, Honduran women lawyers, Honduran activists, Honduran drivers, Honduran businesses, and several free newspapers covering Honduran activities. Radio Tropical Caliente 105.7 provides news about Honduran politics and transmits live broadcasts of Honduran league soccer games (in March 2018, Real España, the Honduran champions, came to New Orleans to play a local team). And yet this is not a hermetic community that closes itself off by national origin. The Congress of Day Laborers, for instance, is an organization that offers information to people from all over Latin America, provides legal counsel, and organizes fundraisers for the families of detained migrants regardless of country of origin. Because what matters is not the birth certificate but the shared experience.

When I first moved to New Orleans, it struck me that in a city with such a distinct global identity—a black city, the birthplace of jazz, the Katrina catastrophe—there was no space for more ingredients in the mix, and that the Spanish- and English-speaking populations lived in parallel worlds, without touching. It reminded me of *The City & the City*, the China Miéville novel in which two peoples occupy the same space, each with their own rules and customs, and the only law they share is the one banning their respective citizens from noting the presence of the other. But here, each community does take note of the other, albeit in sometimes intermittent fashion (Real España beat the New Orleans team 2–0, and the English-language press failed to register the fact, but the local team included U.S. players who play weekly on Honduran teams).

All anyone has to do is listen in order to see how the auditory landscape—the *soundscape*, to use the beautiful English word—has changed. The music you hear walking down the street, as well as the conversations about parties, the heat, and the violence, is happening in Spanish too. The Congress of Day Laborers, incidentally, came out in support of both Black Lives Matter and the young people who managed to take down statues of Confederate generals across the city; and they, in turn, have participated in Congress marches.

The Spanish-speaking population is not a third country, as some have claimed out of ignorance or naivete. What the migrant experience demonstrates is in fact just the opposite, that certain nomenclatures have grown outdated. Even a case like that of El Salvador, whose diaspora is known as Department 15 (the country itself is divided into fourteen departments), underscores the limitations, rather than the expansion, of the nation-state. The transformations taking place are occurring in our imaginary before they are in institutions.

I doubt that Spanish-speaking communities will crystalize into a single official narrative; instead, they are generating multiple narratives that reflect the diversity of solutions that migrants have created, regardless of the nation-state they come from or arrive in. Unlike national narratives, which register who was conquered or needs to be conquered—missions that then memorialize a place—I think migrant narratives speak of how to leave one place, how to traverse another, how to survive; their most notable ideas are not conquest or homogeneity but work ethic, solidarity, reservations about institutions.

It's not a case of *translating* a hegemonic narrative; rather, it's a new *imagining* of the same space: a knowledge that has no single shape or single referent because it hasn't crystalized into some nationalist cliché. The United States is a country being conceived, organized, suffered, enjoyed by speakers who see it less as a place to be occupied than as one to be traversed, even when the journey is eternal.

I don't want to indulge in gratuitous optimism with my description of migrant communities' survival skills or the enduring strength of their languages in the face of nativist onslaughts. (The history of native peoples in the State of Mexico is the history of entire generations made to endure the contempt, racism, and ignorance of their own compatriots. Any mirror held up reflects a horrific image when it comes to assessing how we've dealt with our own linguistic plurality.) Yet there is something in the desperation and ineptitude of those who cling to the narrative of the United States as a monolingual nation that makes me think that even they have realized that there's no way back from this new world imagined in other sounds with other ideas, and that, regardless of what official history books say today, sooner or later, they'll stop speaking of barbarian invasions.

# PLEASE DON'T FEED THE GRINGOS

CLAUDIO LOMNITZ
TRANSLATED BY JESSIE MENDEZ SAYER

A few years ago, when I was in Tijuana for a conference, some colleagues from El Colegio de la Frontera Norte took us to see some of the city's places of interest, including a couple of sectors of the famous border wall. I should mention before continuing that I had always felt a certain admiration for Tijuana's air of bravura. I was surprised to pick up on a sense of freedom (or at least of existentialism) in the midst of that funnel-city, which leans against the border wall with roguish self-assurance, cigarette in hand. Even the famous wall brought to mind images that were somewhat unexpected.

The border wall in this area is actually a double barricade with a road running between them, where towers with migrant-detecting sensors loom, and along which the U.S. Border Patrol SUVs make their rounds. The barricade we could refer to as "interior" (meaning the one entirely within the United States, which does not directly skirt Mexico, but was instead designed as a second obstacle for anyone who has dared to cross the first wall) is tall, made of wire mesh, topped with barbed wire, and is absolutely impassable. The "exterior" wall, that is to say the one that actually does border with Mexico and can be touched by any passing pedestrian, varies in appearance and materials depending on the stretch in question.

The "exterior" barrier of the section that runs along the beach

---

This text was first published in Spanish in three different articles. "Please don't feed the gringos" and "Genealogía del 'Bad Hombre'" appeared in *La Jornada* in 2013 and 2017, respectively; "La importancia del muro" was published in *Nexos* in 2017.

and into the sea is made of iron piling, the spaces between the piles big enough to allow an unimpeded view from one side of the border to the other. Its architectural design is much less violent than that of the solid wall, which not only blocks the vision and passage of undocumented people but also those of squirrels, rabbits, and lizards, all of which exist in less touristic areas.

The wall on Tijuana's beach is covered in all kinds of graffiti: Christian, anti-imperialist, philosophical, romantic, et cetera. Much of this graffiti is in English, and was written by U.S. citizens who live in Mexico or who perhaps pass through Tijuana and feel outrage about their own country's policies. The phrase in graffiti which I liked the most says: "Please don't feed the gringos." The image, a wonderful one, inverts the meaning of the wall. It is U.S. citizens, and not the supposed southern barbarians, who are the caged animals under observation, like those in a zoo. But it struck me that this graffiti went further than simply pointing out how U.S. immigration policy lacks humanity. Given its location, on a border wall with a view through it to the pristine fields on the U.S. side (and the port of San Diego in the distance), the graffiti made me think of Americans (and those who, like me, live in the United States) as domesticated animals.

This is Friedrich Nietzsche's own image of modern man as a pet, properly fed, properly groomed, properly neutered, and properly broken. "Don't feed the gringos," they already have food; it's in a plastic bowl in the kitchen. Order in the United States and disorder in Tijuana are presented here like the boundary between the domesticated human and the (somewhat) wild one.

This same image struck me once again a few kilometers ahead, at the part of the wall that flanks the Libertad neighborhood. Before they built the border walls (in the eighties), this was a place where dozens of migrants would cross every night. As it turned out, our driver and guide had crossed there twice, around twenty-five years ago, and he told us about his experiences with the pleasure of someone recounting an adventure: he had no regrets.

In those days, market stalls were set up every afternoon all the way along the Mexican side, so that those making the crossing could buy some juice or a couple of quesadillas while they negotiated with the smugglers, who ambled around the area like street vendors.

"I have fifty pesos (dollars), will you get me across?"

"O.K."

Back then, the smugglers would send some "bait" ahead of them, a small group of local guys (drug addicts or alcoholics, for example) so that the border police would jump on them. The border force at the time was made up of only two or three patrols for all those people. And as soon as they went for the bait, a group of ten or fifteen migrants would head across with their smuggler, running toward the gullies to hide amongst the hills behind San Diego.

Our guide told us all of this with evident joy, and it was then that another image came to me: the border as an episode of *Tom and Jerry*. And I realized that this image had a connection to "Please don't feed the gringos": in this case, the U.S. citizen is revealed to be a domestic animal (Tom the cat), and the Mexican as a smaller animal, but one that remains in a state of freedom, who does not answer to any master. It occurred to me that the origin of the wall lies in Tom's damaged pride in the face of Jerry's cunning and the invisible repression of his master's law. The poor little frustrated cat went to buy a double barricade from the ACME corporation, the whole package including towers with motion sensors, so that the mice would stop making a fool out of him. Mission impossible.

## The Origin of the "Bad Hombre"

At this stage, we all know that in an English accent "bad hombres" is pronounced "bad jambris," but what exactly does it mean? Does it matter that the president of the United States uses it instead of saying, for example, "bad men," all in English? What are the uses of anglicized Spanish, and what clues can they offer us about the representation of the Mexican in Trump's era?

Before answering these questions, it is worth noting that the use of Spanish terms with anglicized pronunciation is now a common part of the English language, and that they are used by characters as cherished as Bart Simpson ("Ay, Caramba!," pronounced with the English "r"). I also fondly remember a conversation between Elaine and Seinfeld while eating ice cream, when Elaine says (in anglicized Spanish) "Qué rico!," and Seinfeld knowingly replies "Suave!" And of course, there is also Arnold Schwarzenegger's immortal phrase, "Hasta la vista, baby!," which nobody in their right mind would want to remove from the English language.

We therefore must proceed with caution, in order to avoid a "politically correct" critique that measures everything by the same yardstick. Twenty years ago, the linguist Jane Hill published a series of studies about the so-called mock Spanish, which Hill defines as a "jocular register of English" that uses elements that English speakers consider to be Spanish in order to create a light-hearted or humorous effect. Based on a detailed study, Hill concludes that mock Spanish "reproduces racist stereotypes of Spanish speakers," although, she adds, English speakers usually deny that its use has any racist undertones.[1]

I do not wish to argue with Hill about how racist any particular colloquial turn of phrase may or may not be; mock Spanish is used far too frequently and in many forms. Having seen several seasons of the show, I am certain that the writers of *The Simpsons*, for example, feel a certain affinity toward Mexicans. In fact, "reinforcing racial stereotypes" doesn't necessarily imply any antipathy for the group of humans in question; you can reinforce a racial stereotype in order to transcend it, or its use can be ambiguous. To offer up a Mexican example, the song "Negrito sandía," or "Black Boy Watermelon," by

Cri Cri, undoubtedly reinforces racial stereotypes (it's about "a black boy with an angel face" who "turned out to be more foul-mouthed than a parrot from the slums"). Furthermore, the association of the black person with a watermelon is a classic element of white racism toward black people: in the United States, watermelon was a luxury for freed slaves, and so the image of a watermelon came to be used with racist malice, like a sign of the supposedly insurmountable distance between blacks and whites (the champions of racial segregation chose different symbols of luxury for themselves, unattainable for black people). In other words, Cri Cri's song reproduces racist stereotypes. There is no doubt about it. However, this does not necessarily mean that when Francisco Gabilondo Soler (Cri Cri) composed the song in the early forties, he did so to propagate black people's social inferiority, nor that he did so as a gesture of hate. This idea would come later.

In the same way, the "ay, caramba!," the "hasta la vista!," and the "suave!" uttered by Bart, the Terminator, or Seinfeld could propagate racial stereotypes and yet also signal affinity toward or solidarity with Mexicans or Hispanics. This idea would also come later. In any case, regardless of whether racism comes into play, it is important to understand that when we consider the use of mock Spanish, we draw near to the racial border that divides the Mexican and the Anglo. It could be said that whoever utters the phrase is playing with this border, sometimes crossing it in a friendly manner, and other times reinforcing it.

Right. So now we can move on to the topic of the "bad hombre." What does this expression mean? Does it have similar historical baggage, so to speak, as the watermelon in the history of racism against black people? Should Mexicans let slide the fact that the U.S. president refers to the Mexican criminal component using this term, and not be offended? The expression "bad hombre" was common in western movies during Hollywood's early decades. There is even a movie called *Hombre*, starring Paul Newman (1967), where the "bad hombre" (Newman) is a white man who has been raised by Apaches, and who goes on to confront discrimination in the white world. In old westerns, the figure of the "bad hombre" is actually part of the landscape, part of the fauna of the West. Usually the "bad hombre" hides behind rocks or thickets, getting up to no good, and must be exterminated by sheriffs and colonials. The "bad hombre" prowls. He is never a farmer, and certainly never a landowner. In the oldest westerns, the sheriffs also referred to the "bad hombres" using the term *varmint*, alluding to the wild animals that sometimes ate a part of the harvest, or ate chickens. A "bad hombre" is, therefore, like a coyote lying in wait, and must be kept outside of the perimeter of civilization.

The image of the Mexican migrant as a category infiltrated and irreparably contaminated by "bad hombres" who are on the prowl and must be eliminated is therefore loaded with all the brutality of the colonization of the American West. It is the violence of the colony against the former inhabitant, rootless and dispossessed and transformed into a livestock thief. Does Trump's use of this expression reinforce Mexican racial stereotypes? Yes, without a doubt. Is it also an expression of racial antagonism? Again, yes.

## The Importance of the Wall

Let's build that wall! This was Donald Trump's most popular campaign slogan, but what does it mean? Would it make a difference if the United States were to invest in a building project of this kind?

A consensus is beginning to form in Mexico, at least on an informal level, that the wall project is in a way irrelevant. Chihuahua Cement, a Mexican company, has even put itself forward as a provider. You want a wall? We'll build it for you! There are even people who think that building it would benefit Mexico. Are they right?

After all, it is true that a wall already exists. The wall is not new. The United States has been investing in reinforcing its border with

Mexico since 1994, and today around 1,000 kilometers (621 miles) of the border is fenced or walled. This cost around $7 billion, as well as what it costs to maintain it. Extrapolating from this figure, building a wall along the roughly 2,300 remaining kilometers (1,429 miles) would cost around $15 billion, more or less, plus maintenance, without taking into account the cost of lawsuits for violating environmental agreements, or the purchase of land in cases of owners who are reluctant for anything to be built on their property, or the compensation that would have to be paid to the ethnic group Tohono O'odham Nation, whose territory sits on both sides of the international border.

In addition, the United States has invested heavily in increasing police patrols along the border. In 1994, "la migra" (Border Patrol) had 4,100 agents, and by 2015 it had almost reached 21,100. So, has the combination of a fivefold increase in the Border Patrol force and the thousand kilometers of existing wall failed to seal the border? Let's see.

In 2015 the number of migrants caught at the border was just over 337,000 (230,000 were Mexicans), a figure close to 1970s levels, and far fewer than the 1.6 million border arrests made toward the end of the nineties. Besides, for reasons that are demographic as much as labor-related, the flow of Mexican migrants to the United States has been in negative figures since 2009, and has been close to zero since 2005. Lastly, there is the fact that the majority of the undocumented migrants who enter the United States do not do so by crossing the border with Mexico, but via airports and with tourist visas. In 2015, Border Patrol captured, as already mentioned, 337,000 migrants who crossed the border without papers, but they caught 527,000 undocumented migrants who had entered legally with tourist visas.

For all these reasons, there are those in Mexico who argue that if the United States builds a border wall it will not affect Mexico all that much. The great Mexican migration to the United States is basically over, and so this wall would only serve as a political concession to Trump's support base, who would like to see migration used as a scapegoat. The wall would therefore be a colossal ritual of expense, carried out in order to allay fears that in fact have other causes, such as automation, for example. There are even those who speculate that a wall like this one would somehow benefit Mexico (beyond Chihuahua Cement): the wall and the current Border Patrol forces migrants to cross via difficult and dangerous routes, which has allowed Los Zetas and other criminal groups of this kind to control the flow of migrants. According to official figures, over 6,500 migrants have died crossing the border into the United States since 1998. There are also many thousands of Central Americans who have died while crossing Mexico's southern border; some estimate dozens of thousands. Furthermore, according to the CNDH (National Commission for Human Rights), in 2012 around 11,000 Central American migrants were kidnapped and suffered extortion by Mexican traffickers. Perhaps a completely sealed northern border would reduce the number of people using Mexico as a point of transit, and therefore reduce some of these figures. These are some of the speculative ideas circulating these days (always look on the bright side).

There is no question that adding another 2,000 kilometers to the wall that already exists between Mexico and the United States would be a bad use of public funds. Dr. Everard Meade, director of the University of San Diego's Trans-Border Institute, has asserted that the resources invested in the wall would have a far more positive effect on the United States' economy if they invested it instead in improving the quality of the roads and entry points along the border with Mexico, which currently resemble chicken coops. This would also have an important political and symbolic effect. He is right.

To spend another $15 billion on a wall, and billions more on its maintenance, would be to invest heavily in the United States' cultural and political isolation, and would also be a considerable investment in the portrayal of Mexico as a barbaric land, along with all the consequences that could follow. Just like the great ice wall on the television series *Game of Thrones*, this would serve to harden the relationship between the supposed civilization and the supposed barbarians.

In an equation such as this, the risk to the United States would not be insignificant. Just remember the border wall in Tijuana: "Please don't feed the gringos."

# ASYLUM UNDER SIEGE: WHY DOES IMMIGRATION LAW FAIL TO PROTECT WOMEN AND CHILDREN FROM STATE-SANCTIONED VIOLENCE?

VALERIA LUISELLI AND ANA PUENTE FLORES

The women asked:

"What time is it?"

"Are we still in August?"

Others said:

"I've lost track of time since my son and I got locked up in here."

"I was separated from my children on June 9. I don't know how many days have passed."

As in any incarceration space, time moves at a strange pace in the South Texas Family Residential Center in Dilley, the largest immigrant family detention center in the United States. Dilley is run by Immigration and Customs Enforcement (ICE) and CoreCivic, the private prison corporation contracted by the federal government to manage nearly 63 percent of the immigrant jails in the United States. It's one of 120 active immigration detention spaces in the country's rapidly expanding—and extremely profitable—prison–industrial complex.

While these testimonies from women and children at Dilley were recorded in 2018, the fear they express is current. Conditions for families in detention are the worst they have ever been.

---

This text was first published in *The Believer* #127, October 1, 2019.

Twenty-four people have died in ICE custody since 2017, including six children. Migrants are often held in rooms with freezing temperatures and are denied medical treatment. In an El Paso detention center, a midwife wishing to serve pregnant women was barred from entering; the facility cited "security concerns." Such cases are the rule.

The United States has constructed the largest immigration detention infrastructure in the world. On average, forty-two thousand people were detained each day in 2018—the highest rate on record since ICE began tracking the data in 2001. Also in 2018, U.S. Customs and Border Protection made approximately 396,600 apprehensions, a 124 percent increase from the year prior. It's no surprise, then, that cells are overflowing. The most overcrowded facilities are at the border. They feature cages, which migrants call *perreras* (dog pounds). Photographs have shown migrants sleeping on concrete floors, and children going unfed and unwashed.

It is clear that ICE facilities do not provide adequate resources to migrants. But the more important problem, the one we must turn our attention to first, is why detention is a condition imposed on migrants in order for them to begin the process of claiming asylum. While their particular circumstances and stories vary, the women and children held in the Dilley facility have one thing in common: they are fleeing circumstances of grave violence in their home countries, have come to the United States to seek legal protection, and are detained in a federal prison complex while they hope to be granted due process. Dilley holds 2,400 women and children, most from the countries of the Northern Triangle (Honduras, El Salvador, and Guatemala). Despite laws requiring that a detention center that incarcerates children "shall not be equipped internally with major restraining construction or procedures typically associated with correctional facilities," the Dilley detention center is a jail—and is in fact known colloquially as "baby jail." No physical contact between detainees and volunteers is allowed beyond a handshake, and although detainees question the quality of the water, volunteers are not allowed to offer them bottled water.

The majority of the women whose voices appear here arrived in the United States in the early summer of 2018, after the Trump administration enacted its "zero tolerance" policy and family separations began. In the summer of 2018, news of the family separations traveled around the world, haunting the minds of millions with leaked sound footage and brutal images of children being torn away from their parents and put inside cages. After a generalized public outcry, as well as a seventeen-state lawsuit against the government, President Trump put an end to family separations—though some families have yet to be reunited, and many more are still being separated through ICE raids.

The photos and stories in the media are shocking. The public must protest such injustices. But to understand how immigration rights for women and children are being systematically eroded, our attention must shift from accounts of individual victimization and violence to the legal and systemic threats to women's freedom. Over the past two years, the Trump administration has made policy changes as well as amendments to immigration law. Most are made so swiftly and are so technical that the general public is unlikely to keep up.

The futures of the mothers and children detained in Dilley and other detention spaces across the country remain uncertain. The asylum they seek depends on this administration's less visible, more constant, and equally bewildering bureaucratic violence—one enacted on paper, through policy memorandums and amendments to immigration law. While the Trump administration wages loud "shock-doctrine" attacks against minority groups, such as the assault on immigrant caravans, its bureaucratic assault is more silent, more surreptitious, and may even be more toxic.

---

In the visitation trailer at the Dilley detention center, volunteers interview women to help them prepare for their "credible fear" interview with asylum officers. This is the first formal step toward being granted legal protection in the United States. The volunteers have to be cleared by ICE and approved by the Dilley Pro Bono Project (DPBP), part of the Immigration Justice Campaign. A long line forms in front of the registration sheet, where each volunteer and DPBP staff member receives a CoreCivic badge with an ID number. As volunteer attorneys, legal interns, and staff shuffle through the visitation trailer every morning, detainee women and their kids are lined up outside. The CoreCivic guards—sometimes patient, other times cruel—remind them to stand in line and keep quiet. Children who speak indigenous languages, even if they wear badges that say "I speak Mixteco" or "I speak Q'eqchi," are given instructions in English or sometimes Spanish, and are often scolded when they do not understand.

The right to seek and be granted asylum in a foreign territory is articulated in *The Universal Declaration of Human Rights*, signed in 1948, in the aftermath of World War II, by forty-eight member states of the United Nations. The 1951 UN Refugee Convention, ratified by 145 nations, defined *refugee* as "an individual who is outside his or her country of nationality or habitual residence who is unable or unwilling to return due to a well-founded fear of persecution based on his or her race, religion, nationality, political opinion, or membership in a particular social group." The convention also encoded basic rights that a refugee should be afforded, though the specifics of asylum proceedings were left for each country to determine.

In the United States, any person seeking refugee status is usually first screened by an asylum officer, who will conduct the credible fear interview. If the officer determines that the person is eligible, the next step is to sign release papers with ICE. If the asylum officer decides that the asylum seeker's fear is not credible, they will receive an immediate deportation order. The denial rate for asylum has been growing as applications increase. According to reports out of Syracuse University, just 15 percent of asylum applicants pass the initial credible fear review. Of this group, only 35 percent are awarded asylum. A "not credible" decision can be appealed in immigration court, but only with the help of an attorney.

This is where pro bono organizations step in. They prepare asylum seekers for their credible fear interviews and find volunteer attorneys and legal interns who can serve as legal representatives. Since asylum grants are based on fear of persecution on account of "race, religion, nationality, political opinion, or membership in a particular social group," the objective of the preparations is to link a woman's persecution to her belonging to a particular social group.

After initial biographical questions, legal volunteers ask women about their fear of persecution.

To the question "Have you ever been threatened or hurt by anyone in your home country?," women almost invariably reply: "Yes."

The questions proceed.

"Who threatened you?"

"MS-13 gang members. Barrio 18 gang members. The police. My husband. My partner. My boyfriend. My children's father."

"What did he do?" or "What did they do?"

"They beat me. He raped me. He said they were going to kill me."

"Why did they target you specifically?"

"Because I resisted his advances. Because I didn't want to hide the guns. Because I didn't vote for the party they told me to vote for. Because I look this way."

When a seventeen-year-old girl and her mother, both from El Salvador, arrived at the preparation interview in the visitation trailer, the girl asked for water. As she sipped from a paper cup, she said: "I just want you to know that I didn't want to come here. I had a good life, and I was about to graduate from high school, but now I missed my chance of getting my diploma."

Her gaze was steady, intelligent, and her voice soft but firm.

"Why did you leave your country?"

"Because members of the MS-13 gang threatened to kill me."

"Did they hurt you?

"No, they never hurt me. They only threatened me."

"Why did they threaten you?"

After a silence, she explained that she was threatened because one of the gang members wanted to date her and she refused, and because they wanted her to sell drugs for them, and she had also refused. In a way, her problems were not too dissimilar from those of many other seventeen-year-olds—drugs, dates—except in her case the consequences were life-threatening. The MS-13 said they would also kill her mother if she did not comply with their demands, and everyone knows that the MS-13 carry out their threats without thinking twice. They told her mother: "We will throw your daughter's body in a black plastic bag in the palm tree next to your house."

The particular details and circumstances vary, but the stories women tell at the Dilley visitation trailer all touch on abuse and violence perpetrated against them by the men in their communities, in their homes, as well as in the public institutions in their countries. As the journalists Óscar Martínez and Juan José Martínez explain in their book, *El Niño de Hollywood*, women are seen by the MS-13 gang not only as expendable and disposable, but also as a nuisance to a member's commitment to the *pandilla* or *clica* (gang). Women are "an obstacle to achieving gang-purity" that "stands in the way between the *pandillero* and his full commitment to the *clica*." The only form of participation that women have in MS-13 is as *jainas* (girlfriends or wives of gang members). Women who have MS-13 family members—a brother, uncle, or cousin—run the risk of being targeted by opposing gangs because of this affiliation. Gang rape, death threats, and prolonged psychological and physical abuse are everyday occurrences that women recount during their preparation interviews.

Volunteer attorneys and legal assistants have to gather as many details as possible in order to understand how these abuses may qualify the women for asylum.

"How many men were there?"

"Did they have weapons?"

"How close were they to your body?"

"How do you know they are capable of killing you and getting away with it?"

"Have there been other women who were killed because of this?"

"Do you fear they will carry out their threat if you return to your country?"

"Did they also threaten to kill your children?"

"Did they say this to you explicitly?"

"How do the authorities react to these crimes?"

"Did you report this to the police?"

"Why not?"

In an overwhelming majority of cases, when asked this last question, women reveal either that they did not report the crime to the police as a result of fear of further consequences, or that they did report it but the police simply did not intervene. One woman explained: "We didn't go to the police, because we knew they would tell the gang. They work together to keep us under their eye. Even if you know a woman is locked up in her house, and she yells when she gets beaten, you can't go to the police."

If so many women are being threatened, raped, abused, and sometimes killed by gang members, and if some of these women are gang members' own relatives, and if authorities in their countries are not doing anything about it, why is it so difficult for them to get asylum? Why does asylum law not protect them?

The answer is complicated, but it comes down to one fact: asylum parameters in the United States have typically prevented gender alone from being a qualifier for a "particular social group." Gender-based violence, whether domestic or gang related, is not considered linked to state violence. Over the years, attorneys advocating for detainees have found ways to argue why women in certain circumstances—for example, those afraid of persecution who live in a country where the government fails to protect their fundamental human rights—may indeed qualify as belonging to a particular social group. Examples of such litigation include the *Matter of A-B-* and *Matter of A-R-C-G-*. (These are cases that set a legal precedent for the viability of domestic violence claims by asylum seekers; "A-B-" and "A-R-C-G-" are the initials of the women in these cases.) It is through "matters" like these that legal advocates have recently been able to argue that women who are seen as property, who are abused, and who are unable to leave their marriages qualify as belonging to a particular social group and are therefore eligible for asylum.

This legal activism has helped, some. But the progress halted sharply in July 2018, with a memorandum issued by the attorney general at the time, Jeff Sessions. The policy explicitly excluded women fleeing domestic violence and gang violence from asylum eligibility, in a direct attack on the thousands of Central American women and children seeking asylum precisely on the grounds of an intersection (or a collision, rather) of these conditions, from countries where the government cannot and will not hold persecutors accountable, or where state actors are complicit in or even direct perpetrators of such violence. Currently, the *Matter of A-B-* is in legal limbo. This means that it's possible to build an asylum case based solely on domestic or gang violence, but the case is not certain to succeed.

It is now not sufficient to argue that a woman cannot return to her country of origin because of domestic violence. The argument must also prove that she faces another, unrelated threat, such as racial discrimination, or threats to her life because of her political affiliation.

At Dilley, there were times when a woman's story did not meet the asylum requirements, but her interview was only hours away.

Volunteers prepared these women as best as they could, scanning ruthlessly, in a matter of minutes, through the details of their lives to find something that fit the legal definition of a person deserving of protection. In those minutes, it became clear that the entire system was rigged against them. The asylum-seeking mother is a woman who flees her country with her children because, from the moment she was born, society has punished her for being a woman, for being poor, for being indigenous or *mestiza*, for being a single mother, for being a victim of sexual violence, for being politically active, for being a business owner. She has been born into a society and under a government that do not seek to protect her well-being; she has been abused constantly, and she runs the daily risk of being killed. Otherwise, she would not have fled. The larger, underlying problem is that societies and governments fail to recognize domestic violence as a symptom of wider and deeper societal and political violence against women. Women living in poverty and violence, in post-conflict contexts marked by an entrenched patriarchal system, are seen as expendable both to the state and to society. There's a word for these states: femicidal. The only option for women there, if they want to live, is to flee.

Most women detained in Dilley had not suspected that on the other side of the border, in the United States, they would find more violence, more threats, and indefinite imprisonment.

During a preparation interview, one woman recounted her experience before arriving at Dilley: "We crossed through the river. They had clothes for us to change into, but they purposefully left us wet and freezing in the *hielera* [icebox]. Even the children. They all got eye infections, colds, and diarrhea."

And another: "Everything you see in the news is true, because I am living it. When the volunteers came to the *perrera* [cages], they had signs that said 'We love you! Welcome to America!' They were all crying. All the mothers and children in the bus started crying too. Not out of joy, but because the volunteers and the protesters seemed very worried, and that scared us."

Asylum law is currently under siege in the United States. And whatever might be the racial, cultural, or ideological motivations for barring asylum seekers from due process, the results of this administration's policies are clear: an increase in the federal budget assigned to Homeland Security (and specifically to ICE), an increase in border security, an increase in the daily quota of detainees, and, possibly more important, an increase in the construction of new immigration detention spaces. The detainment of undocumented bodies is simply one of the most lucrative industries involved in the business of governing the United States.

The circumstances that lead to the displacement of families from their countries, the framing of immigration as a national-security issue instead of a human-rights problem, the criminalization of asylum seekers and immigrants, and the profit earned from incarcerating them merge into the perfect scenario for mass immigration detention. It has become clear how far the current administration is willing to go—by terrorizing, separating, incarcerating, deporting, tearing apart children and parents, and, ultimately, breaking the psyches of as many asylum-seeking immigrants as possible—to widen and strengthen an already alarmingly robust prison–industrial complex.

After twenty-two days in the detention center, one young woman said: "I won't keep begging, because it becomes more and more humiliating."

Another woman said: "I feel caged here. Wherever you look there is someone watching you. But this is paradise compared to the *perrera*. There, we had to sleep on *colchones* [mattresses] smeared with poop and pee and vomit. They didn't let us brush our teeth."

Another woman said: "I told them at the *perrera* I would sign my deportation. I am not a criminal to be treated this way. I have never felt so resentful. I cry when I am asleep."

Another: "It's been three months since I've been here. If I don't get a pass out of here in a week, I'm going to ask for my deportation."

And another: "Some of us get together and tell stories and laugh. When we laugh it is not joy we feel. We are just trying to survive. We daydream of escaping this place through the toilet."

When asked if she regretted coming to the United States, a young woman answered: "Now I regret it, a thousand times. I think I'd rather die of one gunshot in my own country than let them kill me slowly in this one."

# LANGUAGE SOLIDARITY: HOW TO CREATE A FORCE FIELD WITH WORDS

JHONNI CARR AND ROMÁN LUJÁN

*Life is political, not because the world cares about how you feel, but because the world reacts to what you do.*

—*Timothy Snyder*[1]

## The Situation of Spanish Speakers in the United States

We've all seen it. Horrifying, gut-wrenching attacks that make us burn simultaneously with rage and disgust. A Latina mother berated for speaking Spanish in a Los Angeles restaurant. Two U.S. citizens detained by a border agent, solely for speaking Spanish in Montana. A teenage Venezuelan refugee beaten by a peer on a school bus after speaking Spanish with a friend. A Mexican consulate employee assaulted on a bus in San Diego for speaking Spanish over the phone with his mother. A ninety-one-year-old Mexican man brutally attacked with a brick by a woman while he cried out in Spanish, "Why are you hitting me?" A lawyer in New York threatening to call ICE because people were speaking Spanish in their place of work. Over and over again we hear about violent verbal attacks, threats of deportation, assaults, and even assassination for speaking Spanish while brown.

Ever since Donald Trump launched his presidential campaign on June 16, 2015, there has been a noticeable increase in the number of hate crimes directed at Latinx individuals. Just last year, 485 hate crimes were committed against Latinx people, according to the FBI.[2] Trump famously started his presidential bid by targeting Mexican immigrants: "They're bringing drugs. They're bringing crime. They're rapists. And some, I assume, are good people."[3] During that first speech, Trump also referred to China, Japan, and the Middle East as rivals of the United States. However, those comments were not as pervasive as what he said about Mexico.

The other news that came from that speech was the first mention of his wall: "I would build a great wall, and nobody builds walls better than me, believe me, and I'll build them very inexpensively, I will build a great, great wall on our southern border. And I will have Mexico pay for that wall."[4] This became his most celebrated campaign promise, and a chant that has been repeated at rallies during his political campaign as well as at subsequent events: "Build the wall!" Although he later said that Mexico would not pay directly for the wall and that it actually might be a fence on some parts of the border, the rhetoric of separating Mexico and the United States remains. Trump has effectively poisoned civil discourse in the United States to the extent that Spanish speakers—in particular brown or indigenous Spanish speakers—have been mischaracterized as invaders. Relatedly, there has been a spike of attacks toward people who speak languages other than English in public. These attacks have been more frequent among speakers of Spanish (along with speakers of Arabic), one of the main targets of this administration's bigotry and discrimination.

Fortunately, we now have mobile devices that allow for the documentation of verbal or physical attacks, which can then be disseminated to the largest possible audience. In some of these videos, we see individuals jump to the defense of the person who is being harassed. The mediation of these allies is important because the presence of an English speaker can reduce the escalation of verbal and physical violence. However, while impromptu manifestations of support for victims of language discrimination are crucial, they are also insufficient by themselves, since they tend to occur after the fact, as a reaction. They don't resolve the main issue, which is the mainstream opposition to the use of languages other than English in the public space. We need to find ways to combat the pernicious idea that using Spanish in public is inappropriate or offensive.

Like Trump's wall, languages can be used as obstacles or barriers to freedom and justice. In the same way that you can be judged based on which side of the wall you are on, you can be discriminated against for the language you speak or even the accent you have. The United States has over 56 million Spanish speakers, approximately 41 million of whom speak the language natively, making it the second most spoken language in the United States, after English. The United States is also the second largest Spanish-speaking country in the world, just after Mexico.[5] Nevertheless, Spanish is still otherized in the United States. At educational institutions, it is taught as a *foreign* language, and people who speak it are considered foreigners, even when they are U.S. citizens. Speaking Spanish in this country is still perceived as a rarity by some, even as we begin the new twenties. Or maybe these people, attached to the incorrect idea that English is the official language of the land, try very hard to fool themselves, pretending that the presence of Spanish in the public space is abnormal. For them, speaking a language other than English in public is disrespectful. "Maybe they're talking about me," they say. That's their fear. So they react against the sound of "foreign" words (especially those from cultures they deem inferior) as if they were evidence of an invasion. This, of course, has been exacerbated by Trump's rallying cry that immigrants coming from the Southern border are "invaders." The misinformed mentality of "one nation, one language" impedes the acceptance of all other languages.

Even though hundreds of languages are spoken in the United States, for some Americans, non-English languages are only meant to be spoken at home, if at all; once in the public space, everyone should switch to English. Language zealots consider this to be the correct way to demonstrate assimilation—a willingness to stop using one's mother tongue, one of the most important aspects of one's identity, in order to become a true member of society. Despite the language's long history in the area known today as the United States, Spanish continues to be viewed as an anomaly, and its speakers as people who belong on the other side of that wall. Even worse, those who dare speak the language (or any other non-English language) are potential victims of verbal and even physical attacks. While these attacks "go viral" within hours, in most cases the effect of their dissemination on social media is just to draw likes, retweets, or angry emoticons, without any further action being taken. "Hashtivism" might have its place, but discriminatory attacks will continue to happen until we as a society feel more at ease regarding the use of multiple languages in the public space. According to the Fourteenth Amendment of the U.S. Constitution, freedom of speech includes freedom of language choice.[6] So, what can we do to allow multilingual people to better exercise this right?

Various strategies have been implemented to foster linguistic equity around the world. From a top-down perspective, countries such as Spain, Canada, and Bolivia have declared multiple official languages. Linguistic policies to support and protect the presence and use of multiple languages have also been incorporated into educational systems and local governments. From the bottom-up perspective, grassroots organizations such as Antena, Tilde Language Justice Cooperative, and Caracol Language Coop work to achieve language justice by providing interpretation services, workshops, and publications to inform and promote linguistic equality and inclusion. There are also those individuals who share both the value of equality and an interest in serving as allies against linguistic discrimination, but they don't know what to do besides be ready to react in a moment of public violence. While these reactions are necessary, it is important to have preventative strategies at our disposal as well.

So, what can we do to stave off these violent events in the first place? We need to go to the root of the problem: the entitlement that linguistic xenophobes feel to attack people who speak a language different from their own. They believe that Spanish is "taking over" and claim that the second most spoken language in the country is foreign, just because they don't know it. With this in mind, how do we make Spanish more "known" in the United States, especially for people who continue to deny its importance? Surely those who scream "Speak English! This is America!" aren't going to enroll themselves in a Spanish course. Well, we propose to bring Spanish to them: in the streets, on the bus, in the grocery store. In the following pages, we will present strategies that linguistic allies can enact on a daily basis to go beyond hashtivism and engage in preventative measures that work to protect Spanish speakers and their freedom of language choice.

## A Proposal

To those who, channeling their *migra interior*,[7] are emboldened to police the languages spoken in the public space; to those who use English as a weapon of discrimination and exclusion; to those who seek to alienate whomever they cannot (or choose to not) understand, we say *basta*. If English can be used as a weapon of discrimination, then Spanish (or any other non-dominant language) can become a communal shield, a force field under which we will remain and flourish, and to which we invite anyone who needs safety from harm.

We propose to use Spanish as a force field of words. Whenever we speak a minority language in public to defend others from language discrimination, we engage in linguistic solidarity, or the practice of protecting others by speaking in a given language. We are currently in a moment when English is a hegemonic power attempting to suppress linguistic and cultural diversity under a fictitious guise of assimilation—that in order to become part of a new culture, it is not enough to gain a new language and customs; you must also sever your cultural and linguistic backgrounds. However, in this sociopolitical environment, speaking Spanish (or any other minority language, for that matter) has a twofold purpose. On the individual level, it enriches our lives by providing us with more ways to understand the complexities of the world around us; it gives us access to different forms of thinking, creating, and imagining. At a societal level, multilingualism allows us to foster deeper relationships with other peoples and cultures, thereby enabling us to achieve common goals. In both cases, it prevents us from cultural isolation, bolstering us to face the future as a more cohesive and egalitarian society.

We conceive of language solidarity as a grassroots endeavor that works toward achieving social justice and, in particular, language justice—which has been defined by Jen Hofer and John Pluecker, members of the Antena collective, as the right all individuals have to participate in the public space using the language in which they are most comfortable.[8] Thus, our proposal is simple: speak more Spanish. It doesn't matter if it's your second or third language. Speak more Spanish. And speak Spanish in public places. By relegating the language to the household or the classroom, only to be spoken with family members and classmates, we're reinforcing its status as a "foreign" language.

Let us be clear, we are speaking to allies—those who do not directly experience this form of prejudice, yet want to actively contribute to preventing it. If, on the other hand, you are the target of linguistic discrimination, it is entirely your decision as to when, where, and with whom to use Spanish. If you fear that your physical or psychological integrity may be at risk, your only concern should be to stay away from harm. Currently, when most second-language learners are given the choice to speak Spanish, more often than not they decide against using Spanish in public for various reasons, including shyness, anxiety, or a concern of offending monolingual English speakers. However, doing so might help to prevent an act of aggression. Therefore, to these allies we say: we need you to take a stand against linguistic xenophobia. *Necesitamos que hablen español en público para ayudar a normalizarlo.*

Although some people might react adversely to the proliferation of Spanish and feel entitled to tell you to speak English or something similar, we believe that these actions will gradually enable a cultural shift. When someone intolerant of other languages hears us conversing in Spanish more frequently and in more locations, we believe they will eventually begin to see this practice as common and harmless, and there is a chance that their fear of the unknown might begin to diminish. For the sake of clarity, let us say it again—every time you speak Spanish in public in the United States, you are creating a force field that will protect a Spanish-speaking minority.

Even if we have an accent (we all do!) or took a few Spanish classes ten years ago or learned the language at an older age, those of us who are able to speak the language to any extent should strive to use it in the public sphere so that more interactions in this and other languages happen. As a critical mass we can transform our sociocultural environment to a point that makes public multilingualism more regular and, as a result, safer in the United States.

So, how do you get started? We propose the following seven concrete actions:

1. Start small by having a conversation with someone else about language solidarity. Invite that person to join you in your effort. If you can find someone else to share a common goal with, you will be more successful in the process. It might be easier to start in private at first, with a friend at lunch, in social gatherings with others who have studied Spanish, while carpooling to work.

2. Next, move on to public places. Begin by speaking a few sentences in Spanish every day, maybe at a coffee shop, perhaps at the supermarket. Speak as much Spanish as you can on the metro, at religious gatherings and athletic events, on the phone, while waiting in line at the DMV, at the gas station or the dentist's office. Challenge yourself (and others) to speak Spanish everywhere the language is not expected to be heard or used. If you can inspire a single eavesdropper per day, that would make a huge difference.
3. When we say we are encouraging you to speak Spanish, we want to make a clear distinction between making a genuine effort to speak the language and what has been called Mock Spanish.[9] Peppering your speech with fake Spanish like "no problemo" or "no bueno" and even real Spanish with an intentionally anglicized accent such as "hasta la vista" and "muchacho" is in fact more detrimental than helpful. It depicts a cartoonish version of the language, erasing its complexities and instead projecting Spanish as if it were a simple code. By the way, these words are often related to the topic of partying (*cerveza*) and the idea of laziness (*siesta*), which reinforce stereotypes about Spanish speakers. Therefore, avoid using Mock Spanish.
4. Relatedly, when speaking Spanish, do so at a normal volume and intonation. Don't exaggerate or ridicule words in Spanish, even if they may sound funny to you. Spanish is a complex linguistic system and the second language in the world with the most native speakers, just below Mandarin. Demonstrate your respect for the language and the many Spanish-speaking cultures by speaking it in the same fashion you speak your first language.
5. If you want to speak Spanish with someone you suspect is a Spanish speaker, first ask them if they do in fact speak

the language. Then, ask them if they are okay with speaking Spanish with you. A simple question might do the trick: "Can I speak Spanish with you?" We advise against judging someone's linguistic abilities based on their appearance. For most people in the United States, it is offensive to assume someone speaks a given language and begin speaking it to them without first asking. While we propose greater use of the language in general, our goal is to shift the focus from what native Spanish speakers already do to what non-native Spanish speakers can be doing. In order to make a visible change we encourage you to predominantly focus on challenging yourself and other speakers of Spanish as a second language to use the language in public.

6. This is a not a call in favor of speaking "pure" Spanish—as if such a thing could exist! It is common to mix languages within discourse and even within sentences in all places where languages and cultures coexist. Going back and forth between these different linguistic codes is known as code-switching or translanguaging,[10] and some refer to switching between English and Spanish as Spanglish. So, if you describe what you speak as Spanglish, by all means, speak more Spanglish in public.
7. Insist on speaking Spanish in public even if nothing seems to change. Don't feel discouraged if your efforts aren't noticed or celebrated by others. Don't abandon the endeavor the first time you are criticized for speaking Spanish in public, particularly if you are a second-language speaker. Persevere. Remember that this is not about you. The point is to change culture together, to create a more egalitarian society, and that takes time and consistent behind-the-scenes work. Just know that every time you speak Spanish in public or private you protect someone in this country.

These actions are examples of what you can do to foster language solidarity on a daily basis and are not meant to be an exhaustive list. We encourage you to come up with new ways of protecting others with words.

## Further Considerations

Language solidarity is a bottom-up endeavor, one undertaken by individuals invested in changing the status quo. However, we understand that it is easier said than done. Even in the classroom—the educational environment designed for practice, where mistakes are expected—anxiety runs high, and people dread being called on to share their answers out loud. "How would I be able to go out into the streets with my cumbersome, accent-ridden tongue and mess up verb conjugations . . . in public?!" As educators of thousands of students, to those who ask this question, we could toss Theodore Roosevelt's saying at you: "Nothing in this world is worth having or worth doing unless it means effort, pain, difficulty." Or the more concise version by José Lezama Lima: "Sólo lo difícil es estimulante."

Instead we ask you: Does a temporary embarrassment caused by speaking Spanish put you physically or psychologically at risk? Does using your native tongue make you a target for hateful comments and loathsome glares? Has your employer threatened to fire you for speaking it at your place of work? Have you ever been denied housing or medical services for using this language? The temporary challenges that might arise when you speak Spanish are not comparable with the harassment and other forms of discrimination that native Spanish speakers experience every day. Consider your brief moments of discomfort as bricks that are laying a new foundation of more widespread, normalized Spanish, which will in turn serve as a cultural device—a force field—to protect individuals from violent attacks. You might feel uncomfortable at first, but the fear will subside with time. Remember that you are working to protect other people.

In addition to physical protection, our proposal carries with it a psychosocial effect. Someone who employs verbal or physical violence toward Spanish speakers does so, in part, because the act of speaking Spanish is highly racialized. There is an incorrect assumption that only people of certain physical attributes speak the language. Furthermore, these people tend to hold additional misconceptions: that Spanish speakers belong to a low socioeconomic status and, in some cases, are not legally permitted in the United States. As a result, since they are "not from here," they should not be allowed to use their language in public. So, these individuals will be shocked when they see an influx of allies of all backgrounds speaking Spanish. And this shock, instead of being a source of further hostility, might just as easily become a window for acceptance of other languages and cultures. A goal of this community endeavor we call linguistic solidarity is to boost the "visibility" of minority languages so that the general public pays more attention to their utility instead of attacking their speakers for their perceived appearances. Seeing that speaking Spanish is not attached to uniform physical characteristics could have the effect of informing those who harass others based on stereotypes that people of all races and ethnicities speak the language. Although this might seem obvious to most of our readers, there is still a lot of work to be done in terms of educating the mainstream population of this country regarding racial and class aspects of multiculturalism.

We also want to acknowledge that speaking Spanish in public can be dangerous, not only for native and heritage speakers, but also (to an extent) for those for whom Spanish is a second language. The goal of this proposal is not to put you in danger, but rather to collectively disperse the danger currently experienced by native and heritage speakers, to share it amongst ourselves and to use our different forms and degrees of privilege to dilute it until it begins to dissipate.

In the unlikely case someone reacts negatively to you using Spanish, do not take the bait—as much as you may want to confront that person with similar force (and believe us, our exasperation toward language intolerants was the original trigger for this chapter), the objective is to help them understand that there is nothing wrong with speaking languages other than English in public, that you use Spanish because you can, because it's useful to communicate, and that it is not their business to police your forms of expression. You can also remind them (or tell them, since there is a chance they won't know) that the United States doesn't have an official language, and that speaking whatever language pleases you is your constitutional right. If this person themself is a Spanish speaker, listen to what they say. Is it possible you were using Spanish in an offensive way? Also know that not all who confront you for speaking Spanish will do so in an antagonistic way. Some people will genuinely be interested in your motives, so think about how you can share them with others and explain why you are going out of your comfort zone to speak Spanish.

This proposal is also a call to reconsider how Spanish is taught. As language educators, our goal is not just to teach grammar, but also how to appreciate cultural and linguistic diversity. Usually Spanish classes, especially those at the beginning levels, are organized around the idea of shaping the language learner as a cultural tourist or even a cultural dilettante: someone who will eventually visit a foreign country, frolicking from cathedral to market to museum in order to document their adventures on social media. Hence the commonplace lesson in all Spanish textbooks on how to reserve a hotel room in Buenos Aires or how to order tapas at a restaurant in Barcelona, and so forth. Although learning how to perform practical tasks is essential for language acquisition, it is just as important to develop empathy toward the people who speak the languages we aim to learn. We believe that all language courses should incorporate a module on the urgency of language solidarity in a moment when speakers of Spanish and other languages are considered not only second-class citizens but also invaders and criminals.

## Conclusion

In this chapter, we have discussed strategies to address language discrimination through preventative measures that aim to transform our culture. Unfortunately, when an attack occurs it is generally not feasible to politely ask the attacker to consider the benefits of multilingualism and multiculturalism. In the face of an attack, those of us who have the privilege to do so should be ready to put ourselves on the line to defend people in more vulnerable positions. This is our moral obligation as human beings. However, we also think that, in addition to these direct actions and in order to curtail violence toward Spanish speakers, a preventative movement in favor of the use of Spanish in the public space should also take place right now, simultaneously.

Amid social exclusion, harassment, and physical violence directed at the use of Spanish in public, instead of giving in to those who attempt to coerce others into silence and subjugation, we reject any imposition of linguistic "assimilation" and propose to engage in a collective effort to expand the use of Spanish in public. While this process will not happen overnight, we believe this historical moment calls for a cultural shift. In the midst of the current avalanche of racist, xenophobic attacks, silence is not a viable way to oppose discrimination. Indeed, violence toward people who speak languages other than English should be confronted by speaking up, not only as a consequence of an attack, but also before the attack, in order to prevent it. Speaking more Spanish, however, is not going to produce immediate effects by itself, nor should it be used as the only strategy in achieving language justice. Our wish is that the concept of language solidarity enters the conversation as a sustainable strategy of resistance—a conversation that should take place both in English *y en español.*

Second-language learners need to speak Spanish in the public space in order to generate a common front to address the violence directed at those who don't have their same privileges. Currently, using Spanish in public in the United States without being attacked is a license typically granted to those of a certain skin tone and phenotype. As a means of creating a counterbalance to linguistic discrimination, we challenge all who speak Spanish to any degree to use it. If more people start speaking Spanish in public, the use of this language could be normalized, which, in turn, could contribute to a decrease in episodes of linguistic discrimination. The idea is to chip away at the stigma of using this language and to create a public critique of the racialization of language. Perhaps at first these individuals will react adversely, but in time this movement will be able to counteract that opposition, creating more nuanced responses to the unease. Normalizing the use of Spanish will demonstrate that hearing it in public is not uncommon, something out of the cantina scene in a western movie, but rather a reflection of the multilingual and multicultural reality of this country. As long as the mainstream continues to exoticize the use of Spanish, it will be singled out with negative consequences. Conversely, a larger presence of Spanish in our daily lives will serve to protect those who speak it natively. Our ultimate goal is to change public discourse by making Spanish more frequent and more quotidian so that people who consider it a threat can eventually understand that it is just another language spoken in the United States, along with English and hundreds more.

# RAPE AND THE IDEA OF MEXICO

ALEJANDRO MADRAZO LAJOUS[1]

According to Sinisa Malesevic, if we are interested in the processes of state formation, we need to ask the following:

> How is it possible to make a person feel so attached to an abstract entity that he or she allegedly expresses willingness to treat and cherish this entity in the same way one cherishes his or her close family?[2]

Answering this question entails tracing the links between small-scale solidarity, such as that owed to family and town, and broader social entities, such as states or nations.

This, for the case of Mexico, is what I aim to do in this chapter. Concretely, I want to explore this question through the role rape in the U.S. Invasion of Mexico, in the mid-nineteenth century, played in linking micro-solidarities—such as family or town—to the macro-solidarity that is the nation. The Mexican government used the threat of rape as an instrument of mobilization for the war, but in its aftermath—once rape had actually been inflicted on part of the Mexican population—rape needed to be suppressed from collective memory. This tension between rape's importance and rape's suppression from collective memory resulted in an interesting displacement from women's bodies to territory as the locus of harm and the core of collective solidarity. Rape's architecture as a harm successfully fed into the collective remembrance of the war as a shared grievance for Mexicans, which was symbolized and materialized in the loss of large portions of Mexico's territory. For this reason, I posit that the importance and consequent suppression of rape from the collective experience of the war helps explain the emergence of *territory* as a pivot of collective identity and the defense of the territory as a shared political project for Mexicans since the second half of the nineteenth century.[3]

If we want to understand the formation and consolidation of the Mexican state—as a shared identity, as a shared idea of a polity—the role rape played in the U.S. Invasion should be central to our inquiry.

Now, rape as a central piece for understanding the "Mexican identity" is not new. Claudio Lomnitz, in his ambitious book *Death and the Idea of Mexico*, holds that death is one of three national totems that have, sequentially, served as "figures of collective filiation"[4] for the country. He holds that "Mexico is one of those countries that have had to recognize serious limitations to concerted collective action. It was this awareness of an only very tenuously shared sense of *future* that led intellectuals of the mid-twentieth century to elevate Death to the status of a *national sign*."[5] This tenuousness is not present, however, in our sense of a shared past: we have successfully created the impression that we share a common past, reaching back to the foundation of the Aztec capital of Tenochtitlán, still represented as our national symbol and printed on our flag: the mythic eagle eating a serpent.[6]

That past, however, is generally imagined as having been initiated in and defined by trauma. Trauma, not totem or a glorious foundational myth, is at the inception of the idea of Mexico. The Conquest is iconically imagined as a rape and personified in Hernán Cortés and his slave/consort/translator Malintzin, or Malinche. Octavio Paz famously argued that Mexicans identify as *hijos de la Chingada* (sons of *La Chingada*) and argued that Malinche was the paradigm of *La Chingada*.[7]

> *La Chingada es la Madre abierta, violada o burlada por la fuerza.*
>
> [La Chingada is the open Mother, raped and mocked by force.]

Paz further specified: for the Spaniard, dishonor lies in being a "son of a whore," a woman who willingly gives herself, whereas for the Mexican, dishonor lies in being the result of a rape.[8] Lomnitz contributes to our understanding of the centrality of rape by underscoring it as a function of the centrality of the *mestizo* in the political imagination of Mexico. We imagine ourselves as *mestizo*, mixed blood, because we can't imagine ourselves as either European or (native) American, as both are, in different ways, excluded from (modern) Mexico. *Mestizos*, in the collective imagination that subscribes the official narrative of the Spanish Conquest, are the product of rape:

> Creoles who fear being cast as foreign Europeans; Indians who constantly face exclusion. The nation's official protagonist, the mestizo, is represented as issuing from rape.[9]

Rape as a central image in the conformation of "national identity" has become a trope. Little attention is now paid to further understanding it. I hope to reopen this topic by making two shifts from the way in which it is usually tackled.

First, I want to shift our understanding of rape as stemming from the *narrative* of the Spanish Conquest of Tenochtitlán to the more recent *experience* of the U.S. Invasion of Mexico in the mid-nineteenth century. This shift between *narrative* and *experience* is somewhat arbitrary and subject to criticism (*What makes one a narrative and the other an experience?*), but I will try to explain why I hold that distinction.

Second, I want to use rape—its experience before and during the U.S. Invasion and its later suppression from collective memory—not so much as a component of national identity, but rather as an entry point to explore the processes through which a national ideology was constructed. In this second shift, I'm inspired by Sinisa Malesevic, who urges us to "refocus our attention from the vague, fuzzy, metaphoric, often static and inward-looking concepts such as 'identity,' 'consciousness' or 'psyche' towards multilayered processes that are ideology and solidarity."[10]

While I distance myself from Malesevic's broader claim that "'national identity' is a conceptual chimera not worthy of serious analytical pursuit,"[11] in this chapter I want to take up this shift from a conceptual inquiry about national identity to a process-oriented inquiry about how the development of Mexico's nationalist ideology was enabled.

This paper engages these questions through six different sections. First, I will make the case that it is the experience of the U.S. Invasion of Mexico and the rapes—both imagined and actual—that took place in its context that constitute the foundational trauma that spurred the consolidation of Mexico during the second half of the nineteenth century. This claim cuts against the more established one that locates original trauma in the Spanish Conquest and its rapes, both imagined and actual. Next, I will contextualize the U.S. Invasion in the nation-building process that Mexico was undergoing at the time, so as to understand the importance of this period in Mexican history, specifically in terms of investing in collective solidarity around the idea of a nation, and how the trauma of the Intervention (imagined as rape) affected that process by substituting religion with territory as the rallying point of national solidarity. A third section will turn to how the war was imagined, specifically focusing on how the threat of rape was used as one of the central narratives to mobilize the population in defense of the territory. A fourth section will then look at the experience of the war itself, specifically at sexual violence and how it related to both the racialization of what it was to be "Mexican" and collective identity. A fifth section will address how the war was remembered and use its memorialization as a way of understanding how and why the micro experience of rape and sexual violence played into the macro experience of building collective identity around an idea of Mexico that emphasized territory, not religion. Finally, in section six, I will revise my analysis and home in on the ambivalences and ambiguities of both the experience of the Invasion and the need to suppress them. I conclude with a metaphor that may—or may not—guide us if we are interested in exploring the current relevance of this genealogy.

One note of warning before we continue: for the most part, I will explore rape from the perspective of those who suffered it in their imagination and in other people's bodies, not from the perspective of the direct victim of rape. That is, I will look at rape and the role it plays in Mexican political imagination from a predominantly male perspective, not female. In this project, I'm concerned mostly with understanding political imaginaries, not gender violence. Gender violence is here a means to understanding political imagination. And political imagination is dominantly male, both today and throughout its historic construction. It is men who were the citizens and leaders of the nineteenth century nation-under-construction called Mexico, and it is still men who dominate the public space (though that is quickly changing as women take the streets to protest against sexual and gender violence). Furthermore, rape—insofar as it was a communicative and military tool throughout the war—was perpetrated by men as a means to hurt other men, as I shall explain later.[12] One of the many injustices of rape, up until recent times and maybe still today, is that it is not only perpetrated but also publicly signified mostly by men. That, justly, is changing, but only just recently. My concern here is with genealogy of political imaginaries, not with gender justice. In this sense, my inquiry is more related to historian Joan W. Scott's proposition that gender "is a primary way of signifying relationships of power" or "a primary field within which or by means of which power is articulated."[13] I thought that needed to be made clear.

## Rape

Octavio Paz's famous argument that Mexicans identify ourselves as *hijos de la Chingada* has become somewhat of a platitude since its publication in 1950. According to Paz, Mexico emerged from the trauma of the Conquest, symbolized by the asymmetrical and sexual relationship between the conquistador Hernán Cortés and his Indian consort and translator, Malintzin, or *la Malinche*. Let us read Paz at length:

> Si la Chingada es la representación de la Madre violada, no me parece forzado asociarla a la Conquista, que fue también una violación, no solamente en el sentido histórico sino en la carne misma de las indias. El símbolo de la entrega es la Malinche, la amante de Cortés. Es verdad que ella se da voluntariamente al conquistador, pero éste, apenas deja de serle útil, la olvida. Doña Marina se ha convertido en la figura que representa a las indias, fascinadas, violadas o seducidas, por los españoles. Y del mismo modo que el niño no perdona a su madre que lo abandone por ir en busca del padre, el pueblo mexicano no perdona su traición a la Malinche. Ella encarna lo abierto, lo chingado, frente a nuestros indios, estoicos, impasibles y cerrados.
>
> (If la Chingada is the representation of the raped Mother, it doesn't seem forced to me to associate her with the Conquest, which was also a rape, not only in the historical sense, but in the flesh of Indian women

> themselves. The symbol of that surrender is Malinche, Cortés's lover. It is true that she gave herself voluntarily to the conqueror, but as soon as she ceased to be useful, he forgets her. Doña Marina[14] has become a figure representing Indian women, fascinated, raped or seduced, by the Spaniards. And the same way in which a boy forgives not his mother abandoning him and going after his father, the Mexican people do not forgive Malinche her treason. She incarnates what is open, what is fucked, in opposition to our Indians, stoic, unmovable and closed.)

Putting aside the historical imprecisions of this narrative,[15] it contains undoubtedly one of the tropes in popular Mexican understanding of "national identity" or "national character." It fits well with the traditional national narrative that portrays Mexico's beginnings in Tenochtitlán itself, and with the national narrative as progressive liberation beginning with the fight for independence and continuing through the Reform in the 1850s and 1860s to the Revolution of 1910–1920.[16]

I want to shift attention away from the Conquest in understanding trauma—structurally imagined as rape—as foundational to Mexico and instead draw attention to the U.S. Invasion. Of course, the two historic episodes in the collective imagination are not incompatible but rather are mutually reinforcing: both are military defeats and territorial occupations. Both involved, as wars do, a fair amount of sexual violence perpetrated on the population living in occupied territory. But, in contrast with the Conquest, the U.S. Invasion is often minimized in Mexico, reduced to an unjust war by an overbearing bully. As Peter Guardino explains: "Mexican historical consciousness also often slides over the war. Who wants to remember defeat, especially a defeat that many saw as resulting from weakness?"[17] When we do pay attention to the Invasion, the sexual dimension of the event is notoriously absent, and so it is never related to that founding trauma. It is also seldom understood as foundational to what is modern Mexico.

Why, then, look for the foundational trauma of rape in the U.S. Invasion? Moreover, why delve further into the myth of a foundational rape? Allow me to unpack the answers separately. First, why rape? The short answer—which I hope to address in more detail in other spaces dedicated to the broader project that this chapter is a part of—is because I believe that understanding Mexico through the foundational trauma of rape helps us understand the nature of authority in Mexican political culture, and this is key in understanding our difficulties in establishing the rule of law. Masculinity, specifically macho masculinity, looms large in Mexico and informs the ways in which Mexicans understand and relate to authority.[18] As Paz explains, Mexican masculinity is tied to the foundational trauma of rape. I believe that is also true for authority in Mexico, for authority here is linked to a complex—and not very healthy—way of understanding masculinity.[19]

Mexicans often identify with the underdog.[20] The underdog is both the product and the object of harm, and rape is often signified—in Janet Halley's words—as "a harm par excellence," a fate worse than death.[21] So, rape is also tied to our ever-recurring perspective of the world from the point of view of underdogs. In many ways, our national narrative is one of the resilience and endurance of the underdog. But, more specifically, although rape of bodies is suffered at the micro level by those—at least momentarily—disempowered, the "historic" rape that is territorial conquest alluded to by Paz is something that can be shared by the powerful and the unaffected. Symbolically, the association of rape with military defeat allows for an identification of those in power with those disempowered, uniting both and legitimizing the former. It also links the micro experience of people with the macro narrative of The People, a tracing that Malesevic urges us to undertake.

Moving to the second point, why look to the *U.S. Invasion* of Mexico instead of the *Spanish Conquest* as a historic episode from which to explore rape and, through it, authority? There are several reasons, but the most evident is that it is a closer experience than that of the Conquest. It is closer in time, considerably (1847 as opposed to 1521), but it is also closer as a still persistent threat: whereas few Mexicans are concerned or bothered by what Spaniards say or do today, the place of the United States in the conformation of Mexican political imagination is difficult to ignore, as Donald Trump and his (phallic?) obsession with building a wall has reminded Mexicans with great efficacy.[22]

Moreover, conquest and rape in 1521 was fundamentally an experience of (some of ) the Indian population in Mexico.[23] The idea of Mexico is hardly a project stemming from what is today Mexico's Indian population. It is a western, modern, culturally Hispanic political project that was successfully imposed on the then majoritarian Indian population by a generation of mostly mixed-blood (*mestizo*), well-educated, liberal, urban professionals and politicians during the second half of the nineteenth century—what is known collectively as the Reform generation.[24] These men *lived* through the U.S. Invasion, some of them experiencing it firsthand as soldiers, others as local politicians responsible for contributing to the war effort. The U.S. Invasion, the generational sense of failing as a nation, the loss of territory, and, one supposes, the awareness of sexual violence during the war was, for the founders of the modern Mexican state, a lived experience, not a mythic past. As Richard Sinkin puts it, the U.S. Invasion was the "precipitating event" for the "monumental upheaval known in Mexican history as the Reform."[25] Furthermore, it shaped one of the pivots of the political project that was put to the test with a later foreign—French—invasion (1862–1867), which, successfully resisted, definitively legitimated the reformists and their agenda to impose a political project that had little to do with what the country had been until then. Defense of territory was crucial to the reformists, as liberal newspaper *El Siglo* phrased it:

> The liberal party hopes to achieve its political ideas without foreign assistance and *will sacrifice its principles before compromising the independence of the Republic.*[26]

This statement, considering it was made in the middle of a civil war between parties who fought, fundamentally, over which principles—liberal or conservative—should inform the political project of building a nation-state, is symptomatic of the importance that (the defense of ) territory was assuming in the political imagination. The importance of territory is, I believe, one of the central legacies of the U.S. Invasion to the construction of Mexico. And the link between territory and rape is one of the chords that link the micro experience of people to the macro narrative of The People.

Furthermore, even if we do not accept the idea that, in Mexico, rape is a foundational trauma, rape as nation-building is something that needs to be taken seriously. The weaponization of sexual violence has recently come into focus in academic discussion, but can hardly be thought of as an innovation in belligerent practices. Catharine MacKinnon explains how genocidal rape in former Yugoslavia was a form of nation-building:

> The women are raped to death or raped and made to live with having been raped. This is rape as forced exile; to make you leave your home and never go back. It is rape as spectacle: to be seen and heard and watched and told to others. It is rape as humiliation: for certain men to take pleasure from violating certain women, or certain men, or to take pleasure watching certain men be forced to violate certain women or girls. . . . It is rape to establish dominance, to shatter a community. It is rape to destroy a people: rape as genocide. It is rape as nation-building to create a state.[27]

It would be far-fetched to equate the paradigm of genocidal rape—the post-Yugoslavian conflict—and the U.S. Invasion of Mexico. However, there are elements that are present in the latter that allow us to understand the bridge from micro experience to macro narrative, which will be addressed in a later section of this chapter, including the racialization of the victim, and this, in a moment in which Mexicans did not understand themselves as a race, is also an interesting thread to pursue. The point being that there is good reason to look at sexual violence and sexual exchange—not only rape, as I shall point to near the end of the chapter—in order to understand the political dimension of violence and sex during war and the micro–macro link in shared experiences in general, not only in the specific case of Mexico.

If we accept that rape can be an ingredient of nation-building, introduced not only by perpetrators, as MacKinnon argued, but also—as I argue here—by victims (if successfully spun), then we need to look, even if briefly, at Mexico's nation-building process leading up to the war.

## Nation-Building

Mexico had a hard time emerging in the nineteenth century. The U.S. Invasion took place one generation after independence had come to be formalized.[28] When it happened, "national governments and political leaders in both nascent countries worked hard to make this a war about what it meant to be a Mexican and what it meant to be an American."[29] Until then, in the midst of deep tensions and contested ideas of what the country was and should be, there seemed to be an uncontested notion that Mexico was, first and foremost, a Catholic country. Religious intolerance had been invariably included in all four national constitutions, which varied enormously in almost every other respect.[30]

Catholicism as the axis around which the country must be constructed did not entail only religious intolerance but also a broader notion—labeled "providentialist nationalism" by Brian Connaughton[31]—that understood Mexico as having a divine mission, embodying orthodoxy in religion. Under this understanding of Mexico, the government's role was first and foremost spiritual:

> For clerics and many other Catholics, the government's principal role was to provide the conditions necessary for souls to be saved by guaranteeing the social order and protecting Mexicans from heresy.[32]

This claim needs proper context. It is a mischaracterization to present the idea of a strong, unquestioned national unity around Catholicism as the core of the nation-building process. Rather, there were myriad overlapping values and loyalties that atomized identity—to their hometown, language (Spanish was, by no means, the native language for many rural Mexicans; at best it was a kind of lingua franca), their social class, neighborhood, family, profession, local patron saint, and so forth. In this complex map of overlapping identities, religion was the one tenuous, but undisputedly shared, axis for building national identity.

However, beginning with independence, the groundwork for nationalistic ideology had already been actively laid, even if the specifics of that "nation" had not yet been defined. In a mostly illiterate society, it was through public acts—including Mass and other solemn religious ceremonies—that this groundwork was laid:

> The importance of the nation was stressed not only in print media but also in civic ceremonies and the justifications of judicial decisions. Even impoverished Mexicans who lived in relatively isolated areas were exposed

> to these ideas and began to use them during social conflicts.[33]

Nationalism, however, was moored to religion, both conceptually and historically. Peter Guardino sums it up thus:

> The belief that Mexico was Catholic was very firmly tied to ideas of nationhood: the Mexican War of Independence had been launched by the priest Miguel Hidalgo and sustained by many priests for years, and the idea that Mexico had a particular role to play in the religious destiny of the planet was a prominent part of political discourse. By the mid-nineteenth century, devotion to the Virgin of Guadalupe had become a symbol of this national religious destiny, and Mexicans voiced both pleas for her protection and calls to protect her image during the war. . . . The vast majority of Mexicans believed that only Catholicism and Catholic sacraments could open the door to that afterlife. Although we might see religious diversity as desirable, in the 1840s most Mexicans saw it as evidence that many people were making mistakes that were both terrible and terribly permanent.[34]

The process was under way, and the war naturally congealed the result. It would, however, deeply redirect it. Out of the war, the church would emerge deeply weakened—both financially and politically[35]—and Catholicism would not only be displaced from the core of nation-building, but would soon, for the first time, have to accept religious tolerance.[36] As Mexico emerged from the U.S. Invasion, positions regarding what the nation was and what it should become underwent a quick process in which they became hardened.[37] For the generation of the Reform, which took power within a decade after the war, the church was the main obstacle for the consolidation of the country:

> It had been the church that had financed and promoted the military Polkos revolt during the American attack on Mexico City; it had been the church that seemed to monopolize most of the productive land; it was the church that received more income than the national government; and it was the church that existed as a separate entity within the state with its own courts and privileges. Indeed, for Mexican liberals the church embodied all the worst elements of the colonial heritage, and from them the only hope for national survival lay in a severe reduction of the power of the Catholic Church.[38]

But we are getting ahead of ourselves. We need to establish, first of all, the narratives deployed leading up to and during the war, and then those stemming from it, which allowed for this radical shift in nation-building narratives in Mexico. We also need to understand how the war was experienced as an existential threat, and how rape provides a matrix for the shared experience of survival from that threat even though it needs to be explicitly suppressed.

## Imagining

Existential threats work "entirely in the imagination" according to political and legal theorist Paul Kahn.[39] Let us then explore how the war was imagined before engaging how it was experienced. Let us begin with Catholicism, the pivot of an incipient nationalist ideology until then. The U.S. Invasion was seen as a direct threat to Catholicism. For Peter Guardino, Mexico's war effort itself—the staunch resistance offered by Mexico during the war, fielding one army after another in spite of consistent defeats—would have been inconceivable had American domination not been seen as a direct threat to Catholicism.[40]

There was good reason to imagine the U.S. Invasion as a threat to Catholicism. The direct antecedent of the Invasion, Texan independence, had been fueled in an era of broad American nativism and anti-Catholicism, and support for the Texas Revolution in the United States had pointed to Catholicism at the root of the Texan rebellion, a narrative that had gained leverage in the period leading up to Texan annexation by the United States, identifying Mexican Catholicism as inherently opposed to liberty and progress.[41] As the war began, anti-Catholicism became an uncontrollable "ideological force" that neither the military nor the political leaders of the U.S. government could successfully deactivate (although they wanted to, for they understood correctly that U.S. anti-Catholicism would fuel Mexican resistance):[42]

> Mexicans were very aware of this rhetoric. It made them fear that at the very least the Americans would insist that Protestant denominations be allowed to operate in Mexico, a development that Mexican priests believed would tempt some Mexicans away from the only faith that could lead them to eternal salvation.[43]

Anti-Catholicism was not the only existential threat. Other central aspects of identity for Mexicans were also brought into question. Race, for one. Again, in the context of the Texan revolt, U.S. supporters had cast Mexicans as "a different and inferior race . . . not martial enough to defeat Native Americans [and] too lazy to make the wonderful lands of Texas productive."[44] This perspective was flabbergasting to Mexicans: they understood themselves as a nation formed by *many* different races, but although there was (and is still) much racial prejudice and stereotyping within Mexico, racial distinctions had lost legal relevance with independence.[45] What for the United States was uniform and crucial in determining legal status, for Mexicans was highly plural and legally irrelevant.[46] Being seen as a *race* came as a shock to us.

Race and religion, as well as culture more broadly, were meshed together in supremacist ideology, dominant in the lands and communities in the United States most involved in the war.[47] Mexicans were seen as inferior. As this supremacist ideology did not escape Mexicans, they understood that domination by the United States represented a threat to the central understandings that they had of themselves as a collectivity. The threat was existential; it was felt as potentially degrading the whole country and everyone in it:

> Mexicans repeatedly argued that American racism would lead them to enslave Mexicans, especially those of indigenous or African roots. General Zavala of Aguascalientes warned that if Mexicans did not stop them, the Americans would "stamp on their faces the infamous seal of a shameful slavery like that suffered by that unlucky race they call people of color." Bustamante reported rumors that Mexicans in occupied lands were being branded and sold in the slave markets of New Orleans.[48]

The threat was imagined as looming, among other reasons, because some of the most notorious military men participating in the invasion *were* experienced at what we call today ethnic cleansing. Texan regiments were formed by men who had been involved

> in the ethnic cleansing campaigns that the Republic of Texas unleashed on its Native Americans in the early 1840s. During these campaigns, when any Native Americans attacked settlers, Texans killed whatever

> Native Americans could be found, including women and children from peaceful groups. The men engaged in these activities were called the Texas Rangers.[49]

The Texas Rangers, part of the Texan volunteer units, were notorious during the war, their reputation preceding them—both within the invading army and in the invaded territories—and their weapons, the Colt revolver, distinguishing them. More important, they were assigned specifically to counterinsurgency efforts and became "notorious for stealing from Mexican civilians and conducting revenge attacks on civilians after guerrilla activity."[50] Deployed both in the north and later in Veracruz, these volunteers were particularly present among the civilian population.

How did Mexico respond to this existential threat? Discursively, authorities used it to rally support for the war effort. War propaganda is particularly interesting because it reflects what Mexicans at the time believed was worth defending from that existential threat; in other words, what was threatened. Interestingly, territory—what the invading government actually and explicitly sought—was not a protagonist.

Propaganda for the war consistently centered on

> three threads of argument: They appealed to a relatively general form of patriotism, often by invoking the memory of independence war heroes. They called on Mexicans to defend the *honor and bodies of their wives and daughters.* And . . . they stressed the need to protect Catholicism and its sacred objects from the rapacity and impiety of American soldiers. Dozens of documents combined these last two elements, including an April 1847 proclamation of the Zacatecas town council, which speaks of Americans, "destroying, occupying and burning our cities, trampling on our altars, stealing

> our property, and sacrificing to his brutal customs *our chaste maidens, our faithful wives." Even nuns would not be safe from rape.*[51](my emphasis)

The propaganda drives the threat the invading army poses close to home: occupation would entail desecration of both cherished bodies and sacred places and objects. Patriotism, of course, could not be excluded from any respectable modern war propaganda. It is interesting to note, however, that it focused on the legacy of the previous generation, which had fought for independence, thus dovetailing into family (and therefore linked to sexual and reproductive access to women's bodies). Guardino explains:

> The themes of independence, religion, and the need to defend or avenge Mexican women were each very powerful, and in each case some of that emotional power stemmed from connections to the family. This connection is least obvious in the case of independence, which at a glance seems an abstract political ideal. However, as we have seen, when Mexican leaders brought up independence, they usually pointed out that the parents of the current generation had sacrificed to achieve it, and the current generation could only prove itself worthy by fighting to preserve it. Religion was connected to national identity, but calls to defend Catholicism focused on the much less abstract idea that Catholicism was the only path to eternal life, an idea whose emotional power was at least partially drawn from the possibility of eternal union with beloved family members. Defending Mexican women from rape was defending both their bodies and the honor of the family. These three elements were powerful individually, but propagandists usually

> invoked more than one and often all three, in any given document or speech.[52]

These tropes were successfully deployed to mobilize the defenses at key moments of the war, such as the building of an army at San Luis Potosí to contain the invading army from the north; mobilizing defenses against a second invading army from the east after the fall of Veracruz, and the final defense of Mexico City.[53] They must have resonated with the population.

For reasons I will unpack in the final section of this chapter, honoring the sacrifice of the previous generation and defense of religion could not serve as tropes on which to build a nationalist ideology *after* the war, but rape could, albeit projected onto the country's territory. But before we engage in that interpretation of events, we need to look at the experience of war itself. Specifically, at *how* sexual violence was experienced, for the importance of rape *after* the war had less to do with the *women* who suffered it and more with the *men* who gave it meaning.

## Experiencing

American invaders engaged in abuse while in Mexico. Abuse was both extraordinary—such as public mass rape—and everyday: "The longer the Americans stayed the more people resented them—not only for the central fact of their conquest, but for the thousands of little insults and daily humiliations committed by an uncouth foreigner who considered himself, in every possible way, superior."[54] These "little insults" included calling the men "greasers" to their face, while they also "freely consorted with Hispanic women . . . brought venereal diseases . . . mangled the Spanish language [and] gorged themselves like hogs."[55] Among such little and large abuses, rape stands out.

Catharine MacKinnon explains the communicative power of rape thusly:

> Violating other men's women is planting a flag: it is a way some men say to other men, "What was yours is now mine." He who gets away with this, runs things. Doing this institutionalizes the rulership of some men over other men even as it establishes the rulership of all men over all women. You cannot govern the dead. Better that those you rule live in terror, knowing you have something over them, knowing what you can do to them at any time.[56]

Rape is deeply political, as an act of war. It is also normalized—in war and in everyday life—as inevitable and therefore inconsequential, except for the individuals involved.[57] Yet, if we take seriously our attempt to link the micro to the macro, then we need to keep in mind that the experience of individuals as victims and their relatives, fed into the experience of the political community. Of all that rape is, I want to focus here on how rape is a way of making "women's bodies into a medium of men's expression, the means through which one group of men says what it wants to say to another. . . . It means supremacy: we are better than you. And possession: we own you."[58]

We do know that rape occurred, and often.[59] And we know something of how it occurred and by whom it was perpetrated most often. It happened mostly—but not exclusively—in the north, under Zachary Taylor's army, specifically by the volunteer units. It was part of a broader pattern of abuse, but this abuse was particularly powerful when it took the form of sexual violence.

One important aspect of abuses, including rape, is that they were most often associated with U.S. volunteer units. The relative discipline of regular U.S. Army units was notorious when compared to the way in which volunteer units behaved, particularly toward the civilian population. Volunteers incurred abuses toward Mexico's civilian population in a number of ways: theft, arson, murder, and, of course, rape. This meant that it was foreign citizens who victimized Mexican citizens, and that did not escape them. It was Americans doing this, not the U.S. government alone or a professional army:

> Volunteers often murdered Mexicans who protested the theft of their possessions: a Mexican not willing to let volunteers walk away with a blanket or drive away his livestock without protest could quickly become a dead Mexican. Often, though, the murders do not seem to have had such a well-defined motive. Mexicans were killed in a variety of contexts: on the streets of Mexican towns and cities, on the highways, and even right on the outskirts of American camps, and the reasons are more often than not unvoiced.[60]

Rape stood apart from other abuses. Occurrence of rape is both well recorded and veiled, either through language or through omission, creating a silence around rape which

> suggests that rape was terrible in both cultures precisely because attacks on the honor and bodies of women were attacks on the families that both cultures saw as the foundations of moral society. These attacks also damaged the honor of the woman's fathers and brothers, something volunteers sometimes deliberately drove home by forcing them to witness the attacks. These nineteenth-century American men used sexual violence against Mexicans as a way of emphasizing racial domination, much as they commonly did against African Americans and Native Americans.[61]

This silence confirms the idea that, to many (at least to the men), rape was a "fate worse than death." Why was this so? MacKinnon, speaking of the rape of Muslim women by Serbian men in Bosnia, unpacks the importance of having the rape be public: it becomes a form of "ritual degradation."[62] Let us look more closely at this degradation, through Paul Kahn's study on violence:

> The victim is degraded whenever he experiences the emptying out of a symbolic world of meaning. Degradation is the experience of the collapse of that world, which leaves one literally alone. . . . Degradation works through the use of pain to destroy faith in that which provides meaning and identity.[63]

By raping Mexican women, U.S. soldiers were—among other things—speaking to Mexican men and degrading *them* also:

> Socially, sexuality means intimacy; forced sex violates a person in a way that, as intimate, is seen and experienced as especially violating. Because sex is relational, sexual atrocities destroy relationships. Perhaps in part because it is seen and felt to destroy one's humanity and relational place in community indelibly and irreparably, in a way the victim never lives without, rape is sometimes termed "worse than death."[64]

The place of Mexican women in their communities and their worlds were affected, undoubtedly (and we will explore that more in the closing section), but, importantly, so were their male relatives'. Furthermore, the males' roles as fighting men and citizens were also tied to their role as family men. Mexican men who fought were imagined as family men.[65] Their role as fathers and husbands was exalted by recruitment efforts. What kind of fighters were these men who could not defend their families? Moreover, fighting was actually the entry into citizenship for many of the Mexican men fighting the war. Most men who actually were recruited to fight through the National Guard were legally disenfranchised men, who were offered access to citizenship through enlistment; the war was the forge of citizenship for most in Mexico. If they could not defend their women from rape, their role as family men, soldiers, and citizens was in question. Those who survived the war had, by definition, failed in either effectively protecting their women or deploying self-sacrifice.

Rape as a threat to bodies, families, and the polity (and even eternal salvation) during the U.S. Invasion not only was relevant in itself but also informed the experience of the war of the entire population. As the war reached its climax and the invading army approached the capital, fear of rape was paramount, not even rivaled by the fear of hunger:

> The possibility of mass rape was taken so seriously that in June [of 1847] the city council suggested that the city's hundreds of virginal nuns be evacuated, and on September 6 officials authorized the evacuation of all women, although no mass exodus ensued.[66]

After the capital was taken, what little military action that took place again underscored domination through degradation. Rape continued to be used as a means of communication *par excellence* for punishing civilians. For instance, after the close escape of an important guerrilla leader, the invading army unleashed horror through public mass rape on the population of Zacualtipán in February of 1848:

> The horror began. The soldiers mutilated and burned the corpse of one guerrilla leader. They looted the town,

> stealing anything they could from wealthy and poor alike. The Americans set fire to many houses and killed many Mexican civilians. In the parish church they stole the sacred vessels used in ceremonies, as well as the priest's vestments, and defecated in the sacristy. The Americans later brought a number of Mexican women to the church and raped them there. . . . There is no direct evidence that Lane, Hays, or Polk [Army officer, brother to President Polk] ordered their troops to attack civilians or even gave them explicit permission to do so, but the prevalence of similar incidents under their command suggests that punishing civilians was for all intents and purposes a policy. And, of course, the presence of the president's brother at this particular scene is jarring.[67]

## Signifying

Defeat was devastating and called into question the existence of the country:

> Stunned by the rapid defeat, humbled by the Treaty of Guadalupe Hidalgo, and fearful of the future, educated Mexicans began to wonder out loud about Mexico's continued existence. Obviously the United States could have absorbed all of Mexico had it so desired; clearly, too, there would have been little Mexican resistance to national disintegration. As one pamphleteer put it, "Wherever we cast our view, we see that everything is decaying, everything is degenerating." And Mariano Otero, one of the leading opponents of signing the peace treaty, summarized a general feeling: "In Mexico there is

> not, nor has there ever been able to be, anything called national spirit because there is no nation."[68]

Most of the country was occupied, the northern provinces in dispute irrevocably so; the government had abandoned the capital to the invading army and could barely continue ordinary functioning, let alone significant military resistance; the capital was brutally occupied by the invading army, which suppressed a popular uprising by using artillery within residential neighborhoods[69]; civilian population—as we just saw—continued to be the target of brutal violence outside the capital; and all symbols of the sacred were trampled on, notably the country's most venerated shrine—the Virgin of Guadalupe—which was witness to the signing of a humiliating treaty, the core of which was the cession of over half of Mexico to the United States. The absorption of the entire country as part of the United States was not only a hovering threat, but also an actual possibility being discussed in the United States.[70]

But what did defeat mean?

> For the nation, nothing is more degrading than defeat. Defeat is the disappearance of the sacred from the world. To get to the concession of defeat one must pass through the possibility of martyrdom. . . . The degradation moment is not the injury itself but the failure to convert suffering to martyrdom. That is the moment of the failure of faith and, simultaneously, the experience of the body as nothing but an object of sacrifice for an alien god. Degradation lasts as long as the memory of failure of the sacred.[71]

Paul Kahn holds that the domain of the state—its borders—is where it can demand sacrifice.[72] If we take that into perspective, then we can understand the magnitude of the crisis: after abandoning Mexico City to its fate in the early hours of the fourteenth of September, the Mexican government was hardly capable of demanding sacrifice. It had failed to sacrifice itself in defense of the nation. Instead, people (The People?) sacrificed themselves spontaneously, rising in popular revolt against the U.S. army between the fourteenth and the sixteenth of September 1847—importantly, the sixteenth was the national holiday celebrating independence from Spain in 1821, which added to the devastating symbolic failure of the State. After the violent revolt in the capital and its violent suppression, which lasted three full days, and its lingering effects for three months, people outside the capital engaged in guerrilla warfare, with little or no support from the government.

The government had failed—the Mexican army had, after all, failed to sacrifice itself in the final hour—and was at odds with claiming legitimacy.[73] In this context, there was little of the narratives that had (successfully) mobilized a defense that could reinsert meaning—the sacred—into the political. It would take years—decades—to consolidate a memorialization that introduced martyrdom into the national episode and thus provide meaning and reinsert faith in the political community.[74]

What we need to understand is that the symbols and narratives that had served to mobilize the country for war were either meaningless or unspeakable after defeat. Let us recall the three narratives deployed during the war to mobilize for collective action: (1) honoring the legacy of their fathers, who had given them independence from Spain; (2) defending religion; and (3) defending women from rape (and thus family from dishonor). After the war, the first two were useless. The latter, unspeakable. (Yet, as I will argue, this last one *was* useful.)

Mexicans of the generation that fought the war had failed to honor their parents' legacy: they had lost the territory liberated by their fathers. Having inherited a country stretching from northern

California to Costa Rica, within a generation they were close to becoming the colony or protectorate of a foreign power. Even after the threat of (immediate) absorption was dissipated with the Treaty of Guadalupe Hidalgo in 1848, what remained seemed, literally, not even half the country that it used to be. Being worthy of the legacy of their forefathers, for that generation, was not an inspiring trope for how they could move forward.

As for religion, it was probably the hardest-hit symbol and narrative. This was not surprising, as it had been the pivot of the national project that now seemed lost. But the obstacles for using religion as a narrative for national reconstruction went beyond that. The physical symbols of religion had been trampled—altars sacked, churches desecrated, the shrine of Guadalupe witness to the formalization of defeat—calling into question that Catholicism was what provided the transcendental/sacred glue that the polity required. The institution that lorded over religion was deeply weakened, both materially and politically. The church had financed much of the war effort. However, during the dispute with the government over financial contributions for the war, the church had very clearly reminded the government that its mission was universal and it would not commit self-sacrifice for a temporal polity.[75] Moreover, as we saw, it had actively supported a revolt against the government at a crucial moment during the war, when General Scott's invading army landed at Veracruz. It was cast by the liberals as having betrayed the country, and no longer had the financial might it had used to lord over society for centuries. Religion, too, had failed to protect us.[76]

Rape, finally, had moved from threat to reality. It had become actualized, and not only for those who suffered it and their families. As Paz's language reveals, for citizens (that is, for men) the physical experience of rape (of their women) corresponded with the historic "rape" of their country.[77] Rape was a shared experience and thus could easily become a trope. But not directly. Using MacKinnon's words when speaking of sexual abuse during the Holocaust, "survivors understandably do not want to be pornography."[78] Rape ruins identity: "Sexual atrocities shatter community, the ability to relate and cohere through a common identification, to identify with one another."[79]

And so, we find Mexicans at the end of the war in quite a conundrum: with little to hold the shared identity, they shared the experience of rape both physically and at the micro family/community level and at the macro national level. The country had not disappeared, but it had been degraded through defeat; just as survivors had not been killed, yet they had been degraded through rape. But the degradation was unspeakable, for identifying the fact of sexual assault "seems to entail identification *with* those facts."[80] And survivors do not want to be pornography. This is why the turn to territory makes sense.

Territory was lost, but it had not disappeared, just as bodies had been assaulted and degraded, but had not been killed. There remained *something* to protect. Territory and territorial integrity would emerge as the epicenter of nationalism within a decade.[81] The early leader of the Reform movement, Juan Álvarez, a protagonist of the defense of Mexico City (and the only military leader who attempted to return in support of the popular revolt of Mexico City in September 1847), very self-consciously returned to his region to reorganize his National Guard units in order to fight for land—both the land taken by the invader and the peasant lands taken by local landowners—as the epicenter of national unity.[82]

What relation is there between rape and land? Land, like women's bodies, was the patrimony of men: theirs to possess and draw fruit from.[83] Land was not a commodity (in most cases), but the direct link to collective identity and social solidarity, much like exclusive access to a woman's body is the pivot of familial identity and solidarity. Most land in Mexico then was either church-owned or collectively owned by towns and community members, known as *ejidos*, and understood as the material manifestation of the local community. Most women were the rightful possession of either their husbands to enjoy or their fathers to dispose of.

Thus, land, like rape, invoked a shared experience of both identity and defeat. But unlike rape, land could become the rallying cry and pivot point of a new national project: survival understood as territorial integrity. As we saw earlier, this was the paramount objective of the Reform generation—and also an achievement, for Mexico faced a new invasion, this time from the French, scarcely fifteen years after the end of the U.S. Invasion, that successfully engendered modern Mexico.

Territorial conquest and sexual conquest had been tied to the war from the beginning and in more than one way. This was understood by both the invading army and the invaded population:

> Writers in the aggressive country have rarely been quite so open about their interest in sexual conquest as they were in the Mexican-American War. These writers were referring to the romantic conquest of Mexican hearts and bodies, and sometimes that did take place. Sadly, though, there is much more evidence from both Mexican and American sources that American soldiers, especially the volunteers, brutally raped many Mexican women. These crimes were assaults on the bodies of Mexican women, but they were also attacks on the honor of Mexican families and the patriarchs who headed them. Honor was a crucial social value: in lamenting rapes by the Americans, the town council of Zacatecas called honor "the most precious belonging of society . . . in all its relations with the world and morality." Honor was a possession of Mexican society, but even more it was a possession of particular families, one that patriarchs should defend with their lives.[84]

I want to underline the importance of understanding these experiences from a *male* perspective; call it the *male gaze* of the war experience. In the wake of the war, Mexican men could not grieve together the rape of *their* women. That mourning had to be, if it was done at all, an intimate experience, one that they did not wish to share: rape called into question their manhood and their capacity to be *family* men, proper family men capable of protecting. Mexican men could not exact vengeance upon the perpetrator either, and therefore could not reclaim dignity—could not reinsert the sacred into the world, to use Kahn's words. Men do not engage in collective mourning of an intimate defeat. Revenge could not be reaped, and rape could not be undone. It had to be denied.[85] But the experience of defeat *and of degradation* was now a shared experience, and shared experiences were preciously few, and so valuable for the polity. Loss of territory—the rape of the nation—on the other hand *could* be collectively grieved, and it did not demand vengeance, only resistance, and resistance could be projected into the future and portrayed as successfully carried out or, as in the case of the French Invasion a decade and a half later, actually successfully carried out. Thus, Mexican men's (collective) gaze on the experience of the Invasion, I posit, shifted from the intimate experience of desecration of "their" women's bodies to the public experience of loss of "their" territories. Territory allowed for collective solidarity as well as for the assertion of dignity; rape could not do either.

## Ambivalent Conquests

This brings me to a final point, which is also about denying the experience of the war. Rape of "their" women was not all that demanded denial. Not all women who had sexual exchange with invading soldiers were raped. From the male perspective, that needed to be denied. And not all territory lost was taken. A possible narrative is that it was given, ceded (and the U.S. narrative of the Invasion, then and now, certainly makes an effort to portray the events in this manner), but that has little to no traction in the collective imagination. What is seldom argued, but enjoys better grounding in history, is that the territories *gave themselves* up.

If there is any truth to the ambivalence of both sexual exchange and territorial occupation, it is intolerable to the Mexican male gaze (in more ways than one), even to date. It had to be denied and still has to be denied. But if we want to *understand* our foundational trauma, we need to understand what the Mexican male gaze suppresses. To do so requires bringing to light the female voice and the female experience of our history, our polity, and the border. Maybe in so doing we can shed some light on some of our current troubles, both within the polity and at the border. That is a pending agenda.

Rape has become a metaphor for territorial seizure, even if it was originally the other way around. Little does it matter which represents which, for both are—in the imagination and from the male perspective—assaults on dignity that serve as the blueprint for the roles of victims and perpetrators in which Mexico–U.S. relations are often cast. In experiencing the Invasion as rape and, from that experience, anchoring the national project as one of defending territorial integrity, the men who built modern Mexico denied an important part of the war experience and, with it, a crucial aspect of the relationship between Mexico and the United States. Imagining rape and plunder is simple. But the one fact that keeps coming back, over and over, is the *complexity* of the relationship between Mexico and the United States, between Mexicans and Americans (and between both nationalities and Mexican Americans). So, let us explore what the straightforward idea of rape leaves out.

As Janet Halley exposes in "Rape in Berlin," sexual exchange in the midst of war is not nearly as binary as the (male) narratives that later signify it would have us believe. Women do not necessarily experience rape as worse than death, because sometimes it is not.[86] Some rapes are worse than others,[87] and there is always the possibility of ambivalence of rape:[88] "Women who have sex with enemy combatants will not always believe that they are being assaulted. Sometimes they want it."[89] The experience of war is far from clear cut at the micro level. They may "want it" for protection, to escape scarcity, to evade more or more brutal sexual exploitation, or for comfort in trying times. Little does it matter. The point is that there is ambivalence. Yet "in nationalist normativity, only sheer domination—only the designation 'rape'—makes women's sex with a wartime enemy tolerable."[90] Especially to men, I add.

It is relatively well documented that both during and after the Invasion, consensual sexual exchange between Mexican women and invading soldiers was relatively frequent, particularly after the military operations wound down after the fall of Mexico City. It was also shunned by Mexicans. Mexican men could not bear to think that sexual access to "their" women was anything but forced. Their manhood was already called into question by defeat on the field; they could hardly admit that they were also defeated in "their" women's hearts (or appetites) by the enemy. Like the returning German soldier at the close of "Rape in Berlin," we can imagine that Mexican men could not bear to admit to enemy soldiers' having access to Mexican women's bodies through anything but brute force. Women could only be cast as victims or traitors. There was little room for ambiguity. And so the narratives of rape or treason were the only acceptable alternatives to signifying the actual experience.

As in the case of "their" women, "their" territories had not unequivocally rejected the invader. Why would they? If—as I suggest at the beginning of this section—authority in our political imagination stems from the capacity to possess—be it territories or female bodies—and Mexican citizens (men) and authorities had failed to protect that which they possessed (women and provinces), then authority—of the state over land and of men over women—was deeply undermined. But the truth is that the Mexican government's authority over the lost provinces had been tenuous for a long time.

For long years after independence and before the U.S. Invasion, the northern provinces had flirted with separatism and had, more than once, revolted.[91] New Mexico had turned to St. Louis and, through it, to the Eastern Seaboard as its main business partner with the establishment of the Santa Fe Trail; often U.S. traders consolidated business ties through marriage within the New Mexican elite.[92] When the invading U.S. Army headed by General Stephen Kearny reached the province, local governor Manuel Armijo surprisingly and somewhat unexplainably abandoned its defense after having mobilized the population to an advantage, and capitulated without a fight.[93] California traded more with and was arguably more successfully colonized by the United States than by central Mexico.[94] Texas had been an independent republic for nine years before its annexation to the United States triggered the war.

The truth is that some parts of the territory that were settled and in the process of being developed—such as the strip of land between the Nueces and Bravo rivers in Texas, which served as an excuse for starting the war—were undoubtedly *stolen* by the United States. Yet in other parts—such as what is now northern Arizona—the border actually caught up with the Mexican frontier, which had been retracting for decades, since colonial times.[95] New Mexico and California are equivocal, as both territories were witness to resistance—as in San Diego, San Pascual, or Taos—and surprising capitulations—as in Apache Canyon and Santa Fe. And of course, Texas had been an independent republic for nine of the twenty-five years since Spain's loss of sovereignty over the land.

Placing territorial integrity at the core of the national project not only allowed for the suppression of the ambivalence represented by Mexico's shrinking from its 1821 borders to its 1848 borders, but it also echoed the demand of exclusivity over their women's bodies. Casting territorial loss as theft was the functional equivalent of casting all sexual exchange as rape. It allowed for the safeguarding of wounded male honor. It allowed the surviving males to endure a foundational trauma by removing disgrace and failure from the immediate and personal—the micro—and displacing it to the national narrative, the macro. In doing so, it reinforced a shared experience and underscored the demand for loyalty and exclusivity in the claims to both "their" women and their land. Yet it also denied at least some of the truth of both sexual exchange during the Invasion and the territorial loss resulting from the Invasion.

## Conclusion

Denial serves the purpose of making experience bearable, but it has many costs, and it is often said that war's first casualty is truth. What can we learn of ourselves by revising our history? I want to focus our attention on ambivalence because it underscores the importance of what we deny. Denial is both knowing and not knowing, according to sociologist Stanley Cohen. It is at its core a contradiction. And contradictions are what U.S.–Mexico relations are made of.

Anti-gringo sentiments crisscross Mexican history, but Mexican fascination with the United States is undeniable. It is, like anti-gringo sentiment, a collective experience for Mexicans, yet we deny it. It is an attitude that transcends social class and geographic region, but it appears in very different forms depending on where you stand. Poorer Mexicans risk life and limb by the millions in pursuit of what they believe emigration to the United States promises. Rich Mexicans buy properties across the border, educate their children there or in bicultural schools in Mexican posh neighborhoods, and have even begun celebrating Thanksgiving. Northern *regiomontanos* are caricatured as wishing they had been annexed together with Texas, but southern *oaxaqueños* increasingly populate the streets of California and often learn English, not Spanish, as a second language—second, that is, to their Mesoamerican, indigenous tongue. The Mexican government is indignant when Trump demands that Mexico *pay* for his wall, yet it deploys its army so as to *be* the wall Trump demands to keep Central American immigrants at bay.[96]

If it were only a matter of finding the truth, I would not be so concerned. Myths and lies are what countries are built on. But there is something about our traumas that we suppress that keeps haunting us. At the macro level, we cast ourselves as a nation of resilient underdogs, but in doing so we often set ourselves up for defeat. At the micro level, we claim to be *real men* because we can protect "our" women, but we still confuse protection with possession and so become the symbol for gender violence across the world, as was the case of Ciudad Juárez.

Ciudad Juárez is a good metonym for what has resulted from our foundational trauma. This border city sits across from El Paso, Texas, at the point where the Rio Bravo becomes the border between the two countries. It is named after the mythic President Benito Juárez, the hero of the Reform and founder of modern Mexico, who in his commitment to territorial integrity would govern from there, a barely existent border crossing back then, rather than recognize French sovereignty over an inch of Mexican territory. It is also where the revolt that is claimed as the origin of Mexico's current regime prevailed over the federal army and ended the three-decade-old Porfirio Díaz presidency in 1911. Historically, it is a symbol of both territorial integrity and popular democracy. More recently, throughout the 1980s and 1990s it was hailed as a boomtown: an example of the virtuous interpenetration of the U.S. and Mexican economies that would bring Mexico into the fold of developed countries. It drew on immigration across Mexico for labor and foreign investment for capital to set up *maquilas*, tax-exempt factories where commodities are assembled by cheap Mexican labor and then exported to foreign markets, most notably the United States.

Yet as the twentieth century drew to a close, Ciudad Juárez became notorious for its violence against women and the failure—due to both incapacity and unwillingness—of authorities to contain this violence. Scores of women, often young, single, immigrant women who came to Juárez to work in the maquilas, were found dead, brutalized, and raped in the open fields near the city, without a seemingly reasonable explanation. What they tell us is that Mexican men are more concerned with possessing than with protecting "their" women, and that territorial integrity is more nominal than substantive: it does not entail sovereign acts such as imposing taxes, nor is it a place where the state provides basic public services, such as transportation and public lighting, or effective police and prosecution. Is it really our territory if we don't tax it and we don't provide basic services there? In what sense do we possess it? Are the women who come to work for the maquilas really Mexican citizens, if they are left to face rape and death in the dark?

To understand the *muertas de Juárez* we need to understand both Mexican masculinity and the ways the border defines us, through our past and presently. What identities will emerge from the fields where women's bodies were left to rot? What solidarities will link the micro to the macro in such a context? How does our constitutional imagination inform the possibilities of collective action under such circumstances? The *muertas de Juárez* are a symbol—and were a foreshadowing—of the failures of the Mexican polity toward its citizens, particularly women; they are also a symbol—and a foreshadowing—of the incapacity of the Mexican State to perform basic functions such as providing security for its population and legitimately exercising its authority, as the "war on drugs" has exposed over the last dozen years. Like the war on drugs, the *muertas de Juárez* cannot be understood without reference to our asymmetrical relationship to the United States. But then again, as I've tried to argue in this chapter, neither can we explain Mexico as a shared political project without reference to the neighborhood bully. The border still defines us. It is the result of trauma. So are we. It is also the source of trauma. (And so are we.)

# AESCHYLUS AND THE MIGRANTS

JEAN MEYER

TRANSLATED BY ELLEN JONES

Aeschylus, who fought against the Persians at Marathon, was the first of the three great Greek tragedians. In 463 B.C., his play *The Suppliants* was performed in Athens. In it, fifty daughters of Danaus travel from Egypt, fleeing the sons of an Egyptian king who want to marry them against their will. They disembark in the Greek city of Argos and take refuge at the altar of Zeus. They send word to King Pelasgus that they are scared of being caught and raped by their pursuers, and beg him not to hand them over to these violent men. In order to escape masculine violence and be able to do with their bodies as they wish, they ask for permission to remain in Argos.

The king, faced with the choice of giving or denying hospitality, and with the Egyptian ambassador threatening war if the women are not handed over, exclaims: "I am confused, and fear now grips my heart, | to act or not to act . . . here we need profound and sure advice . . . so this affair will turn out well for us."[1] Fifty "barbarous" young women—foreigners—accompanied by their servants, fleeing rape and possible murder. The "profound and sure advice" comes after the king decides to consult his people to help him decide whether or not to expose the city to the inevitable complications choosing hospitality would entail. The people vote that the young women should be "free | to settle in this land," that they should "not be seized | by anyone and carried off as hostages."[2] No citizen of

This text was first published in Spanish in *El Universal:* https://www.eluniversal.com.mx/opinion/jean-meyer/esquilo-y-los-migrantes.

Argos, nor any foreigner, will be able to remove the refugees; what is more, any citizen who commits the crime of refusing to help will be automatically exiled.

How bizarre, that in this age of #MeToo and other movements fighting against sexual abuse, rape, and femicide, this age of great migrations to Europe and the United States, of xenophobic backlash and walls, this age when those who do not drown in the Mediterranean are denied entry to Europe, and when those who do not drown in the Río Grande might be lost in the Arizona desert, Aeschylus's play should seem a work of modernity and extraordinary courage.

The chorus in *The Suppliants* tells us that the girls are of a "dark and sunburned race,"[3] much like those who arrive in Mexico from the south and cross this country in the hope of getting to the United States, like those fleeing wars and everyday violence, here and also in Central America, the Middle East, Africa. Today's states are truly miserable compared to the city-state of Argos, its people, and its king, who preferred to risk war with powerful Egypt than experience the shame of offending the gods by refusing to grant asylum.

In Aeschylus's tragedy there is much talk about skin color, that physical difference that at first makes people anxious and inclined to refuse; after all, the women are "barbarians," foreigners, nothing like them. But little by little the women's brown skin is emphasized, magnified almost, until it becomes a symbol of victory over fear and cowardly defeatism. So when the fifty (would-be) rapists disembark, arrogant and certain of their victory, they instead suffer a humiliating defeat. Danaus, the father who accompanied his fifty daughters, continues to needle us: when it comes to foreigners, he says, we all have ugly words at the ready. Nothing comes more quickly to the tip of the tongue than a slur.

I discovered this remarkable text, which should be required reading for all leading politicians, when I was teaching a class on the history of Western thought. And it turns out that Aeschylus's, Sophocles's, and Euripides's plays are all about the urgent need to welcome, protect, and understand foreigners. At the end of *The Suppliants*, the chorus asks Zeus to concede victory to the women so that "justice" may "judge their cause."[4] From Abraham to Christ, the books of the Bible repeat this call. It seems we remain deaf to it.

# DROPLETS

PAULA MÓNACO FELIPE
TRANSLATED BY ELLEN JONES

## Rafael

Everything is pinkish stone and bald mountains—some with rocky peaks, others rounded off by a strong, relentless wind. It's always windy in La Rumorosa, a desert 1,232 meters above sea level that stretches between Mexicali and Tecate.

The crowd that set off from Mexicali has become more dispersed, because that's how this caravan advances: chaotically. Each person covers what ground they can. There's only a handful of us in the hut at the top of the mountain, only a few of the dozens of journalists who covered the last stretch of this first great migrant caravan, which began in Central America and arrived in northern Mexico, at the United States border, in November of 2018.

The road twists and turns and twists and turns, steep drops around every corner. It's dangerous, narrow, and very windy. Some families pass us on foot, but the majority hitch a ride up here, to the highest part of the desert. Two boys show up, alone: one of them sits in a wheelchair with bags, sacks, and backpacks hanging off it, and the other is pushing him up the hill. How does a boy in a wheelchair manage to travel thousands of kilometers on a journey that involves leaping onto buses and cars, crossing rivers, sleeping in parks, going weeks without washing, and negotiating hostile cities? How is it that another boy can have pushed him all this way? It's all I can do to take a photo, thinking to myself that they must be brothers or very close friends.

It's a steep climb, but the skinny boy is pushing hard. It's not long before they're out of sight. The Honduran family we're filming—twelve people—manages to clamber into a bus that will take them to Tijuana. My colleagues go with them; it's my turn to follow in an empty car.

Only a couple of kilometers ahead I catch up with the two boys and the wheelchair. I slow down to offer them a lift, and in only a minute or so we've crammed everything in—I don't want to lose my group.

The boy in the wheelchair is called Rafael Peralta Aguilar, and he's from Honduras; the one pushing him is called Miguel Ángel Rodríguez, and he's from Guatemala. They're not brothers, nor are they childhood friends; even though they only met a few days ago, Miguel decided to assume the task of pushing his new friend and travel companion. The bags aren't all theirs either—some belong to another migrant, a man who was cycling but had a breakdown near Mexicali. They offered to take his things to Tijuana, this pair who are pushing and wheeling the entire way.

Rafael and Miguel are short, dark skinned, and thin—very thin. Friendly, soft spoken, and always smiling. They're in their twenties but have the leathery skin of regular fieldworkers. From Rafael's hands, which seem to want to curl into fists, it's clear he suffers from some sort of bone condition. As they're getting into the car, he manages with great difficulty to take a couple of slow steps, battling legs that want to knock together, not strong enough to support him. He explains that he's not completely paralyzed, though he finds it very difficult to walk. He began the journey on crutches but couldn't keep up with the pace; along the way, someone gave him the wheelchair.

Rafael has worked his whole life, ever since he was a child. His physical problems began in his teenage years, when he started to gradually lose mobility. He never stopped working, though, almost always in the fields near San Pedro Sula, where he was born and raised. His most recent job, just a couple of months ago, before setting off on this journey, was installing wire fences. Just talking about it, a smile spreads over his face: the memory takes him back to the lush green of his beloved Honduras. He might be running away, but he still talks longingly of his home country. He earned a pittance there, not enough to live on, and was lonely. His mother died, and with his health getting more complicated he started to feel like a burden on his family—on his brothers, who had their own children—so he decided to leave and look for somewhere else. He isn't just trying to find a way of making money; Rafael is also traveling in the hope of finding a cure for the disease that threatens to debilitate him.

"What disease is it?"

"I don't know."

"What did the doctors say? What was the diagnosis?"

"I never saw a doctor. No doctor ever examined me in Honduras."

There was no doctor or hospital in his community, nor did he have the money to travel somewhere else to get checked over. No care was available. In twenty-one years, Rafael was never diagnosed.

He says this without resentment, his voice still gentle, as though the situation were inevitable or divine. I can't hide my angry surprise, so he adds that it's different now, that when they were offered temporary shelter in Mexico City a doctor came to check him over. They said he was suffering from a degenerative disease, but that was pretty much all.

Rafael also says that he's been here before. He migrated for the first time a couple of months ago and got as far as Guanajuato. The Mexican border agents caught and deported him. Once he was back in his old town, he realized there was nothing left for him there. He didn't even have anywhere to stay, because in order to pay for the journey he'd sold his mattress and his only piece of furniture, which was all he owned. He learned then about the caravan, waited for it to pass through, and joined it. He had traveled almost the entire route, crossing Honduras, part of El Salvador, Guatemala, and the whole of Mexico—he's finally only a stone's throw from the U.S. border, which can be glimpsed every now and then from the road.

The day comes to an end on Federal Motorway Number 2. The light disappears in a spectacular sunset. Rafael gestures at the last scrap of sun, the colors in the sky, the pinkish glow of the stones in the evening light. He smiles, excited. He talks about how beautiful this place is, how lucky he feels to be part of the caravan, how happy he is to be seeing such beautiful places.

## A Bribe or a Bullet

The wall has existed for a while. It has bars, netting, metal panels, electric fencing, sensors, barbed wire, and huge struts you can squeeze a finger through, but not a hand. In Tijuana it extends out into the sea. It also has several layers: an old, metal, three-meter-high outer barrier that the locals jump up onto "for the photo-op," and behind it a new, intelligent wall.

The San Jeronimo–Santa Teresa bridge, on the U.S.-Mexico border where Chihuahua meets New Mexico, is seven meters high and opens every now and again to let thousands of animals through. It's mainly young bulls and cows that cross from Mexico to the United States, born here to be fattened up over there. From the other side comes a huge number of horses.

"Modern! Convenient! Quick!" boasts the New Mexico Border Authority. "Hundreds of thousands of cattle cross every year, making this port of entry the biggest livestock import and export facility on the Mexican border."

The same logic seems to apply to animals as it does to humans here—they are treated like goods. Several people wait on this side, keeping an eye on any movements beyond the wire fencing. Somebody presses a button, and the wall opens to let seven beautiful horses pass, walking elegantly on their slender legs. On this side nobody moves, nobody is allowed near the dividing line. From the other side comes someone on horseback, but they aren't asked for any papers. They aren't even asked their name.

Not far from here, on the border bridge, buses full of horses also pass through without any holdups. They bring old, badly treated animals, injured and wild, known as mustangs. They have no use for them over there anymore, so they send them off for slaughter, to be killed in Mexico. They do it quickly, no photos or recordings allowed.

In the neighborhood of Anapra, on the outskirts of Ciudad Juárez, in the state of Chihuahua, the wall ends suddenly. The same thing happens in Nido de las Águilas, on the outskirts of Tijuana, in the state of Baja California: the wall peters out on an arid hillside. Jumping over looks easy, but don't be fooled: where there's no wall here, instead there are landowners. They're coyotes, cartel and gang members, henchmen, assassins. They'll only let you cross if you pay them what they want. It's expensive: a bribe or a bullet.

## Rober

Rober, some people call him. To others, he's Xicali.

Roberto Márquez has lived for more than ten years by the Tijuana canal, a thin, sewage-clogged waterway right on the border with the United States, hailing distance from San Ysidro and San Diego.

He sleeps under a bridge, on cardboard boxes that he later folds up and hides in a corner. He covers himself with a blanket that he also tucks away each morning, and he washes in the water from an outdoor tap on a street with cars racing by. He walks along the bank of the canal, where dozens of men—most of them are men—are emerging from their own shelters, shelters that are nothing more than different kinds of outdoors. Some sleep under bridges or settle themselves down between bushes, while others spend the night inside the sewers, because even though a stream of diluted shit might flow along their length, they at least provide a roof over your head and some form of protection.

These men are deportees—neglected, lonely beings who exist on the margins of the city of Tijuana. Some are recently arrived, having just been thrown out of the United States, some are looking to get to the other side of the border, and some, like Roberto, can't quite remember how that first day of abandonment somehow became years, a whole decade.

Every morning, the deportees head to the Padre Chava Salesian Canteen, where more than a thousand free breakfasts are served up. The space is a migrant support center set up by the Salesian Society in 1999 and manages to survive thanks to help of various kinds—cash donations, food, volunteers.

"What's happening to deportees is especially cruel because they've already gone and given the best years of their working life over there, only to be thrown out like they're trash—it's like, we're washing our hands of you," says Margarita Padilla, who has been in charge of the canteen for a number of years.

As they move through Mexico, migrants are offered help mainly from a range of religious organizations. But that solidarity doesn't come from the Curia, archbishops, or prelates: it's always members of dissident, anti-traditional movements, such as those who follow Liberation theology, Indian or Latin American theologies, and forward-thinking factions within congregations. There's Fray Tomás and the La 72 migrant shelter in Tabasco (southern Mexico); Father Pedro Pantoja and Bishop Raúl Vera in Coahuila (northern Mexico); and the Hermanos en el Camino shelter, founded by the priest Alejandro Solalinde, in Oaxaca (southern Mexico).

After breakfast, Roberto goes back to the canal. He walks a lot, his steps weary but firm. His body is tough, visibly muscled. He is about fifty and still strong. Sometimes he finds temporary work, though it doesn't come easy, because there aren't many who'll employ someone like him, someone who lives on the street. He earns little, lives almost entirely without money, and when he does have a few pesos he almost always spends them on a fix—a powder that when heated up becomes a liquid, which he injects. It's sold down by the canal, everyone knows where. They say it's heroin, but it costs twenty Mexican pesos—about one dollar. Many deportees use it to pass the afternoon.

When he shoots up, Roberto loses his implacable look, and his stringy, muscled body relaxes, allowing him some respite. When he shoots up, Roberto talks. He talks about how he was born on the border but on this side, in Mexicali. How his father was a coyote whom he accompanied to the United States in 1964, when he was a child. How he lived there for more than forty-eight years. He had a pretty stable life, a wife, children, work, and a house, but one day a relative of his was killed. He knew who had done it and couldn't stop himself: he went to avenge the insult. He killed a man with a knife, and so they locked him up.

In prison, death came knocking for him again. He killed two other men because that's what it's like inside, he says, kill or be killed. I got these tattoos in there, he says, showing his back covered with a virgin and the faces of a baby and two adults. The designs are black, a bit messy, fading here and there. They were done with *baby oil*, he says. He repeats the words firmly, in English: *baby oil*. He tells me how prisoners fiddled with a discman motor so it would work as a tattoo machine and scraped his skin until the dye-mixed-with-oil sunk in. Inside for almost twenty years, his skin was the least of his worries.

His final conviction got him deported—the U.S. authorities get rid of thousands of people that way, preferring to throw them out of the country than spend whatever it costs to keep them locked up. And when he arrived in Mexico, Roberto didn't know where to go. He didn't know any family there, not a single relative, nor did he know the name of the town he'd originally come from. Everyone he cared about was in the United States. That's why he stayed on the canal, that filthy river right up against the border.

When he shoots up, Roberto stares at the wall with all its barbed wire, electrified fencing, cameras, sensors, Border Patrol officers on duty night and day. He looks at the wall and says, one of these days he'll cross it. The day after tomorrow, this weekend, soon.

When he shoots up, Roberto doesn't look like a man who knows how to kill. A tear escapes him as he's overcome with nostalgia. He tells me he has grandchildren he's never met. They're only little. He'd like to see them one day.

## Adrián

In Mexico there are ghost towns, empty because their inhabitants fled for their lives when a criminal group seized control of the area. But there are also half-way towns, nameless limbos. How else would you describe a neighborhood where half the houses are lived in and the other half abandoned? What should we call a place where some people have fled and the rest stay only because they have no alternative?

On the edge of Ciudad Juárez, in the state of Chihuahua, is Riberas del Bravo. Riberas del Bravo is a social housing development with 12,062 homes of fifty square meters each, built to house *maquiladora* workers. The city is badly planned and prone to flooding, with barely a handful of schools and thousands of empty houses. According to the Municipal Institute for Research and Planning, there are almost 100,000 empty houses in Ciudad Juárez, 27,000 of which are in Riberas del Bravo and four other neighborhoods in the southeast. There are thousands of houses whose doors and windows have been stolen. No light fittings or wiring, skeleton homes with whole chunks taken out of them. Houses full of trash tossed out by people taking advantage of their neglect, or overflowing with the litter left behind by those who use them as squat-cum-drug dens. Houses where people dump bodies.

> Three young girls and a man were murdered in their own home, shot with more than 100 bullets in the Riberas del Bravo neighborhood of Ciudad Juárez, state of Chihuahua. According to the Chihuahua Attorney General, the three girls were aged 4, 13, and 14, and the adult with them, their uncle, was aged 25. (*El Heraldo*, August 26, 2019)

Small houses with two bedrooms, a kitchen, and a bathroom. Four walls that once were a vision of progress and now bear the marks of violence. They came to kill the old man who lived in that house there; in this one, some kids saw their older brother get murdered; that one's got a security guard outside because the man who lives there reported some other guys who were bad news. Each house has its own story, though some of them have already been forgotten.

Art collectives have made proposals to brighten the houses up, various authorities have promised to restore them, and cars drive around honking their horns, their drivers offering to sort out people's documents for a decent price. Still, not much changes in these neighborhoods, half-alive, half-abandoned, a mere stone's throw from the United States. Because from the windows in Riberas del Bravo you can see the neighborhoods of Angie, Aldama, and Alameda. You can see them through the wall, which here is made of an ochre-colored wire mesh.

On this side: streets with assaults, shootouts, and murders just waiting to happen. On the other side: El Paso, the second-safest city in the United States. On this side, houses with barred doors and boarded-up windows; on the other side, homes with front gardens and no security in sight.

Adrián Hernández was born in the cotton fields of Valle de Juárez.

He first moved to the city to work in the *maquiladoras* and then emigrated with his girlfriend, Gabriela Castaneda. They went to the other side, the safe side. They had three children there. They were happy. The parents worked and the children grew. The youngest, Abraham, was born with a medical condition, but the U.S. health system always guaranteed him the care he needed.

In 2016, a day like any other, they were in *la trailer*, their mobile home, the most comfortable affordable living arrangements for many migrants, when immigration agents showed up and took Adrián away. They deported him. The family was separated: his wife and children in El Paso, he in Ciudad Juárez. Gabriela is still in the United States, the sole caretaker of their three children. Adrián lives in Riberas del Bravo, that half-alive, half-abandoned neighborhood. He found himself a little house near his parents and nieces and nephews. He painted it a light, soft green, bought a television and a bed. That's where he spends his days, alone, battling the sadness that comes and goes, and comes again.

He works in construction from Monday to Friday and sometimes Saturday mornings. At noon on Saturdays he runs to pick up his kids at a border bridge. They are U.S. citizens, so can come and see him. Adrián hugs them, takes them home, and makes the most of the hours they have. They chat, tell each other about their week, meet up with the rest of the family that's still in Mexico. They watch TV, go for a walk, or buy an *elote*, a corn on the cob. The next evening, Adrián takes them back to the port of entry, and the kids return to the United States, where their mother is waiting for them. They could all move to Ciudad Juárez—they've thought about it—but they choose to stay where the kids have access to education and medical attention, where they can live more safely. Adrián could cross undocumented, but if they caught him he'd go to prison. From the pavement outside his little green house, Adrián can just about see El Paso, where he has a wife he never sees and children he can only hug on the weekend. Thirty hours a week.

## The Alvarado Family

The twins were born on November 3, 1995: Nitza Sitlaly and Mitzy Paola. Their mother, Nitza Paola Alvarado, was sixteen years old. She didn't have a partner and faced giving birth alone, without telling her family, because she felt like motherhood was her responsibility. Two and a half years later, on June 29, 1998, she gave birth to a third child, Deisy.

She was a single mother providing for the three of them, as well as for her parents, who were by then too old to keep working in the fields. She worked several jobs, almost always as an administrator. She managed to buy a house and a truck. Nitza and her three girls lived in Ciudad Juárez, in the state of Chihuahua, but they spent the holidays in Ejido Benito Juárez, in the district of Buenaventura, where the rest of the enormous Alvarado family lives.

It was there that, on the night of December 29, 2009, soldiers from the 25th Infantry Battalion showed up at the house of one of her relatives and took Nitza Paola and her cousin José Angel Alvarado Herrera away. The soldiers were in uniform. A few minutes later, they also dragged Rocío Irene Alvarado Reyes out of her room, beating her. Several witnesses reported the kidnapping of these three cousins, but no one has heard from them since that night: they remain missing.

The Alvarado family went out to look for them immediately. First on the dusty streets, following footprints in the torchlight. Then at the district attorney's office and the army barracks. They found Nitza Paola's truck there but were told no one knew anything about it. They spoke with the neighbors, writing everything down in notebooks. They discovered that many people had gone missing in the area, especially since the arrival of the army and the launch of the military and federal police operation known as Coordinated Operation Chihuahua in March 2008. Some came back beaten and tortured; others never returned.

The Alvarado family went on. They reported what had happened at every opportunity, went every day to the barracks. On January 9, 2010, they managed to get several authorities, including Colonel Élfego Luján, head of the 25th Battalion, to agree to a meeting.

María Alvarado—small, steady-voiced, and at that time a supermarket check-out girl—confronted the colonel. She demanded he tell her where her sister and cousins were. "I'm not scared of you, no, I'm not scared of you," she shouted at them all. It was after that meeting that the threats against various members of the Alvarado family began. "We're going to beat you to a pulp," someone was told over the phone. Someone else was almost hit by a car while out on their bike. Their house was graffitied, people started harassing them. Everyone was worried about the girls—fourteen-year-old Sitlaly and Mitzy, and Deisy, eleven.

They took them to live in Cuernavaca, where they were kept locked up in the house of an aunt, who was petrified. Later, they went to Hermosillo, but it didn't feel safe there either. From there they went back to Chihuahua, but to the state capital, and then to Ejido Benito Juárez. Four cities in four years, constantly having to move because the military wouldn't leave them alone. They said it's become difficult; they can't even enjoy an afternoon in the park anymore. Uniformed soldiers outside their school, soldiers outside the front door every hour of the day. Their Aunt María and their grandfather Ascensión decided the best thing would be to go somewhere properly safe, to another country. They gave away almost all their belongings, locked the house up, and headed to the border that same afternoon, carrying one suitcase each. Nitza Paola's three daughters, her parents, and her sister, who brought her husband and four children—they all fled. Eleven members of the Alvarado family, forced into exile.

They turned themselves in at the Ciudad Juárez border bridge, but even there they didn't find the safety they'd longed for, because seeking asylum in the United States is something akin to committing a crime. When they got to the bridge, they were separated: the grandparents, the aunt, and her children were freed a few hours later; the uncle was transferred to a detention center; and nothing was heard from the girls for two days. Don Ascensión cried disconsolately, thinking that on top of his kidnapped daughter he'd now had his grandchildren taken from him too. The girls were moved to a center for "unaccompanied minors" because according to the U.S. authorities their grandparents, aunt, and uncle could not take responsibility for them; instead, they demanded the presence of the girls' missing mother.

Mitzy, Sitlaly, and Deisy were locked up for nearly three months with barely a few minutes of phone calls permitted. They got out thanks to the Spector family—the lawyer Carlos and his wife, Sandra. They were by that time seventeen and fourteen years old. Two years later, they had finished secondary school, achieved permanent residency, and integrated into the El Paso community. With a group of other migrants, they founded an organization called Mexicans in Exile. They study and work, they pay their bills, and now they have their own car. Deisy speaks perfect English.

The rest of the family, however, still hasn't gotten the right papers to be able to stay legally. They live in fear of deportation but haven't stopped demanding information about their missing relatives. They took the case to the Inter-American Court of Human Rights. In 2018 they were summoned to the decisive hearing, and María, a key witness, asked the United States for permission to go and make a statement. Permission was denied, and so a dilemma presented itself: she could remain safely in the United States, or travel to Costa Rica to make a statement.

She decided to testify. She spoke for her allotted thirty minutes in San José, making the most of every second. Her words, though crucial, were also costly, because they meant she could not return to the United States. She now lives in Mexico, where she is pursued. She is in constant danger, far away from her children, parents, nieces, and nephews.

Despite everything, the Alvarado family won the first international ruling against Mexico for the militarization of security tasks. The Inter-American Court of Human Rights passed the judgment on November 28, 2018.

# BARBARIANS IN THE PRESENCE OF BARBARIANS

EMILIANO MONGE
TRANSLATED BY VICTOR MEADOWCROFT

## I

Out beyond the walls, in the impossible distance, far from the cities, city-states, and modern states, there were, are, and always will be barbarians.

It did not matter that these barbarians were not bound by the idea of a single god, they were the barbarians; it does not matter that the women of these barbarians share the same social roles as their men, they are the barbarians; it will not matter that these barbarians sing, dance, compose symphonies, paint, or narrate fictions, they will be the barbarians.

They were, are, and will be barbarians because they were, are, and will be other; because they were, are, and will be different, enigmatic, and dangerous; because they have not been and will not be the civilized peoples who live within the walls: that agglomeration of sticks, stones, bricks, cinder blocks, and poured concrete that seeks to protect those on the inside, and should repel those without.

Walls, fences, moats, trenches, minefields, free zones, or postmodern walls: as well as the physical manifestation of the fear, hatred, and prejudices of those who—without even realizing—choose to

---

This text was a lecture Emiliano Monge gave at the Cátedra Nelson Mandela at UNAM in November 2017, and later published at the *Revista de la Universidad* in 2018.

live locked inside, all of these constructions have been, are, and will be the very denial of an existence, culture, and even *collective superego* that infuriates those who proclaim themselves the civilized peoples.

The distance from the other, finally, does not just constrict, limit, and condemn: the barrier that is raised before others, whatever form this barrier takes—we should not forget that borders were, are, and also will be symbolic, signifying, and mental: we need only think of the social classes, inequality between men and women, or distinctions still arising from the color of skin—brings with it the empire of sameness, an empire that leads, historically and inevitably, toward fascism.

Otherwise, how else can we explain the rise of far-right movements around the world? Otherwise, how else should we interpret the ascent to power of individuals like Donald Trump, Jair Bolsonaro, or Boris Johnson, completely disconnected, ignorant, apathetic, and even disgusted by, with, and before otherness, which is to say, before anything that is not their own image or likeness reflected in a mirror?

The empire of sameness has infected us and has infected democracy from within. That is why, today, democracy would appear to be suffering from an autoimmune disease, an illness by which the system attacks itself, an ailment that may yet prove fatal: the sickness of *me and mine*.

An affliction whose first manifestation was the festival of borders and whose most recent incarnation, according to Byung-Chul Han, perhaps the most important contemporary Korean philosopher, is social networks: that tool that was supposed to fly across borders ended up being their best imitator and disseminator.

Today, instead of seeing, searching for, and conversing with what is different, people search, on their screens, for those who think like them, who dress like them, who listen to the same music, who laugh at the same joke.

In short, for those who, rather than representing an *other*, represent an *other-oneself.*

## II

Without doubt, the greatest danger to arise from the conversion of the *other* into the *other-oneself* is that walls, both physical and symbolic, no longer prove necessary, since that which is different, rather than presenting a threat or an enigma, has been transformed into an invisible entity.

This takes place as much within the boundaries of a nation as beyond its borders: without noticing, we barbarians, who in another time would lay siege to the palace together, have bought, accepted, and participated in a highly intelligent, well-designed, and perverse game implemented by those proclaiming themselves the civilized power.

Just as they have created ghettos—a white man who only believes in what is white, who seeks out other whites, as shaven-headed as he is, who wishes to form a herd, and, rather than opposing the coffee-colored, the yellow-skinned, or the black, decides that none of them are there, that none of these are real—we, the barbarians, have created our own: a middle-class Mexican academic seeks another middle-class academic from Spain, El Salvador, Australia, Colombia, India, or Argentina, who shares the same reading, thoughts, and beliefs in order to form a herd, under the assumption that anyone who is not his *other-oneself* does not exist.

We live, as Enrique Díaz Álvarez wrote in his excellent book *El Traslado, narrativas contra la idiotez y la barbarie*, in the era of long-sighted men and women: men and women who are able to see what is taking place—or what they desire, or worse yet, need to identify with—thousands of miles away, but are prevented from seeing what is happening a couple of yards from them—or what they do not desire, or worse yet, no longer know how to identify with.

The *other*, who is not the *other-oneself*, has not only become invisible; the *other* has become nobody, nothing, never. And this *other*, I repeat, is not even to be found beyond the fence, the palisade, the moat, the wall, the trench, the minefield, the free zone, or the postmodern wall. No: this *other* who is not the *other-oneself* is a brother, a neighbor, a co-worker, the pedestrian we almost bump into, the woman we buy vegetables from without exchanging so much as a couple of words, your children's teacher, whose face you are unable to locate in your memory despite having seen it on so many occasions, the migrant whom we unwittingly run over, because we barely noticed he was there, because it isn't true that he was there, because there was nobody there.

## III

Because we barely noticed he was there, because it isn't true that he was there, because there was nobody there.

How else except through an adherence to the *other-oneself* and the definitive split from the traditional notion of *otherness* can we account for—just as we must in the case of the far right and figures like Trump, Bolsonaro, or Johnson—the voluntary and collective blindness in the face of a tragedy like the one being experienced by migrants today?

Despite there being no border between the First World and the so-called Third World—where, right now, at this moment, as I read you these words, as you listen to them, there isn't a humanitarian tragedy taking place—it is not just a case of this tragedy *appearing to be* invisible, but rather of it *having become* so.

Nobody, nothing, never: those six Senegalese migrants are not drowning in the Mediterranean Sea; nor are those two Filipino mothers saying goodbye to their daughters, soon to meet with the man who will later sell them in Japan; nor are those Somali families attempting to reach the oil fields of the Emirates, where men and women will be exploited equally until their last breath; nor are all those Salvadorian, Honduran, and Guatemalan teenagers, all of those boys and girls forced to abandon their countries before being swallowed up by gangs, escaping, terrified and disoriented, from their possible Mexican rapists.

Or maybe they are: because despite the invisibility we have inadvertently allowed to become real, despite the fact that the civilized peoples have imposed an adherence to the *other-oneself* among the barbarians, despite the empire of sameness, and despite our long-sightedness, right now, at this very moment, a number of human beings *are* drowning; as I stand here reading, various mothers *are* saying farewell to their daughters, and, as you continue to listen, in this land we call Mexico, some young child *is* disappearing.

The walls, once vertical constructions that later became symbolic, have ended up converted into territories: in the Third World, particularly in places where it comes into contact with the First, the nation-state has given way to the trench-state, whose political system is, evidently, the immune-diseased democracy I referred to at the beginning of this text and whose greatest social conflict is the mass voluntary blindness around which I have already circled several times.

## IV

What is important, then, is to find the way to cure our system, so sick with itself, and, at the same time, return sight to our eyes. That is to say, to give back to the other his or her outline, his or her figure, his or her truth, and his or her existence, while offering ours to any other in exchange.

We need to shatter the empire of sameness in order to escape from the trap of the *other-oneself*. The nobody, nothing, never should become the everyone, everything, always. We must search for, find, and share with those who are not like us, see ourselves in mirrors that reflect those images that, on first impression, seem deformed to us, but that, in reality, complete and improve us instead of containing and diminishing us.

The paths to achieving this are various and disparate, but all, of course, are long and complicated. Each of us, however, should find our own: the manner in which we will escape from ourselves in order to be and to understand those who are near at hand; the manner in which we will refashion the idea we have carried with us of civilization and barbarity; the strategy we will appropriate in order to understand that above accordance there is always difference; that to be, when all is said and done, is to be all others: the *I* only becomes diluted in the singular—it is the plural that affirms it and affords it meaning.

So, what is my path?

Empathy. I am convinced that this, the empathy that can only be found within literature, painting, music, or laughter, is one of the exits available to us.

Because there is no better or faster vehicle for becoming other, for escaping ourselves and experiencing the life of another human being, than fiction. Fiction gives a face to the drowning Senegalese man, a backstory to the Filipino mother and daughter who have just said their goodbyes, a life to the Salvadorian boy who is running along jungle trails, trying to prevent those men from catching him.

But, moreover, fiction has the power to transform a humanitarian tragedy into something much closer to every one of us: a human tragedy. And this, it seems to me, is the key to opening the gate, be this in a palisade, a fence, a wall, or a postmodern wall.

Finally, "the Salvadorian boy who is running along jungle trails, trying to prevent those men from catching him" will never be the same as:

> Óscar, who has only just turned twelve and was forced to abandon his country after the Mara Salvatrucha

issued his death sentence, a sentence his brother, Alexander, must carry out; he runs along trails, thirty yards ahead of the men who are following him and who gradually, stride by stride, are gaining ground: they've been able to eat and drink recently; he, on the other hand, the youngest son of Carlos and Beatriz, he whose skinny, sinewy legs are struggling to support his body, equally skinny and sinewy, hasn't eaten for three or four days. And he's had no more than a couple of drops of water: that's why his lips are completely cracked, that's why his eyes are so deeply set. Ahuuuu . . . ahuuuu . . . Óscar's breathing in the silence of the jungle—at this hour the sun sends to sleep anything that isn't fleeing—sounds increasingly strained: ahuuuu . . . ahuuu. And those men are getting closer and closer: ahuuuu . . . ahuuuu . . . maybe this is why, for the first time, Óscar considers stopping, collapsing onto the ground, leaving everything behind.

## V

I would like to end by focusing in even greater detail on the possibilities of story, now not only in terms of fiction: I, Emiliano Monge, a thirty-nine-year-old Mexican political scientist and writer, six feet and three inches tall, uncircumcised and resolved never to go back to the dentist, fear, understand, and experience *up close* more about the transformation of a human being into a subject divested of even the right to have rights—as Hannah Arendt once wrote—through the story that Alexander, one night in November, after having met on twelve previous occasions and smoked our way through a couple of packs of cigarettes, finally shared with me about the torture inflicted on him by some members of the Zeta cartel, than from the hundreds of pages of essays, academic texts, and even news reports I may have read.

As Alexander described the jungle encampment where they held him captive; as he talked of the persistent birdsong and the sobs of the other men and women locked up with him; as he described the darkness and humidity and heat and smells in the room where men would have their backs broken so they couldn't escape but would still be able to make phone calls to family and friends in the United States; as he narrated before me the rolling up of shirt-sleeves of the bastard who would pummel him, shove a phone in his face, and order him to ask those same family members of his for the four-thousand-dollar ransom; as he told me how, after hanging up, they would beat him with the flat of a machete, the size of which did not figure in Alexander's memory or his account, I was also the captive and the abused. And I knew then that on the day I wrote his story, in addition to the machete's suddenly recovering its size, someone else might also become the captive and the abused.

Because we should be clear about the fact that art and literature, more than conveying knowledge, should aim to convey a personal experience. A novel, a performance, or a painting should be directed toward affectivity rather than intelligence. Novelists and artists might handle the same subjects as sociologists, political scientists, and journalists, but we should never do so with the same intentions. As the Peruvian writer Julio Ramón Ribeyro stated: "The novelist fails when he attempts to compete by communicating knowledge, instead of accepting that what he should be communicating is an experience. Our purpose is to encourage participation, to offer an invitation to the festival of life, but not describe the menu or provide a recipe."

This is why I repeat: if anything can assist us in hunting down the beast of the *other-oneself* and bringing an end to our long-sightedness, if there exists any medicine capable of curing democracies of their autoimmune diseases, if there is any way of fighting back against walls and borders, it is through the stories communicated by art, music, and literature, capable of embodying, within our experience, all of those other experiences that seem distant to us. All of those other experiences that once resembled the stuff of barbarians.

# THE DILEMMA: TO MIGRATE, OR NOT TO MIGRATE

PORFIRIO MUÑOZ LEDO
TRANSLATED BY JESSIE MENDEZ SAYER

*Migration* is defined as the phenomenon by which "people leave their place of residence in order to establish themselves in another country or region." It has taken place since the very beginning of human history; it was how the world came to be inhabited and is the origin of modern nationalities. Whereas in the past these exoduses toward less-populated areas were facilitated, in today's world hostility and even persecution have been unleashed largely against those who came from the global south, or who belong to ethnicities considered inferior. With globalization comes the movement of all economic factors, except the workforce. Goods, services, and capital are moved from one place to another, while the free movement of human beings is fiercely resisted.

More than 258 million migrants around the world live outside of their country of birth, representing 3.4 percent of Earth's population and contributing 9 percent of global GDP ($7 billion a year), which is equal to 45 percent of the United States' GDP. Vulnerability and xenophobia have resulted in the disappearance of 3,341 migrants around the world in 2019 so far, despite the fact that every year 27 million people migrate, 80 percent of whom are girls, boys, and young people who leave their countries, alone or accompanied by their parents.

---

This text was first published in Spanish in two different articles in *El Universal* in 2019: "El dilema: migrar o no migrar" and "Todos somos México."

Migration is a human right enshrined in the founding documents of the United Nations, beginning with the International Covenant on Civil and Political Rights, in which it is stipulated that "everyone shall be free to leave any country, including his own." Accordingly, it determines that the economic conditions must exist that allow people to remain within their own countries. In short, the right to migrate and the right to not migrate are equally consecrated by international instruments.

The Guadalupe-Hidalgo treaties, which marked the end of the Mexican-American War of 1846, granted broad migratory, political, and economic rights to those Mexicans who remained in United States' territory. As the bilateral possibilities of demanding this right were gradually adopted, and despite our country's traditional diplomacy, we decided to promote world instruments that would protect the rights of our countrymen. In 1980 we promoted the International Convention on the Protection of the Rights of All Migrant Workers and Members of Their Families, the "All" underlining the inclusion of those "illegal" migrants who have become known as "undocumented" since then. This instrument was approved in 1990 by the United Nations Assembly, but Mexico did not ratify it until 1999 for fear of the reaction from the United States, and also because they rejected the obligation to allow migrants in. Eventually, the doublespeak of accepting the close of the southern border in exchange for migratory tolerance on the northern border prevailed.

The disproportionate increase in the number of migrants on national territory, whether Mexico be the destination or just a transit country, raises the problem again in menacing terms. It demands a thorough redefinition of principles and methods, which in my opinion must be constitutional, by means of an update of Article 11 in which we must establish our unshakeable resolutions on migration. Mexico, during a prolonged period of its history, maintained a noble tradition of asylum and refuge, not only for the protection of the politically persecuted, as state policy, among which the victims of the fascist coups in Spain and Chile stand out.

We must specify the scope of both asylum and refuge. Both are a form of migration caused by humanitarian factors. The first consists of the protection offered by receiving countries to people who have well-founded fears of persecution on the basis of their sex, religion, nationality, or political opinions. The second consists of the safeguarding of people facing a humanitarian crisis originating from economic, political, and social factors, as well as armed conflicts or natural disasters. This is laid out in the UN Convention Relating to the Status of Refugees of 1951 and the Protocol of 1967, which were not ratified by Mexico until the year 2000. In 2011, we passed the Law on Refugees and Extra Protection, which regrettably grants the Mexican authorities the prerogative to find out the causes of expulsion in every refuge applicant's case, which is impossible and goes against the principles of international law. To make up for the errors of nation-states and protect those being persecuted in their own countries, sanctuary cities have been created, mostly in North America and also in Mexico City, whose constitution grants migrants the protection of the law and ensures they will not be criminalized by their migrant status.

Considering these advances, the servile attitude of our government regarding the Central American caravan accentuates its determination to do Washington's dirty work for it. It seems to be the perfect crime. Nothing would make Donald Trump happier than for southern migrants to be detained in Mexico. We humor him in his ranting and raving and save him having to pay for expensive walls in return for our laughable fences. We helped him win his first election. Now we are offering him a free gift without any kind of reciprocity on his part. There are many loose ends that need to be investigated; for example, the promoters and financiers of this shift, among which various U.S. organizations have been discovered. A manifest expression of slipping borders.

We have proclaimed ad nauseam that our relationships have diversified, but our compliance has been paltry. We have only eight embassies in Africa, compared to Cuba and Brazil, which have set up more than thirty; our presence in the Middle East, Europe, and Oceania is sparse, and is unfortunately on the decline in Latin America and the Caribbean. Our capacity for exportation is meager, and we are in deficit with all the regions of the world except the United States, with whose economy ours overlaps. We maintain a two-faced diplomacy. Close to sixty consulates in North America and eighty embassies around the world. The latter underpin our advances within the United Nations and are a vehicle for the affirmation of our principles. Foreign Secretary Marcelo Ebrard has said that "our country has the backing of the whole world to lead the battle against xenophobia, racism and hate crimes." He also heralds the recuperation of our leadership among developing countries. I would add that the circumstances are ideal for Mexico to become the most influential country in the United States. The priority is undoubtedly to defend the integrity and the rights of our people and their descendants, who by 2018 represented more than 10 percent of the United States' population.

Despite pressure coming from Trump, we have an obligation to intensify our support and solidarity with those who migrate. Mexico has all the necessary arguments to reassert its rights in its negotiations with the United States and to avoid falling for the deplorable concessions by which Donald Trump uses us for his electoral benefit. The right to migrate is therefore essential.

# MAKE ART, NOT WALLS

NATIONAL HUMAN RIGHTS COMMISSION, MEXICO[1]
TRANSLATED BY ELLEN JONES

Images continue to be a universal form of expression that can convey messages both quickly and powerfully. There's a lot of wisdom in the phrase "a picture speaks a thousand words." And the truth is that a large part of our knowledge and understanding is derived from what we see. Until we see it, we often do not fully understand a given situation; until we see something, we may not believe it.

There are many ways of displaying images for our appreciation. Mexico, for instance, is home to the great mural tradition in which images are drawn or painted directly onto walls of different kinds. *Muralismo*, as it is known, was of particular significance for this country during the twentieth century: as an artistic movement it sought to communicate historical events to its viewers in a way that promoted a particular ideological perspective. This new form of artistic expression developed into a "school" of art.

The Make Art, Not Walls project supports this form of artistic expression—public art, but muralismo in particular—by connecting it with the topic of migration. Migrants are, first and foremost, people, and as such they carry culture with them when they move. They sing and they dance; they write and they read; they cry and they smile; they imagine and they also paint. Each of those things

---

This essay was originally published as part of *Murales, No Muros*, by Edgar Corzo Sosa, Elvia Lucía Flores Ávalos, Ximena Pérez García, and Keisdo Shimabukuro Rivera (Mexico City: National Commission for Human Rights, 2019), available online at https://www.cndh.org.mx/documento/murales-no-muros.

is an expression of culture. You might think that migrants would naturally stay away from walls, which represent an impediment to their journey and need to escape. Walls are associated with imprisonment and isolation, with a feeling of being cut off. Walls, because of their very nature, are dams on our liberty, obstacles to free thinking. All these associations are especially pertinent in the case of walls built to stop migration—an idea that our neighbors to the north have been over-reliant on recently. The aim of Make Art, Not Walls is to forge a connection between walls and migration; to position walls not as an obstacle to migration, but rather as a means of its expression.

The project aims, very successfully I believe, to use art to transform walls into an expression of the migrant experience; to enable walls to express the values and cultural knowledge migrants bring with them when they travel, and thus convert them into mural art. The murals presented in this essay are not intended as a form of social criticism, but rather as a cultural expression of the reality migrants are living on a daily basis. It would be difficult, impossible, really, to reflect all aspects of the migration phenomenon in the eight murals presented here; let them be seen, instead, simply as a first exercise in migratory mural art. These murals, created over the course of a number of years, make visible migration as the result of human tragedy: shortages, family separation, violence, poverty. At the same time, however, they also try to express the importance of dignity, equality, and fairness, to which all migrants have a right, because—let me reiterate—migrants are, first and foremost, people.

Without a doubt, the migrant murals presented here act as meeting points where human stories converge. They are like mirrors, reflections in which each migrant passing through can recognize themselves. The emotions expressed in writing or images on the murals are common not only to all those who migrate, but to all people in general. It is enough to stand in front of one of the murals to understand what these people are going through, and to be reminded that at some point or other every single one of us has been on the move.

Make Art, Not Walls comprises eight murals. The majority represent transit migration, which is to say, the movement of people through a territory because they have had to flee their country of origin; others depict destination migration, where the reason for movement is the draw of a specific location. In the first group we find "I Was Here," whose title is evidence of a through-movement—the phrase acts as a footprint left by those passing by. We also find two linked murals on either side of the River Suchiate, the border between Guatemala and Mexico, which bear the lines "There are no borders up above . . ." and ". . . so nothing should stop us here on earth," respectively. Finally, we find "The Great Door" and "The Fire Worm," which depict the experience of forced internal displacement—a particular kind of transit migration in which people decide to flee their country of origin without caring what their ultimate destination might be.[2] These two murals posed a greater challenge, in large part because a lot of children participated in their creation, children who are themselves victims of the situation the murals depict, but who also offer genuine hope for a better future.

As for the second group, which portrays migration toward a particular destination, we focus here on two murals that involved indigenous communities migrating from the provinces to Mexico City. These are "Strength and Struggle" by the Mazahua people and "Otomí Pride" by the Otomí people. Each of them is linked to a different pattern of migration, but both are evidence of indigenous communities' steadfast determination to keep their traditions and customs alive in the great metropolis.

The final mural, "Tales of Struggle, Hope, and Asylum," is dedicated to the concept of asylum. The right to claim asylum is a human right that, when granted, offers a real alternative to the adverse circumstances many people face in their countries of origin. This mural tells a tragedy of a different kind: first, not everyone is able to achieve refugee status, and second, those who do achieve it often find that social integration remains extremely difficult. This mural had a huge number of participants—not only individuals but also organizations and institutions working in this area. Children once again had a large part to play, and as such they are reflected in the mural's imagery.

There is, undoubtedly, more to be done to tackle the causes of migration more directly. However, we also need to confront the issue of migrants returning to their place of origin. We are planning two new murals on this topic in the near future.

I leave this account, which has no other intention than to describe the first examples of migratory Mexican mural art, in the hands of readers, on the understanding that by *art* I am not referring to any erudite, specialized technique, but rather to the cultural expression of people in the process of migrating.

## "I Was Here"

The title of this mural itself is evidence of people passing through—something left behind as a reminder, a trace of the steps they've taken. The title, originally in English, expresses hope of

"I Was Here." Invited artist: Chachachá Collective (Dayron López and Raymundo Roch
Photography by Tres Gatos Films A.C.

arriving at a chosen destination: the United States. It expresses the desire for a better way of life and for more opportunities, the desire to feel safe and to not have to flee poverty and violence. The desire to look for peace and quiet, for work and resources to send back to family members. The main objective of "I Was Here" was to make visible the complexity of migrants' journeys via anecdotes about their passage through Mexico. The migrant phenomenon is complex, dynamic, and changing, and it's an experience that isn't lived exclusively in the borderlands between one country and another: for that reason, in this mural we tried to distance ourselves from borders and pay attention to what happens in the central part of Mexico, in that bottleneck where different migratory flows are concentrated. "I Was Here" engages with the migrant crossing; with the decision to walk, move, or traverse; with what migrants themselves call "setting off on a journey."

In this intermediary space where migratory routes shift, unseen by those who are not obliged to travel them, we also find the indiscriminate trafficking of weapons, drugs, and people. This is one of the main reasons why routes through Mexico end up being violent for undocumented migrants. So, when we talk about transit migration, one of the most difficult things is to fully understand this

intermediary space, between the place of origin and the desired endpoint. Routes change continually; there are always new and complex clandestine flows across Mexican territory. As a result, our only way of examining and understanding what happens on these journeys is through the voices of the people who undertake them; due to their undocumented nature, there is no other way of doing so.

Messages of love, encouragement, and hope occupy many of the mosaic pieces that make up this mural. However, many of them also speak to the diversity and complexity of problems associated with managing the migrant phenomenon: the recruitment of young people into gangs; refugee crises in different parts of the world; families grieving for disappeared relatives; gender and sexual diversity among migrants; health problems; child and teenage migrants; problems associated with the social integration or the upholding of rights of returnees or deportees; the anonymity of people internally displaced due to violence; and the invisibility of the many thousands of economic migrants. Although the mural makes up a single work of art, each panel evokes the life of someone wanting, at a particular moment, to express their story. Thus we find phrases like the following:

> *Immigration is a right, not a crime*
> *No to discrimination*
> *Just because I'm a migrant doesn't mean I'm no longer human*
> *Never forget where you came from*
> *It's so hard to leave your family, those you love; to leave your country, your home*
> *Chasing a dream*
> *In truth, traveling by train is isn't easy, but I'm doing it because I love my family*
> *Don't let anyone stop you from making your journey with courage and faith*

*I was here to give my family a better future*
*Forever strong*
*Even the longest journey starts with the first step*
*It doesn't matter where you go, but rather the person you become along the way*

## "The Quetzal" and "The Jaguar"

Mexico is a key transit route for human mobility because of its proximity to the United States. The main gateway into Mexico for migrants is the border with Guatemala, marked by the River Suchiate. Every day people can be seen making the crossing, hoping above all to be able to reach the United States.

The first rays of sun illuminate the river's gentle waves; the day begins, and the river moves people, along with their hopes, dreams, longing, and regret at having to leave the places where they were born. These are places where, for a variety of reasons, people have not been able to find the work, safety, or well-being they need, and so they decide instead to migrate. The river is a daily witness to the dreams of people traveling with little more than a backpack, a bottle of water, a hat to keep the sun off, and eyes full of hope and uncertainty. Rafts are made of wood and a couple of tires held together with cables or heavy rope. They transport anything and everything. Some take entire families: women and children sit hand in hand while the fathers stand beside the guide or driver of the makeshift boat. For them, this is just the beginning of their journey. They seem to fix on a spot on the other side of the river, their first destination, and one it's not too difficult to arrive at: the border with Mexico. Then again, sometimes they seem not to see anything at all, their eyes drifting over the abundant foliage in these warm, tropical climes. They have no idea what is waiting for them on the other side.

Mexico receives them with promises, with damp, cool, fertile soil, perfect for sowing dreams at the start of a journey. Most migrants arrive in Tapachula, in the southern state of Chiapas, a border city with a unique personality. In this first port of call, migrant status is taken for granted. But migratory encounters are not always friendly. There is disappointment, despair; people who lose their way and are never seen again.

"There are no borders up above . . . so nothing should stop us here on earth." This phrase appears on two murals that depict the crossing of the River Suchiate. The murals involved artistic collaboration with communities on both sides of the border. The first part of the sentence, accompanied by an image of a Quetzal, is painted on the inner wall of a hostel in Tecún Uman, on the Guatemalan side of the river; the second part of the sentence, accompanied by an image of a Jaguar, is painted on the wall of a market in Ciudad Hidalgo, on the Mexican side of the river. The murals are a visual expression of the power of the natural world; the animals represent movement, agility, and the freedom to travel. They bear witness to a longing for a world without borders, and in particular for there to be no border between these two countries divided by the River Suchiate. They represent the deeply felt need to travel in order to find somewhere free from violence and poverty, somewhere people can come and go freely.

Their message begins in Guatemala and continues in the Mexican state of Chiapas. Guatemala is represented by the Quetzal bird, protected in parts of Central America, its brightly colored wings spread wide. Here, it represents freedom and the ability to move easily across borders. Chiapas, for its part, is represented by the image of a jaguar, a powerful animal that has long been emblematic of the region, appearing in many Mesoamerican myths and legends. It is believed that jaguars, or *balamoob* in the Mayan language, protect humans during dark times, and that their presence becomes particularly valuable at critical moments.

"The Quetzal" and "The Jaguar." Nahual Collective (Mariana Santiago, Mónica López, Daniel Castillo, and Amauri Hx). Photography by Tres Gatos Films A.C.

## "The Great Door" and "The Fire Worm"

Tijuana, known as the Gateway to Mexico, is an important entry point on the border wall between Mexico and the United States. "The Country Begins Here" is the city's motto. The easternmost city in Latin America, Tijuana is a key tourist destination on the so-called Golden Coast of California. It hosts innumerable cultural events every year but is also home to *maquiladoras*, or sweatshops, as well as production centers, commercial spaces, and multinational companies, so is considered a global city. Crucially, it shares twenty-four kilometers of border with San Diego, California. It is estimated that three hundred thousand crossings are made daily through the San Ysidro port of entry, and more than a hundred million crossings every year.

Today, Tijuana is one of the world's most dynamic, complex, and important migratory corridors. People of many different nationalities travel through here—people who have regular jobs or are touring the region's border cities, hoping to cross to the United States in order to claim asylum on account of violence, discrimination, or political persecution, or simply in search of a better life. The two countries' economies, cultures, and, of course, experiences of

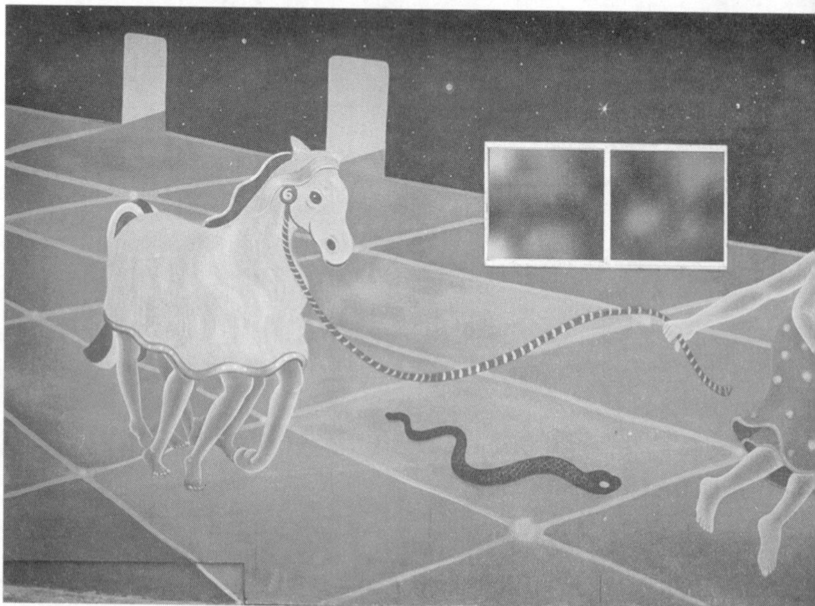

"The Great Door." Invited artist: Pilar Cárdenas "Fusca." Photography: Tres Gatos Films A.C.

migration are inextricable from one another, and it is crucial to avoid discriminatory or xenophobic policies in these areas.

The Tijuana murals, "The Great Door" and "The Fire Worm," aimed to make visible two particularly vulnerable groups among those who make this crossing: internally displaced women and children.

In "The Great Door," the door itself represents fear, while the snake represents the dangers associated with escape, and the horse the way many women must travel, taking with them only the bare minimum, disguising themselves so they aren't recognized, unsure whether they will be pursued or even where they might end up. The mural also depicts migrants' hope of finding a way out of their misfortunes; their longing to find safety, calm, and a good life somewhere else.

"The Fire Worm" depicts displaced children, one of the most

"The Fire Worm." Invited artist: Foi Jiménez Jurado y "Fio Zenjim." Photography: Tres Gatos Films A.C.

vulnerable migrant groups. It aims to explore their current predicament: the uncertainty involved in moving through new and strange places, having been forced to migrate with their families for various reasons. An effort was made to create an image of hope that allowed the children to reflect on their reality as well as to see their future in a more positive light.

## "Memories on the Wall": The Mazahua and Otomí Peoples

Neglect of rural populations and extreme poverty have prompted floods of internal migration from the countryside to large cities. "Memories on the Wall" aims to preserve the collective memory of those rural communities. Internal migration is not new to Mexico; indigenous communities have long felt the need to integrate themselves into urban spaces. Poverty and a lack of opportunities have for many years obliged them to look for a better quality of life in the capital. Today, multiple generations of originally rural communities enrich the multicultural life of this immense metropolis by bringing their traditions, their trade, and their art, thereby showcasing the richness of our country's identity.

We collected these people's stories and used them to create two murals in different housing units constructed by indigenous communities over a period of twenty to twenty-five years. These communities—both of which have deep roots in different parts of the country—are the main actors in this project, and we have been working continually with them since the end of 2014. The Mazahua live in the heart of Mexico City, in a hard-to-find property on Calle Mesones. The Otomí community, meanwhile, has recently acquired a new property, which they call the Mansion, that has allowed them to move out of the sheet-metal houses they occupied until three years ago.

The murals were created in collaboration with the people living in these multi-family housing units and tell the story of their struggle. We listened to their stories, their successes, their customs, and the symbols with which they identify. For them, creating the mural was a way of "depicting the story of their lives," as they put it. The artists and other participants in the project came to know the strength, courage, and resilience of these men and women who refuse to let go of their identity. They learned of their migration to bigger cities, how they abandoned their quiet homes to go looking for a better future for their children, and how they still miss what they left behind.

## "Strength and Struggle": The Mazahua Mural

This mural represents the lives and journeys of the Mazahua indigenous community that migrated to Mexico City. The mural, which was designed to suggest a piece of fabric being woven, tells the story of their life. It begins at the bottom with the image of a woman's hands weaving—an important Mazahua activity that helps bring the community together. Further up, we see other facets of their history of migration. In the first panel, we see Don Antonio in traditional dress, a *sarape* and *sombrero*, demonstrating pride in his origins, but standing next to Mexico City's tall buildings. In this

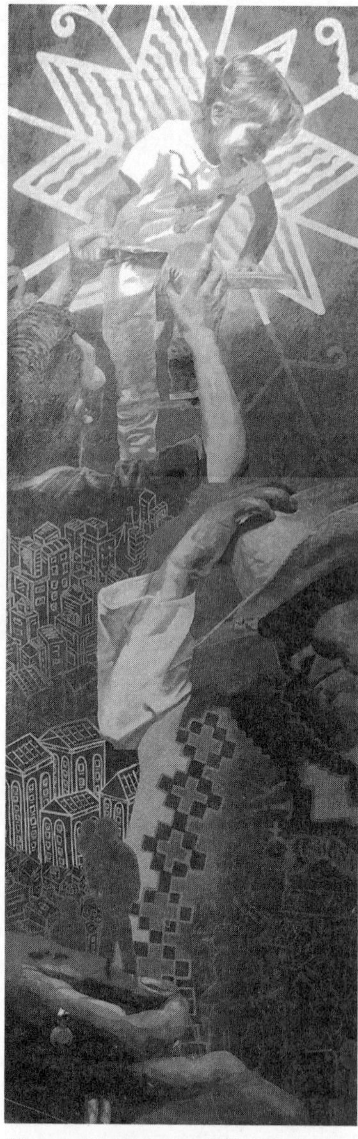
"Strength and Struggle." Invited artists: Michelle Ángela Ortiz, Colective Rexiste, Colectivo Chachacha, Colectivo Nahual, RsES Crew, Osley, Akbal, Roit, MamboSka. Photography: Tres Gatos Films A.C.

way, he represents the rural man with urban experience; the coming together of these two different ways of life. The second panel symbolizes a new generation, a young man who has left behind his traditional dress for casual clothing but who still maintains his Mazahua identity. He is an amalgam of *campesino* and city-dweller. In the third panel, we see a girl, symbolizing the third generation, held aloft by the young man. Her clothing is ordinary—patchwork trousers and a shirt—but the shirt bears the image of a deer, which is the symbol of the Mazahuas.

## "Otomí Pride"

"Otomí Pride" depicts the history of a group of people who left the state of Querétaro in search of better living conditions. It was put together one panel at a time, in the same way a piece of fabric is woven, from the bottom upward. The first panel depicts the strength of women leaving their towns for the city. The women are framed by six ears of corn, each of which represents a neighborhood in the town of Santiago Mexquititlán, in the state of Querétaro. The next panel up bears the image of a smiling child, happy to have a decent roof over his head. His happiness reflects the achievements of his ancestors. The third panel depicts the trajectory of the families that arrived carrying their possessions on their backs, ready to start a new life in the city with almost nothing. In the fourth panel, we see the image of an older woman, a community leader who is urging her people to continue the fight. The strength of indigenous women is overwhelming in this mural; they are the ones that teach, the ones that take the lead, day after day, in order to offer their children better living conditions. They are the ones who pass on the richness of their traditions, and of life itself. The final panel incorporates messages from all the other participants, including those who are not part of the Otomí community. Everyone learned from one another, and so they are all integrated into this project.

"Otomí Pride." Invited artists: Michelle Ángela Ortiz, Colective Rexiste, Colectivo Chachacha, Colectivo Nahual, RsES Crew, Osley, Akbal, Roit, MamboSka. Photography: Tres Gatos Films A.C.

## "Tales of Struggle, Hope, and Asylum"

Asylum is a right—a person's right to ask for protection from the authorities in a state where they are not a national. This might be because they fear for their lives, liberty, or integrity in their country of origin or residence. This right, which in Mexico allows people to be recognized as having refugee status, was incorporated into regulations at a constitutional level as a consequence of human-rights reforms in June 2011. Mexico is internationally renowned for the protection it offers refugees, a tradition that dates back to the period between 1939 and 1942, when the country opened its doors to approximately twenty million Spanish refugees fleeing the Franco regime. That migration event was unique because of, among other things, its unusual magnitude. Between 1934 and 1940, under President Lázaro Cárdenas, the Mexican government passed legal reforms allowing for the entry of Spanish refugees and asylum seekers despite their number exceeding previous limits.

The great exodus of Guatemalans in the 1980s was the last great migration phenomenon contributing to Mexico's solid reputation for granting asylum. The 1984 Cartagena Declaration, an internationally recognized document that protects asylum seekers, outlined five justifications, in addition to ideological, religious, and racial justifications, for claiming refugee status: generalized violence, foreign aggression, internal conflicts, massive violation of human rights, or other circumstances that have seriously disturbed public order. On these bases, Mexico receives people fleeing their countries of origin or being pursued, but in order to protect them they must go through an administrative procedure that is not always quick and to which society is not always sensitive or empathetic. For that reason, "asylum" was chosen as the theme of this large mural.

Murals alone cannot tackle discrimination, racism, poverty, or injustice. However, what they can do is to sow the seed of hope, and if hope can be sowed, then there is always the possibility of healing. People from dozens of different countries participated in creating this final mural, titled "Tales of Struggle, Hope, and Asylum": people from Haiti, El Salvador, Honduras, Nicaragua, Guatemala,

"Tales of Struggle, Hope, and Asylum." Invited artists: Eva Bracamontes and Denisse Escobedo. Photography: Tres Gatos Films A.C.

Venezuela, Colombia, the Democratic Republic of Congo, Chile, Spain, Argentina, Uruguay, Cuba, and Mexico. Just as birds need to migrate in order to look for a better place to mate, to feed, or simply to live, each of those involved in its creation chose a bird native to their place of origin to appear prominently in the mural. Those seeking refugee status imagined themselves traveling on the backs of these birds in search of a better life.

The mural incorporates, too, the image of a woman flying with the wings of a macaw, bearing her home and family on her back. The roots and vegetation sprouting from her shoulders, back, and arms represent the nature or essence of this girl, who is dressed in clothes embroidered in the style of the Mexican state of Guerrero. Her clothing is a reminder of all the Mexicans who migrate to the United States seeking asylum. Behind her come all the birds, each of them representing a different part of the world. The clouds and rain suggest fertility and the possibility of enriching a culture through migration and movement. Among the clouds, there is a rainbow symbolizing the sexual and gender diversity of the migrants. Finally, the sun suggests a future as the migrants are able to glimpse it: one day at a time.

# NOTES FROM "EL CUARTITO"

GUADALUPE NETTEL
TRANSLATED BY SOPHIE HUGHES

The first border I ever crossed was the one that separates Mexico from the United States; I don't remember it, but that's what I've been told. My parents took me to Los Angeles to a renowned ophthalmologist to make an incision in my iris in the hope of letting more light reach the retina of the practically blind eye with which I was born. I crossed that border many times during my childhood, mostly to visit ophthalmologists, but also for family reasons: we had close relatives in San Diego, as well as in Ciudad Juárez. On our journeys there, we would see *campesinos* walking with suitcases or backpacks under the scorching desert sun. My mother always wondered where they must have come from, and she reminded us how lucky we were to be able to travel in an air-conditioned car.

The United States boasted cleaner streets and better kept, newer buildings, but it was also the home of *science*, that goddess my parents venerated, hoping that she would grant us favors. The doctors' appointments would always take place in English. My parents and the ophthalmologist would look at me, ask each other questions, talk, and exchange opinions about me. And there I'd sit, on one of those chairs with little mirrors and blinding lights, not understanding a single word and with no one bothering to translate for me. Two borders separated me from what was happening: the border of language and the border of childhood. The second was the worst. An invisible wall separates the world of children, in which everything arouses curiosity and they are awash with emotions, from the cynical, hectic, and prudent world of adults. Children are more aware of it. Grown-ups not so much.

At some point, we stopped chasing after ophthalmologists. My visual condition hadn't improved in the slightest, but the doctors began putting off finding a solution. When I grew up, medical developments would ensure I'd not only be able to cross the border that separated me from them, the adults, but also make my parents' greatest wish come true: I would escape the hazy, one-dimensional world into which I'd been born and cross over to the three-dimensional world—a world filled with people with bifocal vision. Very happy people, I imagined, given how keen my parents were for me to join them.

Nobody mentioned it at the time, but I sensed that I would also cross another border, the one that separates the world of those with "different capacities" from that of the "normal"—and as such superior—people. For years I really believed that border existed. From where I was standing, normality looked like the United States looks from Mexico: a place where people live without worry, in houses that all look the same, and in incomprehensible comfort and peace, or so it seemed. Even at my tender age I could make the distinction between those who belonged on that side of the invisible yet irrefutable line and those who did not. On my side, for example, lived my deaf neighbor and the college well-being officer's autistic son. In secret, without ever mentioning it, not even among ourselves, we formed a parallel nation. Every now and then one of our fellow compatriots would make a desperate attempt to escape: they'd undergo surgery on their distinguishing feature or fit convincing prosthesis, very close in shape and texture to the missing limb. Looking at them produced a strange sensation. It was at once embarrassing and touching. They almost never managed to totally compensate for their physical difference, and on the rare occasions that they did, something in their behavior would betray their origin. There was always someone who took these efforts to assimilate as a personal affront, but it's also true that those on the other side of the border were constantly egging us on to try: Why don't you operate on that eye? Or why don't you at least use a cosmetic contact lens to make it less obvious? they'd ask me. Why don't you wear heels? they'd suggest to another. Why don't you try covering up that scar with makeup?

As an adult, I went on to cross borders in all five continents, but out of all of them, none were quite as disturbing as the ones that stretch out across either end of the country where I was born. The one to the north is a wound that all Mexicans carry somewhere on our conscience. Not a day goes by when we don't hear the numbers of people who have disappeared in transit to the United States: Central American children sent on journeys of no return by parents trying to spare them from war or destitution, and who pack them off with the promise of meeting again in some hypothetical future; pregnant women who risk their lives for the chance to provide their unborn child with a better nationality than their own. We know about "La bestia," also known as the "Death Train," and about the sexual abuse, robberies, and extortion committed every single day against these itinerant people who travel unprotected, carrying their worldly possessions on their backs. They come from El Salvador and Nicaragua, from Guatemala and every corner of Mexico. We know that there are entire towns in the states of Michoacán, Guerrero, and Puebla with no men left in them because they all went to work in the north. It's reported on the news each morning, and even when we miss the news we just know it, without anyone having to remind us. Crossing that border on a bus is very different from crossing it by plane. On the bus people are stopped for over two hours. Every millimeter of the women's luggage is inspected, and for the men that search extends to their rectum. By plane things tend to be easier, unless your visa isn't in order or you're plain unlucky, as I was on my most recent trip to the U.S.

It was just last week. I was going to San Francisco to take part in an event called the Bay Area Book Festival in the city of Berkeley. It was my third time visiting the country under its current administration of intolerance. I had to get to the airport early because for some months American airlines had been preventing Mexicans from checking in online. During the flight, we were fed a single donut, which I turned down, thinking I'd get myself a better breakfast upon arrival at my destination. As I said, I've spent many hours of my life in U.S. customs and border protection lines, which is how I know that the wait can be long and tiresome. Quite often, as the line inches forward, I will entertain myself with a sadomasochistic game that consists of guessing who among the passengers will be escorted by the security guards for a secondary screening. As soon as I've picked out a candidate, I feel my anxiety levels start to shoot up, and a protective instinct kicks in toward that *campesino*, artisan, or laborer, who, at least to my mind, is going to be rejected at the gates of the empire. On more than one occasion I've guessed correctly. When this happens, I find myself so involved with the singled-out passenger I have to stop myself from abandoning my place in the line and stepping in between the man and the officer escorting him away by the arm. But that particular morning the line was unusually short, and I didn't have time to select anyone; that morning, I was unlucky enough to get a surly officer who didn't ask me the reasons for my trip, but rather what I was there to do, a subtle but eloquent difference. I gave him the name of the festival, and he noted something down on his computer. I was feeling lightheaded, so I leaned on the counter, as I might do in any country during border-check questioning, and the uniformed guy yelled at me to step back. I did as I was told and stood in front of the camera, and again he brusquely ordered me to move. He asked me exactly what a book festival was and if it was a kind of flea market or something. By then I began to suspect that the detained passenger that day would be me, an idea that had never—as absurd as it sounds—crossed my mind. Perhaps I should have felt sorry for myself, but instead I felt stupid for having accepted the invitation to Donald Trump Land, even if that invitation had come from one of its brightest and most progressive enclaves. I set out explaining to the officer the festival dynamic, unable to veil my condescension, just as he couldn't hide his supreme indifference to my story. Before I could even finish talking he had radioed over one of his colleagues, to whom he handed my passport before ordering me to follow him, and then finally calling the next in line.

That is how I ended up in a holding room popularly known as *el cuartito*, a place I'd heard talked about on multiple occasions. It was, at least in that airport, a much bigger space than the name had led me to believe. In it there were fifty chairs arranged in rows, and at the back a counter with a black metal tray into which the police officer tossed my passport as we entered. The first thing that caught my attention was the absence of the order and efficiency I'd come to expect from offices in the United States. Two police officers were killing time at the counter. Every so often one of them would pluck a passport randomly from the tray and call out its owner by his or her last name, regardless of whether they'd arrived before or after the others. Everything about that place seemed designed to make you lose hope. There was no way of finding out what was going on with my case or when I'd be seen. Everything moved very slowly, except for my head, which by then was spinning vertiginously out of hunger and tiredness. Many of the people being held there didn't speak English, and when the police gave instructions about the restricted use of the telephone or asked if someone had an imminent connecting flight, these people didn't even know what they were being told. Most of us were Latinos, from different parts of Latin America, but there were also a vast number of Asians and Arabs. A woman tried to explain something to the policeman in a language I couldn't make out. He barked at her to sit down. I thought how easy it is to detest the police, and above all the American police. It could have seemed obvious to me, as it does to many people, that Americans are the bad guys while we Mexicans are the poor victims, and perhaps I would have come to that conclusion that day if it weren't for a long, eye-opening trip to Guatemala I'd made years earlier, back when I was a student, when I'd witnessed the Mexican police acting as the first filter to prevent Central Americans reaching the United States, with the same sadism exhibited by Border Patrol at the airport. If the northern border is a wound carried by all Mexicans, the southern border is a burden we are all but unaware of.

In the little room, an indigenous boy was dozing on his brother's shoulder. The older one was a minor too, and they both looked poor and defenseless, like the kids you see trying to earn a living at traffic lights in Mexico City. I thought about the little girl I used to be, that girl who crossed borders so effortlessly, oblivious to all the children who risked their lives to do the same. I also thought about the minors who travel each day on the Beast, and the Cuban kids who board those rafts without their parents; I remembered Alan Kurdi, the three-year-old Syrian boy who appeared dead on a Turkish beach, and all those who survive and must get by in refugee camps. What do children know of politics, of governments and their borders? How is any of this their fault? This is just a lucky dip, I said to myself, as unpredictable as the official who dealt with me being in a bad mood that morning, or having an aversion to writers. It is pure chance that some people are born in Mexico and others in Syria or El Salvador. And it is chance that ensures that, before we even learn to speak our mother tongues, our lives are predetermined by borders. I took out the little notebook in my bag and jotted down this last sentence. Then I started writing down everything I was seeing. I noted, just as someone was probably doing from behind a hidden camera, every movement and gesture of every single person there. I told myself, by way of consolation, that this whole sorry incident could be written up as an article about the different borders I've been stopped at. It's an aberration, I wrote, that a place like this exists at every border, but since that is the way things are, every single human should be obliged to pass through one at some point in their lives, to see for themselves what other people go through.

Half an hour later, one of the officers shouted at the boy slumped asleep on his brother, who made effusive efforts to wake him up. The poor kid had barely opened his eyes when the police started interrogating him in English. His brother repeated again and again in almost unintelligible Spanish that they had a visa. That should suffice for none of us to be harassed by the officials, I thought—if not, what are the consular services for? But it was clear that the customs officials didn't feel the same way, which is why they were so ruthless toward those children, to the point of making the little one cry. All of us in the room held our breath. The place had become a pressure cooker. A woman, also in uniform, and who I hadn't seen before, appeared from the other end of the corridor and asked the officer to stop bothering the young boys. *Tenemos un viso*, the older one repeated. The woman flicked through their passports until she came upon their visas. Then she handed over the passports with unusual warmth and opened the door to let the boys go.

Calmed, I made a note of the scene. I told myself that they'd soon return my passport to me and that I, too, would be able to get out of there. I thought about the students waiting for me in Berkeley, those smiling, slightly naive gringos who put their hearts and souls into changing the world; I thought about how the world's police form their own separate nation, but also that there are bad cops and others who aren't so bad. All this I wrote down in my notebook, and I wrote down—I'm reading it now—that this is the only border that makes any sense to me: the one that separates those who do everything in their power to help others from the rest of the species.

# POLITICS OF EXCLUSION, POLITICS OF INTEGRATION

JUAN CARLOS PEREDA FAILACHE
TRANSLATED BY SAMANTHA SCHNEE

In order to examine and evaluate specific situations, it is helpful to use a strategy of transitions, moving from the concrete to the abstract and back. The aim is—among other things—to achieve a clearer vision of where thought meets action. As a consequence, abstract models are often designed in reference to specific situations, to analyze and assess them. In our case, there are two political models—or rather, one political and one pseudopolitical model—that attempt to evaluate a specific situation empirically: aggressive exclusionary politics and the politics of democratic integration. In this essay, I look at these as opposing political models of nation-states in relation to the treatment of social groups. But this distinction, in my view, is not exclusive to large groups; it can be also applied to smaller groups such as families, associations, and so on.

## I

In antiquity, the construction of walls and ramparts was a measure frequently used to protect a city or a region from outside attacks (consider, for example, the Great Wall of China and Hadrian's Wall). In the late thirteenth and early fourteenth centuries, when Marco Polo imported gunpowder from China into the West, walls and ramparts lost much of their purpose. However, in 1961, the Soviets built one right through the center of Berlin, which came to be known as the "wall of shame." In addition to the wall, which measured three meters high, there was a so-called "no man's land," an area that in some sections measured up to 140 meters wide, mined and electrified, guarded by armed soldiers and fierce dogs. This wall was built not to protect the land but rather to prevent people from entering *or leaving*. Thus, while previously used to protect, today walls and ramparts are used as a tool of exclusionary politics. Let's consider what kind.

Using the concept of "constitutive outside"—in the sense that "something is always excluded" and "whatever is excluded in one way constructs what is included"—we can distinguish at least two kinds of exclusions: demarcation exclusions and aggressive exclusions. The first type refers to the placement of limits on the exercise of civic duties and rights. Examples include: children not having the right to vote; cars driving on the right side of the road in Mexico; and the fact that animals can't apply for jobs in philosophy departments.

Of course, behind exclusions that appear to be merely demarcations, is often hidden "the temptation of the Wall" (the temptation to build an *exclusionary* wall); for example, the supposed exclusion by demarcation of preventing women and workers from voting. Indeed, throughout the nineteenth century and part of the twentieth, social movements have redefined these types of exclusion as "aggressive" ones. Similarly, the condemnation of non-heterosexuality has evolved from a exclusion by demarcation to an "aggressive" one. Aggressive exclusions represent walls to tear down. In some parts of the world, these walls are in the process of being demolished for the first time; in others, people are fighting to demolish them again.

So we see that the practice of exclusion creates something that is separate. But it can be a temporary demarcation, such as limiting children's right to vote, or it can be an aggression. When the latter is the case in politics, it blocks things off, isolating what has been excluded. That's why aggressive exclusionary politics—that is, politics that have succumbed to "the temptation of the Wall"—try to isolate a group from a variety of ills that the excluding power seeks to avoid, like quarantines in days of yore, which sought to contain epidemics of contagious disease. It follows that, when people or social groups are subject to aggressive exclusion they are not only no longer treated the same way as others, but they are treated as inferior or dangerous, or both. Why else would they be aggressively excluded? Aggressive exclusion is rooted in negative judgment, which dehumanizes people. The rights of specific social groups are revoked, those groups are sidelined and, sooner or later, stigmatized: "Those people don't deserve respect"; or, more bluntly, "Those people are a bunch of criminals"; and "Those people are trash."

That's why aggressive exclusionary politics imply a double process: at the same time that outward-facing hostility excludes some (think of xenophobia and racism), those who are included are accorded privileges. Moreover, those who are included develop pervasive authority over those who are excluded: "We—and what is ours—the traditions and heritage that belong to us, take precedence. Others—the excluded, everyone else—have little value. They're not important, and, furthermore, when you think about it, they're dangerous. Many of them are thieves, burglars, and murderers who spread terror, so we have to fight them with all the means at our disposal."

As vague as this sketch of a political model of aggressive exclusion or modern wall politics is, both exclusions and inclusions create a *deluge of properties*; from a critical perspective, a national State triggers an *avalanche of ills* when it adopts such a politics. I call it a "deluge" because each property represents an ill, which gives rise to other properties that perhaps aren't inevitable in the strictest sense; nonetheless, one negative property often leads to another, and another. . . . Therefore it's worth looking at some of these properties.

The first property of a politics of aggressive exclusion by a nation-state is building *fiercely guarded frontiers* with customs and border controls that seek to construct impermeable borders around a land. These create external exclusions that often target those who attempt to cross the borders of these nation-states that have succumbed to the temptation of the wall. For example, when a rich and powerful nation-state is faced with the members of a foreign social group who, due to political persecution, or violence in their homeland, or lack of work, have emigrated to that nation-state, eventually these people are barred from entry once and for all, even separating children from their parents.

These nation-states soon find strong justifications for their exclusionary politics—in the drawn-out declarations of government bureaucracies, in the mass media, and often in daily conversations. The emigrants cease to be "desperate people seeking security and the chance to earn a living" and become "delinquents." Or worse, they become "intruders whom the army must attack without hesitation because they want to do away with our way of life, our institutions and our liberties." Under the cover of such fantasies—that's the best you can call them—the politics of aggressive exclusion acquires a second property: *obsessive persecution*.

The properties of aggressive exclusionary politics aren't just directed outwardly; they affect more than the people they repel. As has been noted, the process of exclusion also creates a group that is included. And so we see a possible third consequence of exclusionary politics, which, from a certain point in time, creates *processes of internal exclusion for certain groups descended from anyone who came from "outside."* What am I referring to? Ultimately, the purpose of a nation-state using exclusionary politics is to exclude from its lands anyone who doesn't belong to that national State: those who are not "native"—by "blood," by birth, by legal "adoption." Nevertheless, if circumstances favor the spread of social discontent, modern Wall politics does more than demarcate a border. Barriers are built not only along borders—against other nation-states—but walls (or the mere talk of walls) are also built inside a nation-state—

invisible walls that are nonetheless visible to the portion of the population that is affected by them. It is acknowledged that those who dwell within closely guarded borders are heterogenous, but different social groups within the borders are valued differently. For example, although some descendants of citizens of the countries being excluded by such politics may have lived in the nation-state for many generations and may have even served their host country—from joining the armed forces to making important contributions in science, technology, and the arts of their new nation—they may be harassed or even intimidated. Perhaps these first-, second-, or third-generation descendants preserve some of their traditions or even their mother tongue. One effect of exclusionary politics is that if the family speaks their mother tongue at home it's looked down upon because it's not the official language of the nation-state. Sometimes things go too far and it is said that these groups speak like animals.

However, the construction of internal walls doesn't just affect the descendants of foreigners the nation-state aims to exclude. A possible fourth property of aggressive exclusionary politics is to promote the exclusion of "everything that is not authentically of this land." All too frequently the dramatic use of the word "authenticity" becomes a cover-up for lies and persecutions. That's how we encounter *hate that spreads contagiously.* Then it's no longer enough to exclude foreigners from the nation-state and harass their descendants; these contributing members of society—people whose skin isn't white, or people who practice a non-majority religion, or people whose sexual orientation is not mainstream, or people who don't speak the country's language perfectly—begin to be excluded and removed from good jobs and positions of power. The temptation of the wall—the exclusionary politics—is insatiable: eventually hate targets people or groups who are critical of aspects of the nation-state and the society they're living in.

What can be said about this model of exclusionary politics

and its deluge of properties which define the ills I have tried to describe—*fiercely guarded borders, obsessive persecution, processes of internal exclusion affecting groups of descendants who have come from "outside," hate that spreads contagiously*? Frequently this model can be applied empirically only in part. In quite a few instances social resistance actually prevents the deluge of ills, and that's how to stop the transition from the first property to the fourth one: from excluding immigrants to harassing dissidents. Unfortunately, history demonstrates how easily aggressive exclusionary politics leads to dehumanization and even criminalization. As a consequence, if this kind of politics is not met with resistance by at least part of a population, at some point the temptation of the wall leads to a slippery slope; it leads to the legalization of persecution—even torture and murder, if necessary. In this direction it's not surprising when aggressive exclusionary politics evolves into a politics of death.

Of course, the fourth property of aggressive exclusionary internal politics usually manifests itself even more gradually than the third one: at first, people or social groups are denigrated with irony and contempt, then, little by little, they are treated hatefully and, if necessary, imaginary transgressions—horror stories—are invented.

As a result of the avalanche of ills that aggressive exclusionary politics creates, if the social atmosphere has become terrifyingly conducive, and all democratic resistance has weakened, this politics—characterized by a level of repressive violence—becomes a politics of terror. Sadly, when a society has reached this point—history demonstrates that this has happened and continues to happen repeatedly—it becomes extremely difficult not only to halt but to resist the despotism that evolves into economies of death.

## II

Are there any alternative models to aggressive exclusionary politics or modern Wall politics? It's worth considering the model of democratic politics of integration. The model of aggressive exclusionary politics has been found to cause an avalanche of ills, which become ever more pervasive, feeding on harassment, hate, and violence. On the other hand, politics of democratic integration present a series of *tensions*; or, perhaps, a series of variations on one single tension.

Indeed, any politics of democratic integration is ruled by a *root tension*: if the politics of a society isn't capable of creating sufficient integration, society breaks into groups that are at odds with each other directly or potentially. But if this politics promotes too much integration, it degenerates into subsumption—in the sense of homogeneous incorporation—with a tendency toward despotism.

Before discussing this root tension it's worth considering the difference between the two ways in which human beings try to build community: the bonds of subsumption and those of integration. Let me take a step back to elaborate on this difference by distinguishing between two types of bundles. I propose that a bundle by subsumption is one in which the diverse constituents of the bundle disappear once the bundle is formed. Dough is one example of this kind of bundle: flour, water, and eggs blend and become one in the dough. In the strictest sense, the model of aggressive exclusionary politics aspires to the *ideal* of a bundle by subsumption. The properties I have discussed earlier refer to progressive exclusions which, along with the instruments of xenophobia and racism, attempt to create a population in which, over time, there are no differing desires, beliefs, inclinations, interests, ways of life, and, least of all, dissidents. A population embodying the ideal of subsumption (or homogenous inclusion) is characterized by members who do their best to follow the rule: *"More of the same is always good, and anything different is always bad."* (For example, the pejorative use of the word "populism" refers to this kind of politics: "masses" without institutional branches, serving a charismatic leader making arbitrary and unscrupulous decisions.)

In contrast, a bundle by integration is one in which diverse constituents retain varying degrees of independence within the bundle. A football team is a good example. The members of the team are both independent and dependent on the team. Players may have differing skills but ultimately depend on each other as much in victory as in defeat because both are a function of whether their interactions succeed in scoring the greatest possible number of points against the opposing team. Nevertheless, each player has specific skills that differentiate him from the others and make him better or worse than his teammates. On the other hand, each player has a life, his own desires, beliefs, inclinations, and interests, which are often at odds with, but do not negatively impact his participation on, the team.

Let's apply this analogy to how politics relates to a population, and how, in some cases, it reorganizes or reconstructs the population. The model of subsumption—of homogeneous inclusion—has been linked directly to modern Wall politics characterized by xenophobia and racism. By contrast, a politics of democratic integration has to be able to accommodate different interactions between citizens. As part of respecting citizens' rights, the vast differences in their desires, beliefs, inclinations, and interests must also be respected. Because there's no doubt that the best-known characteristic of human animals is that their ways of life, and everything that constitutes them—their expectations, need for trust, need for recognition, desire for freedom, desire for happiness—can vary dramatically. These divergences, which may sometimes be radical, create political tensions that are variations on the root tension. We can subdivide these into *personal tensions, social tensions*, and the constant *overlap* between them.

Personal tensions, or tensions in and between people, are caused by quarrels, disagreements, confrontations, conflicts of interest, clashes, oppositions, and even violence. To prevent these disagreements from becoming self-destructive or devolving into fatal wars, every individual must face the choice between the two alternatives discussed herein: aggressive exclusionary politics or politics of democratic integration. In the latter it's important to create institutions capable of mediating interpersonal differences—negotiating, conversing, agreeing, devising plans for compromise, but also helping to redefine these conflicts time and again. It follows that all politics of democratic integration have to be able to catalyze conciliating inner conversations and create institutions for mediating interpersonal conflicts. But that's not all. These politics must be accorded authority and efficacy to make them successful—to prevent conflicts from becoming too deep and destroying these politics of democratic integration.

One common overlap between personal tensions and social tensions can be defined as tension between individual interests and the common interests of society in general. Or, as this tension is expressed in many traditions: the rough and necessarily partial integration of the intimate, the private, and the public. It's well known that every person, every social group, large or small, and every family or extended family has their own differing beliefs and interests, as well as specific needs they seek to fulfill. But there are also more general needs. For example, safety is one, though it's often overlooked. Frequently the struggle against uncertainty for an individual, a family, or a group is compatible with common interests such as social trust. On some happy occasions consensus is reached, but more often this consensus may be achieved only "in principle."

No one can deny that consensus weakens when measures to combat violence and lack of security are proposed in order to restore social trust. Such weakening of consensus doesn't just concern short-term programs such as improving safety on the streets by increasing the number of police and supporting them with personnel from the army. Opinion also differs vastly when it comes to long-term programs such as fighting inequality and poverty, promoting employment, and giving grants so the neediest young people can continue their education. People and social groups often criticize such programs: "Increasing police supervision not only increases the violation of human rights, it's the best-known path to despotism." Sectors of business and industry will also object: "Fighting inequality by increasing the minimum wage destroys competition." Faced with these and other attacks, how does one negotiate to build at least partial consensus to fight lack of security and restore trust?

I have considered one example of how politics of democratic integration can negotiate the tension between individual and general beliefs and interests—the case of addressing a widely accepted need, such as security, as a condition for social trust. Difficulties multiply about plans and values where no consensus exists in a society. Consider corrective programs such as "affirmative action" to counter traditionally sexist or racist practices, or strategies to address climate change or the legalization of drugs. ("Is it possible these plans to combat climate change actually eliminate the jobs of people who eke out an existence, living in misery?" "Do plans to combat climate change not endanger the tourism industry and its employees?") There's no doubt that a politics of democratic integration will encounter obstacles to accommodating both individual and general societal interests at each step.

However, neither individual interests, nor common interests, nor the beliefs of any segment of society are permanent givens. We are endowed with a second nature that is in part a product of society and never ceases to change from generation to generation. This second nature is created by concrete experience and the interpretation of these experiences, and also by arguments, models, and general theories. Therein lies the value of not losing sight of the strategy of transitions: to frequently move from the concrete to the abstract and back. That's why a politics of democratic integration should also try to redefine the common interest and show that it can be aligned with individual interests, which are also being redefined.

In addition, many tensions are first and foremost social tensions.

They compound the problems overwhelming the backbone of a society: its natural resources and its economy. One tension that causes frequent unrest in society is the differential between legal equality (proclaimed in many countries by modern laws) and huge economic inequalities (which exist in every economy). Isn't it true that economic disparities, especially when excessive and therefore humiliating, repeatedly disturb and even distort many rights such as the right to health and a proper home, or even the basic right to vote? Isn't political manipulation and propaganda that "persuades" people to vote one way or another a common vice in such societies? For people who are radically disadvantaged in economic terms, aren't legal and political equality merely decorations, created by those in power to confuse and distract them? A politics of democratic integration must create, through public policies, integration process that do not entail economic humiliation. If not, such politics are ineffective.

And so, we return to the root tension: how far should a politics of democratic integration go to maintain quality of life for individuals and society and, at the same time, honor justice and the common weal, without making society overly uniform?

## III

I return to the notion of the root tension: if the politics of democratic integration is not capable of achieving sufficient integration, society falls apart, but if it over-integrates then parts of society are subsumed and, sooner or later, the temptation of the Wall becomes irresistible. Let's consider the second condition: a politics of democratic integration must respect the *differentiating articulations* of a society; groups must be integrated, not subsumed. One can never forget that integration is achieved by bringing together diverse groups and respecting differences—uniting via discussion, negotiating with patience, sharing experiences that are often vastly different. Let's not forget that in any integrated bundle each of the constituent elements retains some degree of *autonomy.* The word "autonomy" causes some fuss, because it refers to the *differentiating articulations* of society. But why all the fuss?

In daily conversations the word "autonomy" refers to the way different entities (nation-states, social groups, institutions, people) are organized and operate following, more or less, their own regulations. We may identify several dimensions in a preliminary account of autonomy. The negative *external* dimension of autonomy is the capacity of an entity to decide without becoming fully determined. When an entity displays negative external autonomy, it simply has some proper space to analyze and deliberate without constant interference. But this space is relative, limited by the powers the entity sits between. There is also negative *internal* autonomy; at the institutional level this is the distance different parts of an administration put between themselves and their peers, with which they sometimes enter into conflict within the administration. On the personal level, it's the difference between desires, inclinations, and deep-rooted beliefs which often contradict good judgment.

At the same time, autonomy has a positive dimension or, if you prefer, the complementary aspect to its negative ones. When relatively free of interference, autonomous entities act in accordance with their own rules, pursuing their chosen objectives. It's important to emphasize that differentiating between the negative and positive aspects of autonomy doesn't mean there are two kinds of autonomy; they're both aspects of the same process.

Societies' differentiating articulations—autonomies—are usually constituted of diverse entities. It's helpful to keep in mind that there are two basic types, which establish clear yet frustrating limits in any complex society: social and personal autonomies. Frustrating limits? That's not much of a surprise. Even if you imagine a well-integrated democracy, when some segments truly operate by their own rules—both personal and social—this autonomy creates serious challenges for governments, private enterprises, traditions, and the rest of society, even for families and their customs. Why? Let's return to the concept of constitutive outside: "whatever is excluded in one way is also included in another." These limits define social and personal autonomies and put constant pressure on them, challenging the way in which the *continuum* of public, private, and personal power (which overlap) is exercised.

## IV

Let's consider *social autonomies* for a moment. It's worth making the distinction between formal autonomies, or autonomies whose rules are explicit and legally reinforced, and informal autonomies, which have either rules derived from explicit rules or implicit rules that are recognized to varying degrees by society. One well-known example of a formal social autonomy is the distinction between the branches of government: executive, legislative, and judicial. This traditional separation of powers exists to facilitate decision-making and lawmaking on the one hand and, on the other, to monitor and uphold these activities. At least that's the theory behind modern politics. But the reality is that this separation of powers often creates conflict. (It's a well-known fact that the exercise of power, like family relations, favors homogeneity in order to prevent fragmentation.)

Another example of social autonomy is universities and other centers of knowledge in many countries. Experience has shown that the pursuit of knowledge—which sometimes requires improvisation and exploration in dangerous directions, and which sometimes involves making mistakes—risks losing sight of new and interesting discoveries without spaces relatively free of interference. In such a case, the epistemic virtues of curiosity and the desire to investigate lead to behavior in keeping with the maxim "*More of the same is always better and anything different is bad.*"

Moreover, if a democratic society upholds this ideal, it's important to protect the informal differentiating articulations, or quasi-autonomies, such as decentralized organizations like the Commission on Human Rights—if such an organization exists in a society, and it aims to avoid conflating human animals and citizenry, which deprives immigrants, refugees, and exiled people of rights. Then there's the example of quasi-formal or informal social autonomy that is no less important or, in some cases, more important: the press and mass media in general. This autonomy derives from a right essential to any integrated democracy: the right to freedom of expression. But the power of the media can be so strong that it becomes a "fourth estate" in addition to the traditional three branches of power. Why is it so powerful? In large part due to its diverse and often contradictory voices—at least in a democracy or something resembling one—steadily feeding and modifying public opinion. It's a machine of mass production of beliefs, desires, inclinations, and more. The media provides an endless stream of information and debate. However, the selection of this information itself orients or disorients desires, beliefs, inclinations, and conversations within the self as well as with others. And then there's the onslaught of commercial advertising that muddles it all even further. At this point it becomes unclear whether we're being informed or whether we're being manipulated to buy things we don't even need.

To complicate things further, words like "press, "mass media," and "journalism" are used to describe vastly different institutions, as different as the individuals who work in these fields and their objectives. At one extreme you have the large conglomerates of mass media, both national and international, which build Walls: they play an important role in politics and even government, creating or destabilizing, often with hidden economic or political agendas. Among their ranks you'll find well-paid journalists who are just following orders, expressing views they have adopted for their own financial benefit. They opine and opine and opine; they never stop. You can turn off the television and throw out the papers and magazines, and you still won't be able to avoid them, because their echoes continue to reverberate throughout society, capturing minds as though the true occupation of journalists were to act as *Footsoldiers of Spin*. At the other extreme of this heterogeneous *continuum* there are journalists and segments of the media who, often with little means, risk their lives to pierce these Walls: they carefully investigate atrocities to testify against injustice, crime, and horror. Generally speaking, the journalists in the former of these two sources of information (really disinformation) are nothing more than *mercenaries*. They are the *Footsoldiers of Spin* who don't bother to make the distinction between fact-based reporting and opinions, or so-called fake news, if it serves their personal interests. The other kind of journalists can be attributed the noble status of *witnesses*.

Witnesses can be described according to three uses or definitions of the word *witness*. A "witness" is someone who testifies in a lawsuit; it follows that, faced with various, conflicting descriptions of an event in society, a journalist-witness conveys information that is critical for their readers, or their viewers, to be able to make a well-informed assessment. The conveyance of this information is critical because a journalist-witness, or meta-witness, has taken the time to investigate the events in question. At the same time, when reconstructing events as history, a journalist-witness tries to relate events in such a way that their root causes come to light. A journalist-witness treats events as "natural occurrences." The investigation's aim is to sketch out explanations subject to debate.

That's why journalist-witnesses, or meta-witnesses, are the critical historians of events *that are happening now*—the immediate present. Like other good critical historians, and like historians in the past who did not adhere to the concept of "history set in stone" or "official history," journalist-witnesses don't just opine based on the facts "at hand," they *investigate* the context and timing of events, and they take the time to *investigate* the causes—often complex—in the past, present, and future. To achieve these ends, journalist-witnesses often must shuffle through the most sordid social garbage, and, on occasion, have the courage to live in extremely dangerous circumstances.

When I define the difference between *journalist-mercenaries* or *Footsoldiers of Spin* and *journalist-witnesses*, on the one hand, and between *opinions* and *investigations* on the other, I'm of course oversimplifying things. In reality there are many levels and gradations, contradictions and deficiencies that differ from country to country, and between regions in the same country. It's well-known that the mass media either belongs to the nation-state or to corporations. That's why it's often said that in both cases they're *mercenary institutions*. Because either the nation-state pays journalists to praise its accomplishments and cover up its errors and corruption, or corporations behave similarly to serve their own interests.

But we must be careful. If we adhere rigidly to these extremes we may succumb to the logical fallacy of all or nothing. Not all the media, state-owned or private, lacks impartiality to the same extent. One might even say that in no country, at any point in history, has the media ever enjoyed the luxury of being impartial and homogeneous. Once in a blue moon in some societies the media—even *mercenary institutions*—hire *journalist-witnesses* in an attempt to broaden and diversify their audiences; they hire different voices, including dissidents who undertake painstaking investigations without fear of offending dangerously powerful people.

That's why, if you live in a highly developed society with a powerful collective memory that does not hide from mistakes in its own past or from self-deception, brazen lies make for bad business. (Except for people who are addicted to sameness, which is another way to refer to fanaticism, few people will watch a newscast or buy a paper that they know from experience will *always*—what a word!—repeat the same accusations against the same people and praise the same people repeatedly. Boredom also has a negative impact.) If you accept these views, it's hard to avoid the disappointing conclusion that in most cases a population has a mass media with the degree of bias they deserve.

Despite all that, I cling to my arguments like a compass in a storm. Notwithstanding the many distinctions and nuances one must draw in the midst of confusion—and in such issues, confusion is often so dense that we end up punishing those who are the least to blame—the differences between *journalist-mercenaries* or *Foot-soldiers of Spin* and *journalist-witnesses* and between *opinions* and *investigations* guide us with repercussions that echo far and wide.

## V

Let's move on to *personal autonomies.* These are boundaries that should be part of any politics of democratic integration as much as or even more than those of social autonomies. Personal autonomy is the root of dignity of every human animal—regardless of the color of their skin, their sexual orientation, their language, or their religious and political beliefs. Respect for each and every person's dignity is the non-negotiable condition for different peoples to live together.

It's no accident that the concept of personal autonomy is often linked to self-governance and self-construction, too. But in what strange way is a human animal "capable of self-construction"? Not from nothing, not without materials at hand, and not in isolation as an *absolute self-construction*. Social and personal autonomies are not forms of autarchy. On the contrary, human animals can only build their societies and construct themselves with the materials they're given, which are external to themselves and contingent, or *relative self-constructions*—like a bricklayer who builds his own home with materials he has earned through laborious effort. Because if we correctly affirm that we build our second nature, at the same time we can't deny the fact that we use materials from our first nature and the second nature which others have passed and continue to pass on to us.

Clearly, the relativity of these constructions becomes obvious in negative situations, especially under awful circumstances verging on the atrocious violation of human rights that occurs in any despotic situation. Such violations weaken and even break the human animal's will to resist evil and other obstacles, just as much as the capacity to recover from any kind of harm, whether psychological or physical. Subjection to torture, the murder of loved ones, living in a climate of kidnappings and endless extortion—these are not just betrayals of human rights when they occur, they undermine one's sense of control of life in the days and years that follow; they also weaken one's self-confidence, particularly the capacity to use reason. But these capacities are the very basis for social or personal self-determination. (Part of the trouble that journalist-witnesses cause derives from their investigation of these violations—these occurrences that prevent people from constructing themselves.)

It follows that the relative self-construction of human animals depends on processes that may be divided into two types: processes of socialization, of agreements and disagreements with both positive and negative customs of a society; and processes of rationalization. In the latter, people learn to accept and reject their own desires, inclinations, and habits, as well as the beliefs of people around them. They use good and poor justifications which are, in part, also learned from their environment. But we human animals won't accept any rationale just as one more imposed conditioning. We assume—we cannot stop making assumptions—that accepting a well-justified desire, belief, inclination, or habit does not merely mean actualizing social conditioning. Based on such inevitable, first-person assumptions, we assume that we learn on our own—sometimes painfully—to discover reasonable desires, reasonable beliefs, reasonable inclinations, and reasonable habits, just as, after receiving education, we learn to discover *for ourselves* that eight plus eight is always sixteen.

Of course, these many *differentiating articulations* of society—social and personal autonomies—are not islands surrounded by impenetrable Walls, islands that have nothing to do with the sea surrounding them. On the contrary, such *differentiating articulations* reflect the social and personal conflicts surrounding autonomies and which often corrupt them. For example, in social autonomies there are plenty of journalist-mercenaries who are complicit, doing whatever they're asked to do and formulating apologia for the governments or corporations they work for. But the frequent corruption of things of value is just further proof that they're valuable, worth fighting for. (Worthless things inspire neither falsification nor corruption.)

That's why it's so important to learn to deal with such corruption and to fight it without questioning the immense value of what has been misrepresented: both formal and informal, and social and personal autonomies, the various *differentiating articulations* of a society. Because, among other things, these *differentiating articulations* also reinforce other forms of value and strengthen the possibility that principled, incorruptible people exist, those unprotected and endangered guardians of the right to truth.

That's why these types of autonomies can provide good training for learning to say "no." That's why it is important to support them. Their existence is an unmistakable sign that integration hasn't gone so far as to create "masses": subsumed bundles that stifle. If this is the case, there are still corners, paths, margins, and hideaways, interstices where freedom can be experienced.

Of course, this is how politics of democratic integration demonstrates its complex character, complete with winding labyrinths that sometimes lead nowhere. All politics of democratic integration must not only negotiate a variety of tensions—which are often difficult to prevent from degenerating into chaos—but they must also toggle between two levels.

Its operations on the first level—quotidian governmental politics—have to go hand in hand with operations on the second level—*metapolitics* that are highly alert to the miscarriage and abuse of power. These metapolitics rope off the different *differentiating articulations* of a society: the places in which a government's plans meet its limits—the limits that both social and personal autonomies impose.

Nonetheless, it's important to reemphasize that to prevent the many *differentiating articulations* of society from succumbing to the temptation of the Wall, we shouldn't overlook the fact that *all* autonomies are *relative* and, even more importantly, they are by definition *relational.* We become more and more autonomous in a society of autonomous people.

So we can see that autonomies, these *differentiating articulations* of society, create both separations and bonds: they mediate the spheres of the public, the private, and the intimate, that compose the way of life of these beings—humans—who, despite their numerous differences, and their fears and even hate of other human animals, continue to attempt to live together, successfully or not. Often they do so kicking and screaming, with lots of conflict—the desire to submit or be submitted to—creating betrayal and blind desperation.

But we must resist the seduction of the *Footsoldiers of Spin*; there lies the road that eventually leads to the construction of Walls, the antecedents of war and other horrors.

## VI

If we take the time to look back, it's easy to see that we did not only begin to investigate abstract models of two opposing kinds of politics that must be contrasted empirically. Such models also indicate "positionalities" toward life: the direction of wants, inclinations, personal desires, morals, and even expectations. Maybe that's why it's possible to illustrate these directions with two characteristic images, as images also enrich our understanding.

Aggressive exclusionary politics or modern Wall politics, which build barriers and create avalanches of xenophobia and racism, attempt to create a homogeneous population segment. But at the same time, that segment of the population becomes even more subordinate through faithful dedication to some public or private power. The aim is to prevent its members from realizing that they live in a walled world, through endless repetition that, in effect, *"More of the same is always better and anything else is always bad,"* or *mirror politics.* (Or, better said, a "pseudopolitics" of mirrors, which—with the necessary support of the mercenary mass media—confuses this politics with its nefarious counterexamples: politicking and neodespotism that denigrate, weaken, and eventually eradicate the politics of democratic integration.)

In contrast, a politics of democratic integration is faced with a complicated puzzle of tensions and autonomies, both personal and social, which eventually look outside themselves to find compromise and workable solutions, frequently redefining its objectives—*window politics*: politics for observing and listening, both carefully and insightfully, the surroundings and beyond—and sometimes even further to investigate, justify, and fearlessly imagine, with a nomadic attitude.

# A WALL THAT THREATENS BIODIVERSITY

CISTEIL X. PÉREZ HERNÁNDEZ
TRANSLATED BY LISA DILLMAN

Biodiversity doesn't understand political divisions. And that's a fact that U.S. and Mexican scientists are now confronting as a result of U.S. President Donald Trump's insistence on continuing with his border wall project to separate the United States from Mexico. The plan is for a 3,200-kilometer wall, of which 1,050 kilometers of barriers and an additional 800 kilometers of roads have already been built.

In October 2018, eighteen scientists from both countries joined voices in the viewpoint paper "Nature Divided, Scientists United: U.S.–Mexico Border Wall Threatens Biodiversity and Binational Conservation" to ask the U.S. government to halt or modify the project.[1] Authors included international experts such as Edward O. Wilson and José K. Sarukhán, and the paper, published in *BioScience*, received an additional 2,556 signatures from scientists around the world.

Specialists point out three ways that the wall's infrastructure and security operations threaten the region's biota: 1) the U.S. Department of National Security has the authority to waive any environmental laws that might stop the wall's construction; 2) the wall requires the alteration and fragmentation of wild flora and fauna habitats, the project lacks environmental impact analysis,

The first version of this text was published in *Letras Libres*: https://www.letraslibres.com/mexico/ciencia-y-tecnologia/un-muro-que-amenaza-la-biodiversidad.

and alternatives that would be less damaging to biodiversity have not been explored; and 3) millions of hectares of protected areas established by governments, ethnic groups, NGOs, and landowners from both countries, as well as several million dollars invested in conservation programs, are now at risk because their objectives might be undermined or resources diverted to the construction of this barrier, while binational collaboration and scientific research in the region would be harmed.

The wall would negatively impact five hotspots—places with an exceptional concentration of endemic species at risk of extinction by habitat loss—as well as several protected natural areas and six different types of ecosystem. It would also divide the populations of 1,506 species, 62 of which are classified as Critically Endangered, as per the International Union for Conservation of Nature (IUCN). One of the most significant effects is that the border wall would impede connectivity between many sections of natural landscape and isolate the populations of nonflying native terrestrial and freshwater species—over 25 percent of them—that live along the border, including the jaguar (*Panthera onca*) and the ocelot (*Leopardus pardalis*), which would render reproduction between individuals on opposite sides of the wall impossible.

Three species on the list that appeared in the aforementioned paper are the hedgehog cactus, the Crotch bumblebee, and the Sonoran pronghorn. Their cases illustrate the border wall's threat to their existence as well as that of hundreds of other species.

## *Echinocereus chisoensis* (Chisos Mountain pitaya or Chisos hedgehog cactus)

This cactus is endemic to the Big Bend region, located in the Chihuahuan desert between the states of Texas, Chihuahua, and Coahuila.[2] In 2011, it was declared a Natural Area of Binational Interest, which both strengthened the relationship between Mexico and the state of Texas and increased conservation investment.

*E. chisoensis* has a very limited distribution, is relatively scarce, and requires very specific ecological conditions. For instance, it only inhabits dry riverbeds, deserts, and chaparrals. During the first years of its life, this cactus needs other larger plants for cover in order to survive. In addition, its flowers require a very specific pollinator, the *Diadasia rinconis* cactus bee, in order to produce fruit and seeds.

Due to illegal poaching, habitat fragmentation and modification, and the presence of invasive plants, it is now threatened or endangered and has been on the species protection lists published by the most important U.S. institutions since 1988. In 2010, fewer than 1,500 specimens were counted, and threats to the hedgehog cactus have not declined.[3]

The roads and construction routes required by the wall will degrade and reduce its habitat, and possibly also the number of individuals, which could in turn lead to a new decline in populations, bringing the cactus closer to extinction.

## *Bombus crotchii* (Crotch bumblebee)

The *Bombus crotchii* bumblebee is a species at high risk of extinction, categorized as Endangered on the IUCN Red List.[4] Its distribution is limited to scrub and grasslands from eastern California to El Progreso, Sierra de Juárez, in Baja California. Specifically, its habitat in the area adjacent to the wall is recognized as a biodiversity conservation hotspot.

An important part of its habitat on both sides of the border has been degraded by rapid urbanization and extensive agricultural intensification. Additionally, the species is suffering from the effects of climate change and excessive use of pesticides, as well as intense competition with the European honeybee *Apis mellifera*. In the last twenty years, its numbers, already low, have declined 67 percent.[5]

These bumblebees are social insects that live in colonies and nest underground. They are important parts of the natural ecosystem due to their role as pollinators of native plants and crops, such as alfalfa and sage. It is likely that all threats to the Crotch bumblebee will increase with the wall, given that their habitat could be reduced once again and their populations fragmented further still.

## *Antilocapra americana sonoriensis* (Sonoran pronghorn)

This herbivore, similar to a deer or antelope, is endemic to North America. The unique *Antilocapra americana sonoriensis*[6] variety has a population numbering under one thousand individuals,[7] which lives isolated in the Gran Desierto de Altar reserve, in the Sonora and Arizona borderlands, and on several Chihuahua ranches. In the nineteenth and twentieth centuries, it had a wide distribution but was almost eliminated as a result of increased mining and agriculture in its habitat, as well as poaching.

The Sonoran pronghorn inhabits open plains, hillsides, mesetas or plateaus, and broad riverbeds. It eats herbaceous plants, shrubs, cacti, and grasses. The pronghorn can survive long periods drinking only dew and moisture from the plants it consumes. It is an important prey for coyotes, pumas, mountain cats, and golden eagles, meaning that the pronghorn is a vital part in the food chain. Additionally, this small herbivore is considered a "sower" because it leaves the seeds of plants it consumes in its tracks, together with fertilizer (feces and urine). A short time later, the seeds germinate, and herbaceous plants and shrubs grow once more in the places where pronghorn made their way.

The Official Mexican Standard (NOM-059-SEMARNAT-2010[8]) and the Convention on International Trade in Endangered Species of Wild Fauna and Flora (CITES) categorize this species as Endangered. Interest in preservation of the Sonoran pronghorn has allowed multiple collaborations between the state of Sonora, the Arizona Fish and Game Department, and the U.S. Fish and Wildlife Service. In 2017, binational collaboration led to an aerial census of the Sonoran pronghorn, although the results have not yet been published.

The main threats facing this species are poaching, drought, and predation. Its vulnerability is increased with installation of barbed-wire fencing in its habitat, which is unsuitable, as it reduces the pronghorn's mobility, speed, and escape routes.[9] Building the wall in the Sonora-Arizona borderlands unquestionably represents a serious threat to the species, as it divides populations that are already reduced and limits its ability to escape predators.

## For a Biodiversity Without Walls

The border wall would have a strong negative impact not only on flora and fauna species but also on nature's contributions to people (what used to be called "ecosystem services"); in this case, people in both countries.[10] It has been documented that the following would be directly affected: 1) regulating contributions, such as pollination of native plants and crops done by greater and lesser long-nosed bats (*Leptonycteris nivalis* and *L. yerbabuenae*) and other species, as well as pest control undertaken by species including the *Tadarida brasiliensis* bat, which regulates pests that attack cotton crops in Texas and Arizona; 2) also, biodiversity maintenance as well as the nutrient cycling and seed dispersal undertaken by species like the Sonoran pronghorn; and even 3) *non-material* contributions, interlinked with cultural contexts, such as those afforded by the monarch butterfly (*Danaus plexippus*) and species sought by bird watchers. Undoubtedly, the loss or reduction of these contributions also has an economic impact.

To avoid this bleak picture, experts recommend that the project incorporate the conservation and mitigation actions outlined in U.S. environmental law; conduct species identification, as well as identify habitats and resources threatened by the wall's infrastructure; and hold training sessions for border agents so they will be able to identify researchers working in the region. They have also stated that the U.S. government needs to recognize and prioritize the ecological value of the region, as well as preserve the economic, political, and cultural value of the areas surrounding the wall. For its part, the Mexican government must also insist on revisions to the project in the name of biota conservation and nature's contributions to people. The U.S. government has already shown some positive response. For instance, it prevented the destruction of two environmental research and education centers, the National Butterfly Center and Bentsen State Park, both adjacent to the border, when the original project planned to eliminate them. This action provided cause for hope that nature would not be divided or destroyed by the wall. Yet, in October 2019, at the Organ Pipe Cactus National Monument, on the Arizona-Mexico border, hundreds of cacti and other plants were removed and bulldozed, including several giant desert saguaros (*Carnegiea gigantea*), as a result of wall construction activity—the erection of a nine-meter sheet metal barrier. A variety of specialists agree that many of these species cannot be transplanted or relocated, which makes it very likely that most will not survive.

There is still no easy solution to the problems caused by this enormous project, which seeks at all costs to build a barrier that will be nothing but a continuous line of devastation. Scientists and conservationists are currently fighting against the clock to stop the looming ecological catastrophe, and they are practically alone. There is no question that they need every possible form of support, including that of the Mexican government, so their arguments against the wall can, in the end, be heard.

# BACK TO TIJUANA

LEONARDO TARIFEÑO
TRANSLATED BY VICTOR MEADOWCROFT

## I

You should never return to the scene of the crime. But, what if there is only a crime when you go back?

I must have been thinking something along these lines on the afternoon in May when I returned to Tijuana's "tolerance zone," the place I'd gotten to know years before people in the United States started talking about the "wall" that surrounds it. A timid sun was grazing the doors of the cantinas, spying on the secrets of noisy alleyways, and caressing the overly made-up faces of the young girls offering themselves among drunks, uniformed police officers, and women who relied less on blush and more on experience. Lost inside that labyrinth, I knew I was looking for something I didn't want to find. Are books with open endings the most dangerous? This was the question that was troubling me. Particularly as I'd written one.

"Art allows us to maintain the illusion of an elegant ending, but in life there are no endings, in life there are only tragedies, partings and losses," says the Argentinian writer Ricardo Piglia in *La forma inicial*. This sentence encapsulates a suspicion I'd been unable to express, which is why I cite it in the last chapter of my book *No vuelvas* (2018), a journalistic account based on the stories of deportees I met in Tijuana during years of investigation, near misses, urgent friendships, and crossings at the border of my personal limitations.

Or, in the words of Piglia, "tragedies, partings and losses." Had I not already witnessed many of these in this city wounded by the "wall"? Yes, but which was which? Clear delimitations do not exist in border zones; in their place there is the flow of exchange, the permanent intermixing of life, the chiaroscuros of portraits resistant to brushstrokes in a single color. The border calls for a meeting with the other; this is why it appeals to our sensitivities and ends up dividing us into that which we are and that which we could be. It is a place of transit toward the best and worst of ourselves. And, once there, the "tragedies, partings and losses" are dependent on the scenography in which each of us learns to recognize ourselves: a bridge, a mirror, a wall.

This might all sound very metaphorical, but I experienced it in the flesh at the Padre Chava Salesian refectory, one of the few places in Tijuana where deportees, many of them already made homeless, can feed themselves on the one free meal they receive per day. Since 2015, I've paid numerous visits to this refectory, located only a few feet from the three fences separating Tijuana from San Diego, to interview some of the more than a thousand people expelled from the United States who arrive every morning in search of hot soup, bread, and something approaching a dose of consolation. The fact, as I quickly learned from their own accounts, was that local police would detain people as soon as they crossed the border from the United States into Mexico because they knew they were carrying dollars. Since, at the time, Barack Obama's government was expelling a Mexican to Tijuana every ten minutes, the spoils became too tempting for authorities to ignore. If their compatriot-prey resisted, agents would confiscate their documents, beat them, and threaten them. In less than fifteen minutes, a deportee from the United States was transformed into an undocumented immigrant in Mexico. And with no documents, separated from their families, persecuted by the police, and finding themselves in a city many were visiting for the first time, they were unable to get jobs and quickly ran out of money for the basic necessities, like food, shelter from the cold, and a place to sleep.

During that winter of 2015, on a very cold morning and following various frustrated attempts at interviews, I came across María de la Luz Guajardo Castillo at the refectory, a fifty-seven-year-old woman who was detained after an incident of domestic violence in San Diego, where she had lived since 1999. María de la Luz was clutching a grubby woolen hat in one hand and two plastic bags in the other. Seated next to me, looking hunched and unwell, there was no way of convincing her to let go of the things she was holding, maybe out of fear that someone even more desperate might snatch away what little she possessed. In whispers, she explained that her partner had been an alcoholic who was married to another woman, a combination seen as unacceptable by her brothers, who lived in Guadalajara. "He drank a lot and would smack me around," she told me. "In the fridge there was nothing but beer. You could say I'm familiar with mistreatment at the hands of men. And for causing a disturbance, because of all the noise and shouting, one day they sent me to the guys at ICE." I immediately wanted to know more: when and why had she gone to live in the United States, had anybody helped her, and how had she planned to survive in a strange city. But she had other needs. Without waiting for my questions, she interjected: "But tell me, young man, would you be able to help me find my daughter?"

I'd gone to Tijuana to gather testimonies for the piece of investigative journalism I'd embarked upon, not to help any one person in particular. But if I didn't offer my help to those who so desperately needed it, what good could my investigation do? From one of the plastic bags, María de la Luz retrieved a small pile of crumpled papers and spread them on the table, pieces of an uncertain puzzle where she played out her future. On the back of a flier advertising vacant rooms she'd written, in pencil, the telephone number of a hospital in San Diego where she'd left her sick son, as well as the name of a doctor. The piece of paper she was unable to find was the one containing the phone number and email address of her eldest daughter, María Elena Martínez, who lived in Tampa. That's why she wanted me to look for her, so she could let her daughter know what had happened and where and in what conditions she was living.

Today, I understand that the border exposes the best and worst of oneself. It placed before me the challenge of trying to help without feeling adequately prepared to do so. And, just as in that moment I felt obligated to rise to that challenge, I now feel compelled to speak of what I saw when I went back to Tijuana one afternoon in May and found myself lost in the "tolerance zone," clinging to the single certainty of having written an open-ended book.

## II

I met Emma Sánchez on a rainy morning in 2015 in Parque de la Amistad, the Friendship Park, a section of Tijuana's border wall that, despite the double fence and surly vigilance of the Border Patrol, transforms every weekend into a binational meeting place. Wearing the pink T-shirt of the Dreamers' Moms non-profit organization, Emma would arrive every Sunday to wait by the side of the fence in case any mother with children on the "other side" required the assistance that, years before, had been extended to her by other women in her situation, those expelled from the United States who—just like her—later joined the Dreamers' Moms team.

The Parque is a strange place. The fence separating families with children on one side from parents on the other crosses the mountains before ending up in the sea. From nearby you can hear cumbia music playing in neighboring restaurants, a beach party atmosphere that belies the tragedy apparent alongside the thick bars, the impossible embraces, and the evident distress nobody wants to show. Tourists take selfies with the fence in the background, clink their beer bottles together, and stroll through a landscape of separated families, political hatred, and social devastation. Anyone taking the path leading from the sea to the edge of the park will hear whispers that tell of lost jobs, unfulfilled promises, premature surrender, and improbable dreams. The day I met Emma, I crossed paths beside the wall with a family who had brought along mariachis to celebrate a birthday, a group of deported veterans of Mexican origin who'd fought in U.S. wars, and an emaciated young man with a three-day beard who was waiting to see his family on the "other side."

"Of my thirty-nine years, I spent twenty-nine of them living in the United States," this young man told me, shortly after introducing himself as David Díaz, from Puebla. "I crossed over very young, with my family, at Nido de las Águilas. Now I've left behind my wife, my four kids, and my grandson in New Jersey."

After showing me photos of his loved ones he keeps in his wallet, David gave me a brief summary of his life. Until his deportation, two months earlier, he'd worked for a moving company, been a member of a church, and never had any problems with the authorities. "They detained me for carrying a fake driver's license," he confessed. "The lawyer told me this misdemeanor is usually punished with a fine, not deportation. But what can I do about it now? Wait. She says she can get me four years' probation."

*"And, in the meantime, what will you do?"*

"I need to stay in Tijuana until I can go back. There's no other way. If I left, how would I see my family? Freshly deported, leaving the Port of Entry, I was approached by some brothers from the Fiesta Pentecostal Church, so now I work there, do repairs, assist with whatever they need. And on Sundays I join them here, at the park, to help out however I can."

*"But you need help too."*

"We all need help, who doesn't? I won't tell you I'm not desperate. You can't even imagine what it feels like when days and months go by without seeing your family, and with nobody telling you when you'll be able to see them again. Every night, before I go to sleep, I ask myself if what I did was really such a big deal. But coming to this place is good for me, you know? It makes me feel I'm not so alone."

Not far from David, sitting on a bench a couple of feet from the fence, was Emma. She is a petite woman with huge dark eyes, friendly and coquettish, the type who smiles and changes the subject when you ask their age. She was born "many" years ago, she says, in Apatzingán, Michoacán, and raised in Guadalajara. She moved to Vista, California, to work as a dental assistant. There, in Vista, every day on the way to the school where she was studying the language of her new country, she would go past the door of the mechanic's workshop that employed the man who would eventually become her partner. She didn't speak English, and he didn't understand Spanish, but love led them first into dating and then to becoming a married couple with three kids. "My husband handled all the paperwork, and it took a long time for the immigration appointment to reach me, perhaps because he notified the post office about our change of address rather than the Immigration Services," she explained. "The fact is, when I left Ciudad Juárez in 2006, which is where I was asked to present myself, they told me my visa was no longer valid and that it would be ten years before I was allowed to return. The news hit us like a bombshell, and we were left not knowing what to do. My husband had to go back to Vista; I went first to Guadalajara, then to stay with a brother in Los Cabos, until eventually my husband rented me a little house in Tijuana, so he could visit me. And I've been here ever since, with no family, only my friends from Dreamers' Moms."

*"And the rest of your family in Mexico?"*

"My family never call me. I have an aunt in the U.S. Army, but she told me she was prohibited from coming near the park while she was serving. After that, she deleted me on Facebook. She doesn't want people knowing she has a family member in my situation, as if I was someone you needed to be ashamed of. All I've got is my children and my husband. He's a Marine veteran and comes to see me every Sunday or every fortnight, but he recently had open-heart surgery and isn't well enough to do so much traveling. And, you know, at the time I requested a humanitarian visa so I could be there during the operation, but they denied me that too. They told me they could only grant it if he was dead or on the verge of dying."

That morning, I had arrived at Parque de la Amistad with the secret intention of meeting María de la Luz again. As I hadn't seen her since we spoke at the refectory, it occurred to me that she might show up in the area alongside the fence, where many deportees go every Sunday to meet with caseworkers. If I found her, I could introduce her to Emma and the rest of the Dreamers' Moms, activists who would be able to help her far more than I could. But, although I searched and waited right up until the last moment, I saw no trace of her. With no work, documents, or assistance, deportees live permanently on the brink of homelessness. And when they begin sleeping on the street, finding them becomes a tall order. Exposed to violence, abuse, and misery, they aren't even guaranteed to survive their risky day-to-day existence. Some, like David Díaz, find the help of a church. Others, like Emma, join forces with those who once helped them. And many, like María de la Luz, turn into ghosts the rest see without really seeing, transformed into gray shadows with plastic bags that appear only for a second before the wall of indifference makes them disappear again.

## III

Emma Sánchez arrived at the book launch for *No vuelvas* in Tijuana with Michael, her husband, squeezed into his military uniform. The event was taking place at the Tijuana Cultural Center (CECUT), in the middle of an unseasonably cold May. When they came in together, I was on stage. We exchanged smiles, and I wondered whether this greeting was the real ending to a book that, in telling a story that is constantly changing, struggles to preserve the "illusion of an elegant ending," as Piglia puts it. Only now, as I write this, do I think that the ending is yet to be written, as occurs with all dreams that are inhabited by some form of hope.

In the first row of the auditorium sat Armando Estrada, a friend from Tijuana who had given me plenty of assistance during my investigation. From his office in the CECUT, Armando had led a musical education project for deportees, which was abandoned because many of them, like María de la Luz, had disappeared completely, devoured by the wall of indifference that cuts through the city. However, far from becoming disillusioned, Armando had reimagined the project, directing it at an audience made up of kids who'd grown up in the "tolerance zone," many of them the children of drug addicts, traffickers, or prostitutes who didn't count educating their kids among their priorities. While working on *No vuelvas* I met many of these boys and girls, all between seven and twelve years old, and had accompanied them for some of their shows. Music was not going to save these kids, but it could help transport them to worlds different from the one destiny seemed to have mapped out for them. It could open doors. This was my friend's gamble, his open-ended dream.

When the chairperson opened the floor to the audience, Emma rose to her feet. She explained that a short while before she'd received permission to return to her home, in the United States, ten years after being deported to Tijuana. With a strength I didn't recognize, she recalled before the whole auditorium how she'd been unable to raise her children in Mexico, because the fact they were U.S. citizens meant there were legal impediments to their even receiving their vaccinations; her husband had raised the children on his own, as best he could, and throughout that whole decade he'd never stopped helping her. "Now we all live together, but we went through a very difficult time," she continued. "I wouldn't have been able to come this far without the support of my husband; I suffered a lot, but so did he. Though they divided us, we're still together. I don't want you to think that everyone in the United States is like Donald Trump. There are all sorts. We're living proof of that." Outside the auditorium, I asked her about María de la Luz. Emma had never seen her among the deported mothers who arrived at the Dreamers' Moms' offices. But, she assured me, sooner or later they all made their way there. "It's a matter of time, like what happened with me, like this whole story," she told me, in an embrace.

Down one of the corridors, Armando was waiting for me. "Let's go for a drive, I want to show you how things are," he said. On leaving CECUT we came face-to-face with the wall. "Always more fences, but people haven't crossed here for years," he told me. "What do you say? A show of strength or of weakness? Is it a monument to their own power or to their fear of the other?" True to my role as a journalist, I preferred to withhold my answer and ask the questions myself. I wanted to know about the reaction in the city to the arrival of the latest contingent of Haitian migrants and what had become of many of the deportees who appear in *No vuelvas*. Nacho, who'd been imprisoned in the United States for a crime he didn't commit? Ismael, the homeless man who carried a thick dictionary in his plastic bag? And the kids from the music workshop? Armando sighed as the car advanced along the fringes of the "tolerance zone." "See? This is where the Haitians ended up," he told me. "They're hard-working people, but they live right beside the drug-trafficking center. If they get killed, no one cares. The state doesn't handle it. And there are hundreds of them!" Then Armando spoke of Nacho, of Ismael, of the nun expelled from the refectory for demanding the city government be held accountable. With more melancholy than actual sadness, he told me how the music project had had its funding cut and was only able to keep going thanks to volunteer musicians, since the new authorities preferred to allow other students use of the CECUT's instruments.

"You said the deportees are like ghosts. And that's true, but it's not just them. This happens with the poor in general. We see them go past, but we don't pay attention to them. I'm talking about racism, classism, here and on the 'other side.' The same happens with the kids from the workshops. The question is: do you really want to see them?"

Armando parked the car in the "tolerance zone." Not too far away were the houses of the eleven- and twelve-year-old girls I'd met in 2015 as part of the music workshop. Getting out of the car, my eyes met with those of two girls of the same age who were offering themselves outside the entrance to a cantina. Now I tell myself that you shouldn't go looking for a story you don't want to find. Just trying to reach the end is enough.

# CLAY MIGRANTS

EDUARDO VÁZQUEZ MARTÍN
TRANSLATED BY ELLEN JONES

Alejandro Santiago was born in 1964 in the Oaxacan town of San Pedro Teococuilco—now called Teococuilco de Marcos Pérez—and died before his fiftieth birthday in 2013 in Oaxaca City. Those who knew him say that he spent his childhood in the countryside, in Zapotec country, where he spoke the language of his people and ran joyfully down its dirt roads. During his childhood, this boy—son of Isabel and Juan—learned to play games, games that taught him to hold on to his inner child for the rest of his life.

The writer Braulio Aguilar Orihuela—Santiago's friend, collaborator, and biographer—recounts how, after studying at Bellas Artes, Santiago became part of the Taller de Artes Plásticas Rufino Tamayo (the Rufino Tamayo Plastic Arts Workshop), where he met Rufino himself, and later the Taller Libre de Gráfica Oaxaqueña (the Oaxaca Free Graphic Arts Workshop), directed by Juan Alcázar, where he met Zoila López, his lifelong partner and the mother of their two children: Lucio and Alejandra. At barely twenty years old, he held his first exhibition and sold every single item; following this sign of good things to come, he pooled all his resources and set off to explore other cities, visit museums, and see the world. In 1998 he moved to Paris with Zoila and his son, Lucio.

Two years later, in 2000, Santiago returned with his family to Oaxaca. Back in Teococuilco, the artist experienced the desolation of a town that has lost almost everyone to migration, where there are many more absences than there are presences. Driven by the need to understand his people's fate, Alejandro Santiago set off on a

Photo by Antonio Turok.

journey to Tijuana. There he made contact with coyotes, who would take him over the border to follow in the footsteps of so many other Mexicans and migrants from around the world. Once in the United States, he assumed the status of "illegal" and experienced the life of a migrant for himself. One day he was gazing at a sea of crosses along the border; someone assured him: there are 2,500 of them.

Back in Oaxaca, Santiago decided to erect 2,501 bodies, each of them distinct, each with its own story, its own flesh and soul. Like the first beings created by the ancestral deities of the *Popol Vuh*, who preceded the men of maize, Santiago's migrants are made from clay. The work is an attempt to repopulate the empty spaces left behind by those who have emigrated; to fire in clay the shadows cast by those who are gone, shadows cast on the homes and hearts of those who remember and miss them. It is a work about the ghosts who, like Pedro Páramo, remain among us, refusing to untether themselves from their land.

This act of transformation, of transit between the worlds of the living and the dead, of restoration and healing—appropriate for the grandson of a *curandera*, a Zapotec "witch"—ended up becoming a process of collective work that eventually involved the whole Santiago family as well as about forty young people and Teococuilco residents. In a ranch acquired specifically for this project and baptized "Where the Zopilote Bird Dances," a small community created around Santiago's sculpture project dedicated itself to molding the bodies of its new residents, just like the ancient gods did, while the artist designed ovens to fire the pieces and decided on the pigments and paints that would bring the figures' skin to life. With a machete, with his hands, even with his teeth, the artist intervened in the bodies before they were fired: he inflicted pain on them, left them with scars, marked them with traces of life.

Wild-eyed faces covered in white desert dust, mothers and grandmothers with breasts exhausted from feeding their offspring, men made leathery by the sun and wind, women who wander the world unshod with children on their backs, some pregnant, all naked, genitals exposed—sheer fragility—resisting and persevering, each with arms crossed over their chests like the arms of the dead but faces full of the thirst, hunger, fear, desire, and hope of the living. Families and solitary individuals, adults and infants living out their nomadic fates, searching for new routes that might bring them to us, returning our gaze when we look at them, answering us when we address them, asking after those who were left behind, those who were lost on the way, while silently telling their story, the story of a great odyssey made by humanity in exile, by those who confront every hardship and remain willing to get back on the road again, however dangerous it might be, in search of better horizons. If you look closely, listen carefully, you can hear them. It sounds like a murmur, a far-off song: the quiet echo of those who had to leave.

*2501 Migrants*, despite its demographic density, creates a space for the personal testimonies that statistics erase. While recognizing the millions of humans who every day leave their place of birth behind—driven by hunger, by the threat of violence and the sacrifice

Photo by Antonio Turok.

Photo by Antonio Turok.

it requires, by the lack of opportunities provided by society—each piece's dramatic expression also gives an individual migrant back their human face, a face that is unique and unrepeatable.

*2501 Migrants* was exhibited in early 2020 at San Indefonso College, where 501 figures are on display. The exhibition marks the thirtieth anniversary of the National Autonomous University of Mexico's North American Research Center. The center's mission is to create knowledge that focuses on understanding national and global problems, and to respond to the challenges facing humanity in a world where capital and goods circulate practically freely but human beings are subject every day to increasingly hard borders and increasingly high walls. The pieces making up this exhibition—pieces rooted in the artist's own subjectivity and empathy—clearly contribute to the construction of an urgent, humanitarian vision that stands in solidarity with those who, every day, are leaving their homes, setting out on the world's roads and seas, crossing borders with dirt from their homelands ingrained in their skin but their eyes fixed on a new life.

In a reflective piece about this work, the poet Natalia Toledo reminds us that Alejandro Santiago was, like every Zapotec, a descendant of the clouds, and that for that reason his nature was shaped not by the political boundaries delimiting nations here on Earth but rather by the winds that flow through the skies. Like so much indigenous cosmogony, Zapotec metaphors can also be understood as universal images. As such, saying the artist was Zapotec is another way of saying that he was human—that, like the rest of us, he was part of the water cycle that flows around the planet and gives us life. We are living beings made of clouds that, when they open, allow us to drink, feed the rivers, moisten the Earth where our fruit grows, and put into potters' hands the liquid that makes it possible to mold clay.

# INVENTING THE ENEMY: THE BORDER IN THE TRUMP ERA

JUAN VILLORO
TRANSLATED BY SAMANTHA SCHNEE

## I. Where Dreams Are Returned to Sender

On Sunday the twenty-sixth of June, 2016, I was in Playas de Tijuana. There, the metal wall that separates Mexico from the United States extends into the horizon, disappearing into the ocean. In a place with such strong waves, you might think there would be lifeguards in the bay, but no, there's a different kind of guard. Through the high fence you can see a Border Patrol truck waiting to arrest anyone who tries to swim across. On the Mexican side, the barrier has been painted in a rainbow of colors. Graffiti reads: "This is where dreams are returned to sender."

On Sundays, families spread blankets on the sand to share food and drinks while they wait for their relatives who come to see them from "the other side."

These visits with loved ones take place with the fence between them. Their feelings cross through cracks and holes: an immigrant living in California rolls up dollars to pass to relatives, who reciprocate with music from the north of Mexico (a musician in a sombrero plays the *bajo sexto* while another plays the accordion); a young woman dressed to the nines protects herself from the sun with an umbrella and speaks softly to her boyfriend, who reaches out from another country to touch her through the fence; an old man enjoys a beer proffered to him from the Mexican side (he drinks through the fence with a straw).

The music tells the painful saga of immigrants: the sorrow of departure and the difficulty of return. Although the songs are melancholic, adults trade stories that culminate in laughter and children kick balls around, using the wall as a goal, or they play with stray dogs adept at fetching sticks and stones thrown into the ocean.

A sign warns that there are sharp blades beneath the water. A tower decked out with cameras, sensors, and radar rises further afield, on the American side. On this closely guarded coastline, only the fish can get around without visas.

The sheets of rusty metal that form this barrier—part fence, part wall—are the detritus of war. They were used during the "Desert Storm" in Iraq to help tanks move across the sand and have been repurposed to separate Mexico from the United States. It's not just an insurmountable obstacle; it's an installation, a symbolic object that declares the intent to halt immigrants.

These Sunday gatherings show just how many have made the crossing. A few miles away, in another California, there are jobs to be had, but the rules of immigration resemble those of a cruel video game: if the crossing is difficult, those who succeed will accept any type of abuse as their "reward."

Everything about the wall in Playas de Tijuana is surreal, starting with the irony of spending one's day off work behind bars. But the atmosphere isn't oppressive. Tears and laughter have a defiant quality. They shouldn't be happening, but they do. However, the absence of an oppressive atmosphere isn't the most surprising thing; it's the fact that it can all happen in a place like this.

There's a map of Mexico on the ground. It's near where the people gather, but no one sets foot on it.

## II. The Viral Candidate

Meetings at Playas de Tijuana represent the "normalization" of the border crisis, which for decades has subjected the lives of those who attempt to reach the promised land to great danger. In his eight years in the White House, Barack Obama deported more than three million Mexicans—the highest number in history—the friendly face of unjust policies that would have continued under Hillary Clinton and that paved the way for Donald Trump's delusional ranting.

Wealth begets delusion, and the ego of the businessman born in Queens, New York, in 1946 is no exception. Behold the most powerful tweeter on the planet, the host of television shows about survival of the fittest in the economic jungle. In 1987, Michael Douglas brought the despicable Gordon Gekko to life in the movie *Wall Street*, directed by Oliver Stone. The motto of this financier was "Greed is good." Capitalism had evolved from the Protestant work ethic studied by Max Weber to the display of shameless and ostentatious wealth, the obscene exhibition of wealth that Trump represents (if you have any doubts, just remember that the bathroom on his private jet is outfitted in solid gold).

Author Philip K. Dick both feared and admired the originality of former Libyan leader Muammar Gaddafi, who went into battle dressed like he was going to the disco. Extravagance can make an autocrat memorable, but it doesn't redeem him. When Trump appeared as a character on *The Simpsons*, it illustrated another spectacle: in real life he had already become a caricature. But let's not forget that his view of the world is delusional, because he has access to the red phone.

In the third millennium, ideologies find themselves in crisis and politicians who don't care whether they appear motivated by principle or by satisfying their own obscure, personal desires in the name of their "homeland" or "hometown" are everywhere.

The great paradox of nationalism is that it's not about loving a country as it is, but an imaginary country. America's greatness is over, pronounced the magnate who became the primary propagator of this lie on social media in 2016. In his bizarre version of the cosmos, Muslims and Mexicans were responsible for the United States' decline. The *New York Times* and CNN predicted he would lose spectacularly, showing how out of touch with reality they were. Welcome to the era of fake news! Accordingly, in 2016 the Oxford English Dictionary made *post-truth* the word of the year, defining it as the deliberate use of lies.

In an environment where public opinion is driven by Facebook and other platforms, where truth is conflated with conjecture and conspiracy rather than with the traditional media, Donald Trump has become the highly resistant virus of the digital era.

## III. The Enemy Inside

Primo Levi wrote, "Our neighbors, that is, our enemies." On an episode of *The Sopranos*, the main character of the show discovers that his neighbors are afraid of—and to some extent enjoy—living next door to a gangster. To feed the morbid curiosity of the household next door, Tony Soprano fills a box with sand, wraps it up, and, in a confidential tone, asks his neighbor to look after it. He accepts the package with a mixture of terror and pride, imagining that it contains something dangerous. In a single gesture, Tony both ingratiates himself and poisons their lives.

It's not easy to live with the other, in large part because it's convenient to consider them inferior. Umberto Eco once took a Pakistani's taxi in New York. When the cabbie learned he was Italian, he asked Eco, "Who are your enemies?" Eco answered that for the time being his country wasn't at war with anyone other than itself. His reply disconcerted the driver: a country without adversaries also lacked an identity. Could the Italians be so insipid? When he got out of the cab, Eco compensated for his country's surprising lack of belligerence with a tip. But a few minutes later, he decided that in reality Italy faced a multitude of enemies (most of which were domestic) but lacked the clarity to identify them. The cabbie's chagrin was deeper than it seemed: the other can act as a target for hate and mistrust, but also, by contrast, defines who we are. Eco's essay "Inventing the Enemy" was the result of these reflections; Eco writes, "Having an enemy is important not only to define our identity but also to provide us with an obstacle against which to measure our system of values and, in seeking to overcome it, to demonstrate our own worth. So when there is no enemy, we have to invent one" (tr. Richard Dixon).

Unlike Italy, the United States has not hesitated to identify international adversaries in order to justify its domestic policies. Nazis, Communists, Islamic terrorists, and drug traffickers are the successive villains in this narrative. During perestroika, Eduard Shevardnadze, the Minister of Foreign Affairs for the Soviet Union, visited the United States and said, "I'm going to do the worst thing that could happen to them: eliminate an enemy."

But enemies are as perennial as paranoia, and recently they're imaginary: Mexicans. According to Donald Trump, the country that inspired the adventures of Speedy Gonzalez should stay in its hole. On January 11, 2017, he announced his intention to build a wall sixteen meters high to prevent the influx of illegal immigrants, and he added that we, Mexico, would pay for it.

Enrique Peña Nieto, then president of Mexico, said he wouldn't pay a penny. Obviously, Trump wasn't referring to the cost of the bricks, but rather to protectionist business policies, taxing the money that immigrants send home, and deporting Mexicans (300,000 of them imprisoned). There was nothing Peña Nieto could do, and unluckily he had unwittingly helped Trump.

In a gesture of blatant brown-nosing, our president invited the Republican candidate to Mexico during his presidential campaign.

The idea was proposed by Mexico's Secretary of the Treasury, Luis Videgaray, a friend of Jared Kushner, Trump's son-in-law. The magnate used this unique opportunity to demonstrate his presidential qualities and to humiliate another country on its own turf. The 2016 election was so competitive that it's not an exaggeration to say that this visit contributed to Trump's victory. The local backlash resulted in Videgaray's losing his job. But when the Republican party won, the ousted politician returned as the Secretary of Foreign Affairs. In a further act of subordination, Peña Nieto facilitated the extradition of the most notorious drug kingpin on Earth, Joaquín "el Chapo" Guzmán, the day before Trump took office. These "goodwill" gestures did nothing to soften the sworn enemy of the "bad hombres" south of the border, because Trump's politics aren't based on reality; they're predicated on the creation of an imaginary enemy to make it appear he's protecting his country from a terrible threat.

Like Tony Soprano, Donald Trump knows how to keep his neighbor in line by handing him a suspicious package. Unfortunately, the recipient of this box was the Mexican government.

## IV. The Land of Ghosts

In the movie *Pulp Fiction* some thugs attack a diner. Everyone freezes, their arms in the air, and there's a tense silence. Suddenly, there's a sound: someone moves in the adjacent room. "Mexicans, out of the fucking kitchen!" one of the thugs yells. He hasn't seen anyone; he just assumes that, if there are people in the kitchen, they're Mexican.

For decades, the United States has depended on invisible laborers to make their food and wash their dirty dishes. Like the assailants in *Pulp Fiction*, Trump is asking them to leave their workplaces. Will they return to Mexico, where their jobs were even worse? "I'm leaving on the train of absence/I've got a one-way ticket," one of the most popular Mexican songs goes. But the ones who are absent haven't left their homeland in search of adventure. They've followed the road of necessity and brought their culture to Chicago, Los Angeles, New York, Phoenix, and other cities. In a way, they belong to a third country—neither the United States nor Mexico—a hybrid place: Mexamerica, the portable homeland of immigrants.

Millions of Mexicans in the United States are like the ghosts in the novel *Pedro Paramo*, half-beings, frontiersmen who have neither documents nor places to stay. The Border Patrol didn't see them, but we didn't see them either. It's possible that the only good thing about despicable Donald Trump is that he has finally made us take notice of the hidden, the displaced, the dishwashers, the Mexicans who are now bereft of Mexico.

Jorge Bustamante, founder of the Colegio de la Frontera Norte, has demonstrated that if our economy hasn't worsened it's thanks to the emigration of workers. The amount of money they send home to Mexico is on par with our nation's oil and gas revenues. But these people who are keeping our country going can't participate in elections. Excluded from our progress, they can't participate in our politics either. And the attempt to create absentee voting for those living abroad has remained just that, an attempt.

For decades the United States encouraged immigration to boost its economic development. The words of Emma Lazarus are inscribed at the foot of the Statue of Liberty:

*Give me your tired, your poor,*
*Your huddled masses yearning to breathe free,*
*The wretched refuse of your teeming shore.*
*Send these, the homeless, tempest-tossed, to me:*
*I lift my lamp beside the golden door.*

From 1892 to 1924, around sixteen million immigrants passed through Ellis Island, where the Statue of Liberty stands. Some days, up to five thousand exhausted people set foot on this promised land.

Little by little, the welcoming atmosphere cooled and the opening in the golden door became narrower. In 1914, while this climate was still favorable, Franz Kafka, literature's greatest predictor of catastrophe, perceived a change in the Statue of Liberty. When the main character in *Amerika* nears Manhattan, he sees the monument shining in the Atlantic's reflected light; in this confusing brilliance, her hand raises a sword, not a torch.

Today, the border between Mexico and the United States resembles this Kafkian version of the Statue of Liberty. A place for walls and swords.

Naturally, the Mexican government deplores the maltreatment of the millions of people who are trying to reach places where they will look after lawns and care for the elderly. But the reasons they leave are no less deplorable. Disinherited twice over, these Mexican nomads lighten the load of two countries but have rights in neither.

At the very margins of civic life, frequently viewed as a threat, immigrants are the modern version of the beings that ceased to exist with the invention of electricity: they're ghosts.

## V. We Are the Wall

In 2018, Enrique Peña Nieto's party lost the election, and the "Fourth Transformation" promised by our new president, Andrés Manuel López Obrador, began to address the strictures imposed by Trump.

But in this spectacle, facts matter less than the way they are presented. In June 2019, Mexico and the United States reached an agreement that both sides celebrated as a triumph, though it has different implications on both sides of the border. The Mexican president claimed to have defended our dignity and moral integrity, while the United States celebrated the implementation of its immigration agenda.

For several days Trump had stridently threatened to impose tariffs on Mexican imports. He agreed to refrain only if Mexico committed to stopping the flow of undocumented migrants, including those from Central America. At the negotiating table, a security strategy was offered in exchange for economic stability. Trump's government dictated the conditions, mixing apples and oranges.

A quarter century ago, López Obrador, then the leader of the Party of the Democratic Revolution (PRD), was vehemently opposed to the North American Free Trade Agreement with the United States and Canada, which went into effect on January 1, 1994. But in order to prevent financial disaster, he found himself in the position of supporting this agreement. In doing so, he did not protect the whole country, as he insistently proclaims, but rather the few wealthy businessmen who profit from exports. There's no question that the domestic economy would experience paralysis if trade with the United States were encumbered, but there's also no question that the same would be true on the other side of the border. No one wins by disrupting Mexican exportation. But one of the privileges of power is taking risks. Washington can make big bets on its balance of trade, whereas Mexico isn't in a position to add to its list of problems.

The call to diversify our economy is as old as the map of Mexico itself, but the dependent nature of our economy has proved stubborn. Although our development programs change, the best tomatoes are still sent to the United States.

Despite their starkly contrasting ideologies, Trump and López Obrador have some things in common: they're both strident, capricious populists, with close ties to evangelism, who claim to have information different from the media's and present themselves as outsiders. One extolls the virtues of rampant capitalism while the other never stops criticizing the neoliberalism he also shields. The character and the positioning of these two leaders are more similar than they think. They're playing on the same chess board, but Washington is playing with white.

The promise that Mexicans will build the wall has come true. Trump didn't have to get army engineers to do it. The new accord makes Mexico responsible for stopping the flow of immigration. Strictly speaking, we are the wall. And it runs from Chiapas to Chihuahua.

Half a million Central Americans have entered Mexico illegally. Will they be deported? Will they be given jobs to prevent them from continuing their journey to the United States? The abuses suffered by everyone who tries to pass through our country have been documented in movies like *The Golden Dream (La jaula de oro)* by Diego Quemada-Díez and books like *La bestia* by Oscar Martínez. Foreign Secretary Marcelo Ebrard has been given the difficult assignment of enforcing the accord without violating human rights. This unusual position has extended his responsibilities from those of foreign secretary to those of secretary of the interior. And so, domestic politics are reconfigured to address the chaos abroad.

According to figures published in *El Universal*, 2019 has been the most violent year in Mexican history. Between January and October, 28,742 murders were recorded, in addition to the 833 femicides. López Obrador has been unable to staunch the bloodbath he inherited from previous governments, dating back to the "war on drugs" initiated by Felipe Calderón in 2006. One of the new government's main initiatives was the creation of a National Guard, intended to unify the command of various armed forces. But due to the accord with the United States, they won't be able to focus on the urgent issue of national security; instead, they'll become a border patrol responsible for stopping migrants who are trying to reach the Arcadia of their dreams.

In 1979, *Alien* created terror in movie theaters, portraying the encounter between a spaceship of people from Earth and a dramatically different creature, an interstellar monster. The movie's compelling tagline was "In space no one can hear you scream." Like desert sands, the obscure origin of these words has stood the test of time. In the treacherous realm of language, people who arrive in the United States without their documents in order are referred to as “illegal aliens.” Forty years after the premiere of Ridley Scott’s film, the tagline that referred to an inescapable horror has become the reality of immigrants: outside their homeland, no one can hear them scream.

# OF NOMADS AND HEROES

JORGE VOLPI
TRANSLATED BY SAMANTHA SCHNEE

Juan Goytisolo said that humans are not like trees—unlike them, we can move around. This ability to relocate from one place on the planet to another, to its most recondite corners, is precisely what makes us human. All people, even people who consider themselves sedentary, are the heirs of generations and generations of men, women, and children who, fleeing hunger, poverty, or violence, dared to traverse endless plains, dense jungles, and heartless deserts, crossed mountain ranges and canyons, and sailed uncharted rivers and seas, all in search of a better life. Those who had the courage to leave their fatherlands and mother countries behind, to abandon the known for the unknown, to venture into wild and hostile territories, are the very best among us. The great survivors of our species. Unnamed heroes. In this sense, we are all immigrants. And we should take pride in that.

In a bizarre reversal, today more and more people would like us to believe the opposite: that immigrants are potential bad guys, infiltrators, and sinister enemies, bent on corrupting our race, undermining our security, and contradicting our customs; in the best-case scenario they're considered *aliens*, foreigners with evil intentions, and at worst they're labeled *criminals* and *murderers*. We don't need genetics to prove that all humans have the same value, but today we know without a doubt that we all come from the same origins. Humanity isn't just some pretty story we've made up; it's a reality manifest, at the deepest level, in each and every cell of our bodies.

One of the most pernicious fictions, on the other hand, is the need to create borders between us: lines drawn arbitrarily by those revolving through the halls of power, intended to divide people into *us* and *them*. *Them*: the barbarians we should always keep an eye on, just as in that famous poem by Cavafy. The same barbarians who have been the pretext for installing walls, fences, and barbed wire. The same barbarians who have been used to excite nationalism—another dangerous fiction—to scapegoat in difficult times, to promote fear of others, to dignify our basest instincts and justify our own barbarism.

This obscene perversion of morality harkens back to that of the Nazis in their time, when the persecution of Jews, gypsies, and homosexuals ceased being despicable and became right and just. It's the same policy advocated by Donald Trump and his minions today: stopping immigrants—the undesirables who dare to cross our sacred borders—becomes an imperative. Any strategy may be employed to succeed. The first, in the case of Mexicans, is to take advantage of the landscape: the dry, hostile desert in the north and the dense jungle in the south. Next, the creation of armed forces to pursue and detain immigrants, who quickly turn into delinquents: from *la migra* to the National Guard, or the guardians of the nation, both American and Mexican. And as if that weren't enough, there are concentration camps where those who are considered illegal—men, women, and children—are incarcerated, in addition to new measures making the right to obtain asylum more difficult.

And then the apogee: the wall. It doesn't matter how impractical or useless it is; just like the Great Wall of China—at least in Kafka's famous story from 1917—it's more of a symbol than a real obstacle. A symbol of discrimination par excellence. And, as a symbol, in the eyes of Trump and his minions it should run the full length of the border and seal off the wild country to the south of the Rio Grande, which we Mexicans call the Rio Bravo. But faced with the impossibility of paying for his insane project, the American president has made Mexico his wall and Mexicans his jailers.

In this new, tragic reversal, we have changed from a country of immigrants, who fought to protect themselves from the barbarians in the north, into a country that's a holding tank for immigrants from the south—eschewing the role of safe third country—a place whose government is capable of celebrating its success in reducing, in just a few weeks, the number of people who pass through our lands to reach the U.S. border, using the same policies that have been used against our own countrymen: fences and barbed wire, arbitrary mass detentions, forced deportations. It seems that, in the face of Trump's brutal oppression, there's no alternative, but at the very least we should deplore the fact that we are hostage to a tyrant instead of filling our quota with pride.

# WALLS OF AIR

YAEL WEISS
TRANSLATED BY JESSIE MENDEZ SAYER

*For Alejandra Carrillo*

That man had many things he wanted to prove to me. The first was that he lived across the street from Tijuana's Salesian refectory, in another part of town. He took out his voter ID and pointed at his address with his index finger. In front of us, on the street, the migrants were waiting in line for their food. In the background was the wall, or, as the locals called it, the "line." The man told me that from his house he could see the caravans as they arrived because he lived on the route into the city shown on all the maps. He had watched the first of the current wave of Hondurans file past. He also told me that he once lived in Kansas, but that they had deported him for driving a friend's car without a license. Over there, on the other side, his two daughters and his wife had stayed behind; he had not seen them in nine years. He took some dirty and tattered photos out of his wallet and offered them to me by way of evidence. In front of us, in the line for food, which must have been at least two hundred meters long, there were only men; the women were lining up separately in shorter queues in order to avoid any unwanted contact. The man introduced himself as Fabián, but when he was about to take out his ID to show me again I stopped him with my hands. On the other side of the human line dividing the street lengthways in two, a Tsuru with speakers on its roof was playing evangelical music. I slipped away from Fabián so I could go and freely observe the man in the stripy T-shirt and New Balance trainers who, standing on top of the car's trunk, was overseeing a parallel act of food distribution. I could make out "Jesus is our Lord" on the back windshield in slender white letters. The Tsuru's sound system included a wired microphone, which the striped man was using to rebuke the five or six columns of people lined up behind the car for blocking people's way. Crowds were swarming up and down the street. "The straightest line goes first," he was shouting. Thanks to those walking triumphantly away clutching their polystyrene plates, I saw that rice and beans was on the menu, the same meal handed out every day by the Mexican navy. The criteria employed by the Tsuru man to decide which line would go next were indecipherable. As soon as one moved forward, another line of people that seemed to emerge from the ground would appear in its place. When there was no more food, the unchosen ones broke ranks with long faces and reluctantly accepted the fliers being handed out by the holy man's acolytes.

Fabián reappeared by my side. For the sake of saying something, I pointed out that the queue down the middle of the street had not moved an inch. He told me that he had actually gone to see the front of the line and that the soldiers were still preparing the food. He was struck by the size of the ladle they were using to stir the pots; it was an instrument capable, he said, of serving five plates at a time, much bigger than the ladle in the Salesian refectory. We swayed back and forth on our feet a while longer, from heel to toe and back again, with our hands in our pockets, as we watched the spectacle of a two-hundred-meter-long queue and the people crossing from one side of the line to the other. Fabián remarked that he could see many of Tijuana's lowlifes among the Hondurans. He recognized them, he explained, because he used to own a store a few blocks from there. He took out his phone to show me a few photos of his old establishment.

"But what would a lowlife from Tijuana be doing here?" I asked him with a touch of cynicism. After all, it was often said that the people of Tijuana wanted to drive the caravan out of the city and that the Hondurans' problems were not their responsibility. When asked about the caravan, they would say how wonderful the Haitians were in comparison, how hard working and honest they had turned out to be. One taxi driver's chitchat included a story about some men who had come from Haiti who were now going around in fancy clothes and driving Mercedes, all of it earned through their sweat and tears. He smacked his steering wheel afterward, satisfied with having demonstrated that the American dream could exist anywhere, even in Mexico, although he had not been able to achieve it himself.

"Taking advantage, stealing stuff, joining forces with the Honduran lowlifes, seeing what they can get," Fabián replied after I had almost forgotten what my question had been. He was as captivated as I was, attentively observing the faces of those who walked past him.

"But there's nothing to steal, these people have nothing," I said. Then I went on to say that migrants accumulated absurd quantities of worthless things in their tents. The camp, behind the white bars, looked like a garbage dump. I immediately regretted saying this because I wasn't even sure it was true. I had never entered the Benito Juárez baseball field where the migrants slept, crammed together.

Luckily my hollow allusion to this stockpile of donations and useless objects was of no interest to him.

"I have a carpentry workshop big enough to fit a lot of people inside," he suddenly assured me. "It's true, I'm a carpenter, feel my hands."

Without hesitating, I touched the callouses on his upturned palms, and then examined my own; much softer than his but a little rough, they have always been that way. A few young men started running toward another of the street's exits, but those in the line stayed where they were so as not to lose their place.

"Now what's going on? Let's go!" Fabián said.

"They must be giving away food or clothes," I explained. "The cars that arrive with donations park over there," I said, pointing toward the other street. At least this time it was first-hand information. I had seen those vehicles and all the ways in which their occupants gave things away: some would shyly roll down the windows of their cars just a little, others would open their trunks and raucously hawk their wares. Many of the donors belonged to some church or another and would take the opportunity to deliver a sermon or spread propaganda. I had spent more time on this street than Fabián had.

"I'm going to go and see," he said, before disappearing forever. "I like to see these things. Before I came I was watching the news on the television, this whole mess with the Hondurans, but I decided to come and see for myself."

This last clarification needed no callouses nor documents to back it up. *I came to see for myself* struck me as the simplest and most exact way of describing what I too was doing there.

Very early on Sunday, November 25, 2018, Central American migrants began to organize a protest. They planned to march together to the El Chaparral border crossing, one of the gateways into the United States, with the intention of gathering there in plain sight so that the northern country would finally take notice of this caravan made up of women, children, and men of working age and thereafter grant them entry, refuge.

From seven o'clock in the morning the most eager among them, with their flags and signs, began to gather. On both sides of the long line of people who were still striving to get some breakfast, dozens of young men were spraying graffiti, making signs, and wrapping themselves in binational emblems; there were flags from El Salvador and Guatemala as well as from Honduras, but they were always combined with that of the United States. Standing in front of a television camera, a man was saying that if God were on his side he would cross the border that very day. He abandoned the interview as soon as his wife and daughter appeared, carrying plates that had just been heaped with beans. They hunkered down and ate quickly because the march was about to start.

The contingent's largest three flags were right at the front: one from Honduras, one from Mexico, and one from the United States. To one side was the banner in honor of those who had fallen along the way. So many made up the exodus and so long had their journey up to this point been that some had died and others had been born, a few had gone their separate ways—a man by my side was grumbling about having been sent packing—and others had met and fallen in love. By nine o'clock in the morning a broad and dense column of people was finally ready, but before the march began, prayers were sung. Their worship was fervent, and then the crowd surged forward in high spirits. Families were carrying backpacks and luggage, airbeds, and pushing strollers bulging with sweaters. Two girls were on scooters, and there was a boy on a bike; there were also older men walking with sticks or crutches and others in wheelchairs.

However, one kilometer ahead, the riot police with their transparent shields were blocking the entrance to the vehicle bridge that led to the El Chaparral border crossing. The march was stuck there for a while, singing and asking to be allowed to pass under the intense ten o'clock sun. The "line" was in sight, its metallic belly covered in graffiti on the other side of the Tijuana River, entombed in underground pipes and notorious for providing shelter for the city's junkies under its bridges.

Suddenly, some brazen protesters decided to break the police line by going underneath the bridge and started to run beside it toward the Tijuana River. Everyone followed them. The riot police tried, without success, to contain the emboldened mass that was chaotically crossing the channel toward the border. Since the protesters were unfamiliar with the geography of the area, they searched haphazardly for entrances into the United States, and a few groups split off from the central column and attempted to climb the wall at different points. The American helicopters monitoring the march suddenly tripled in number in a matter of minutes, like kernels of corn popping in the air, and the authorities announced the close of all entrances into the country. Chaos erupted on the streets of Tijuana because the hundreds, perhaps thousands of cars that were already queuing to cross the busiest border in the world had to go back in reverse.

I advanced, along with the press, behind a large group. Those at the front had torn down the fence separating the road from a vacant lot at the foot of the wall. The families of migrants clustered together upon arrival, unsure of what to do. Some jumped onto abandoned cargo carriages and watched how the bravest, or most reckless, of them climbed up to the very top of the border wall only to freeze upon realizing there were border agents waiting on the other side. The helicopters rumbled over the heads of this small, stubborn, and indecisive tribe. After an hour of this spectacle, during which some saw the promised land from above and others only imagined it, the migrants began their retreat.

Around twenty Mexican riot policemen had positioned themselves next to the violated portion of fence in order to prevent more people from climbing up toward the slope where hundreds of hopefuls were congregating. The path from the road to the wall was tricky due to the rocky ground's almost vertical incline. It turned out to be easier to scramble up the slope in a hurry—which the migrants did with strollers, sleeping mats, blankets, and children in their arms, the reporters right behind them with their television cameras—than to come back down again. Surprisingly good natured, the riot police helped the Central Americans come down from the slope, passing their belongings down in a chain while the women and children used their hands to hold on to one another and slow their descent.

Like an image that sums up the head-on collision between the real and the imaginary, I can still see an incredulous riot policeman under the merciless sun and an average temperature of 30°C, holding a bear-skin coat in his arms. No doubt its owner had heard that it got very cold up north, and did not want to risk being miserable in the snow.

As a result of the stampede, fifty people were arrested by American forces (those who crossed the first border fences), and there were a couple of injuries from the gas bombs dropped from the sky, and even more from the rubber bullets. But the corollary was the cold reality: behind the first wall there was more wall, more bars, and cameras and spotlights and movement sensors, as well as soldiers armed to the teeth, and police helicopters; it wasn't just a question of jumping and scurrying off into the land of the free. This border was not like the ones in Central America or like the one between Mexico and Guatemala; this one is impenetrable.

That morning, the caravan lost all the momentum it had built up over October and November 2018. It had been the first one to attract global attention, thanks to its size. It is important to remember that its members had come from a long way away, and their volume and enthusiasm had grown as the journey went on. In San Pedro Sula, in Honduras, around three hundred people had formed this caravan's embryo. The very same day they began to walk, their number grew to one thousand, and by the day they crossed the first border that number had already doubled. In Guatemala, the caravan swelled with thousands of Guatemalans, Salvadorans, and other groups of Hondurans who had begun their migration separately. The fact that many reporters joined their ranks made this massive exodus visible to the world and protected them along the way. All the doors opened to allow them through. At Mexico's border there was minimal resistance, an attempt at maintaining order, but a few hundred people tore down the fence that serves as a gateway between both countries with shouts of "Yes, we can," while others went around the obstacle with the mass crossing of the Suchiate River. They advanced through Mexico, which sheltered them in refuges created specifically for them, the mobile population: they were given clothes, food, maps, encouragement, and advice. In the big cities, they were housed in stadiums, and it was ensured that donations from civilians reached them; they were even provided with buses for a ride up north. By the time they slammed into the U.S. border wall, these thousands of migrants had built up the inertia of a colossal snowball. It was a devastating blow.

Their strength of faith also entered into the equation. God accompanied these migrants in their hearts and surfaced on their lips every morning when they continued on their journey. Some called the caravan Exodus because in many ways it was one, in a biblical sense. It was made up of slaves to poverty, violence, and crime protected by the state. But in one night the slaves packed up what could fit in their backpacks, got their children ready, and said goodbye to the eldest among them who could not make the journey to the United States, the promised land where freedom, functioning laws, and well-paid work were guaranteed.

In Tijuana, on the morning of Sunday, November 25, 2018, when the members of the Exodus started heading toward the Chaparral border crossing, many of them were carrying what they valued the most. Deep down, they believed they would not be coming back. They held their wives' and children's hands, and swapped numbers with friends in case they got separated along the way. But despite their prayers, the Red Sea did not part, the miracle did not occur, and God stood them up. That day, it became clear that the caravan, at least in its caravan form, would never cross. Each of them had to petition for asylum individually and wait for their cases to be resolved, which could take months or even years. If they had enough money, they could arrange a clandestine crossing with the smugglers, putting their lives at risk. There was also the option of scattering across Mexico in search of work and a place to live, navigating organized crime networks and discrimination, or returning home with their tail between their legs and facing, in many cases, certain death.

On the afternoon of November 25, while the news channels played the images of the morning's breakout attempt on repeat, some volunteers from Mexican non-profit organizations made an appearance around the migrant camp, as well as a few citizens who knew all about clandestine and legal crossings for the simple reason that they lived in Tijuana. They came to help the Hondurans get their bearings, explain to them what the border was really like, what to expect, how to behave, where to put down their names to petition for asylum, what to say to immigration officials, what not to say, where to look for work while their case was reviewed. It was immediately obvious because of their makeup which women did not belong to the caravan, since the majority of those who walk for weeks on end exposed to the elements wear nothing at all on their faces. Since the baseball field could provide only minimum standards of hygiene and no privacy whatsoever, many used the rearview mirrors belonging to the cars parked on the street to brush their hair, squeeze a pimple, or make sure they were still themselves. The television cameras and reporters grew in number, searching the agitated crowd for interview subjects like harpoon-wielding hunters in a pool teeming with fish.

Some special correspondents from a U.S. television channel were getting their film crew ready, with microphones and spotlights, to interview a woman with four children—a sufficiently emotive character to pluck at heartstrings. I joined the small group that was forming behind the cameras to listen to the interview. It was like watching the news without a screen.

"I was there but I turned back before crossing the river because they were already spraying us with teargas," the woman answered. "We went to the back of the march because I couldn't do anything risky with my kids by my side. I had to bathe them, and there's so much mud, the youngest one slipped and cut his knee."

Since the interview was not live, there were constant interruptions. An obese woman who appeared to be the boss kept pulling on the interviewer's shirt and muttering in her ear in English, during which there would be a few seconds of silence. The interviewer asked over and over again why the woman had come and why she wanted to get into the United States; it was unclear if she found the answers unsatisfying, if she was hoping the woman would contradict herself, or if perhaps she just wanted a better shot.

"My children don't go to school, ma'am. In the United States, I want to work and I want them to study." The children were playing with some plastic dolls on the floor by the interviewee's feet, oblivious to what was being said about them.

"Are you aware that it is very difficult to enter the United States?" asked the reporter, her tongue skidding over every Hispanic "r."

"They have to help us. We have nothing, we only want to work," the woman begged.

"Are you aware that the process is very lengthy?"

"I'm asking you to please help us," the interviewee kept saying in a pitiable tone while the obese woman pulled on her colleague's shirt. "This camp is full of diseases, my children can't go to the toilet because they are overflowing, full of trash and infections. It's impossible to live here."

"What message would you like to send to the people of the United States?" the reporter asked after listening to her boss's whispered words.

"That they let us through first—us women who came alone with our children, we are not criminals, we are the most in need, for the love of God we need their help."

The technicians lowered the spotlight and the camera, the reporter and her boss started to argue, and the woman with four children, without much of a goodbye, sat a few meters away, on the edge of the sidewalk, to continue waiting. Most of the people who had been listening to her dispersed, in search of another happening, another expression of collective feeling. By my side, a young man who had been part of the audience was still gazing at the empty stage where the interview had taken place.

"What do you think?" I asked him.

"Terrible," he said. He looked up at me, and I could see his brown eyes underneath the peak of his cap.

His name was David, and he was also from Honduras. He told me that he belonged to the group that had started the caravan, that they had been inspired by the caravans formed by families searching for their disappeared loved ones in Mexico and Central America.

"The day before, we got together to sleep near the bus station, but word got out and many came to join us that same night, others along the way." David looked up every now and then. His eyelashes were curly and almost blond, as if he had burned them accidentally with a lighter. He was angry with the woman with the four children.

"Those women got this far because of us, because we protected them along the way, because we gave them a hand. We helped get on and off the freight trucks, we made sure they ate first and always had the best sleeping spots. It was far more dangerous for us, they kill far more men," David assured me. "And now they want to be let in first? We're a caravan and they want to destroy it."

I argued that it was easier for him to travel, that he could work here in Tijuana or wherever in order to save a few pesos, whereas that woman had four small children she couldn't leave on their own. David admitted I had a point but didn't agree with me entirely. He felt strongly about the power of the collective pressure they could apply as a caravan, without splitting up. I did not want to tell him that the United States was the leading authority in every-man-for-themselves, that it was there that the coldest form of individualism reigned supreme. As for me, I liked the idea of a world filled with people like David, who volunteered every morning to collect the trash that the caravan left in their wake.

"We leave a trail of mess behind us wherever we go. People will never be on our side if we carry on like this," he said.

We talked for a long time. There was nothing else to do in this camp condemned to wait. He had left his children behind in Honduras because the journey was far too dangerous; his plan was to send money from the United States so that they could go to school.

"Smokes for sale; smokes for sale, smooooooookes." A young guy was walking around with two open cartons, selling individual cigarettes on the street, which was as packed as usual, divided in two by the food line.

I saw that David was hiding his face under his cap, so I left him alone. But as soon as I had moved away from him, I regretted it. I had not asked for his contact details so I could write to him later on and find out how he was doing; I had not even taken a photo to remember him by. I ran back to the spot where I had left him, but he was no longer there, and I never found him again, not that day nor the next, amongst the thousands of migrants.

One of the most in-demand characters for the press was the young man with the bandages wrapped around his head. A thick band of cotton was wound around his forehead, and a white rectangle covered his nose. One of the teargas bombs dropped by the helicopters on the morning of the twenty-fifth of November had fallen on him. Underneath the bandages, the young man had fourteen stitches, administered in one of Tijuana's public hospitals. He called all of the interviewers "*papá*." He told the camera what happened, *papá*, and insisted he wasn't daunted, *papá*, that be it today or tomorrow or in a year's time, he would get into the United States. He was nineteen years old. No, he wasn't at the front of the stampede, *papá*, he preferred to see how the first of them got on, but he wasn't right at the back either. The most important thing, he declared in front of the

Televisa cameras and then the TV Azteca cameras as well as their neighboring country's equivalents, was to not give up trying to get to the other side, *papá*. He had his whole life to do it, *papá*.

Nearby, marquees had been set up where requests for voluntary repatriation could be carried out. There was a line of people waiting to ask for information and sign up, and small groups were talking in low voices. From the food line, which curled past them, the hungry silently watched those who had lost hope. Spirits dampened with every hour that went by after people began to hear about the asylum procedure and how many months it took to process. Many women with children wanted to go back; one of them was saying that she regretted bringing her children all this way, that it wasn't what she had pictured, that it was far too hard and they had suffered enough.

"Smokes for sale; smokes for sale; smoooooookes," the vendor insisted.

Those in charge of the voluntary repatriation lists confirmed that eighty people had registered that day and they believed that was a decent number for day one. As the week goes on, they assured me, with all the complications and scarcities in the camp, many more will follow. I asked after a woman with three daughters who had just stood up from one of the chairs without writing down her name. They told me it was the second time she had waited in line and sat down to ask to be taken back that day, but she was asking for protection because back there they wanted to kill her. Unfortunately, this was beyond their capabilities. Those already signed up for repatriation formed an isolated group, waiting to be transferred to another refuge. They must have been separating them from the rest to try and avoid their changing their minds at the last minute, but also so that when the buses were about to leave, other passengers would not try to board en masse without having registered.

To get into the camp and receive the plate of beans and the tin of chipotle chilies, you had to show them a bracelet similar to the ones worn by guests at all-inclusive hotels: a strip of plasticized paper in a phosphorescent color, impossible to remove without breaking it. David had told me that he was hesitant to get his, because doing so meant registering with the authorities. Any migrant without papers instinctively fears handing over their name. But to spend the night on the streets of Tijuana as a Honduran illegal was far too risky; it meant falling prey to the police or to any local in need of a pair of shoes.

The migrants' ID bracelets were a double-edged sword. On the one hand, it protected them, because only they were allowed into the camp, no native thieves, no angry locals (such as those that had attacked them with sticks on Playas de Tijuana). However, it also singled them out as residents of the ghetto. Outside the baseball field, on the road that had been cordoned off by the police, 95 percent of people were wearing the bracelet. But the farther away you got from the reserved area, the rarer they became. Thanks to this distinctive mark, I knew at first sight that one of the guys working at the secondhand clothes market, in another part of the city, was part of the caravan. I lingered at the stall to see what this kid was like, how the locals reacted to his accent, and how they related to one other. I discarded the women's clothing because I was too lazy to try it on and pretended to be very interested in the items for babies. It was just my luck that the boy knew nothing about the merchandise and, instead of answering my questions, yelled "*Girl!*" to call over the owner of the stall who had given him the job, who must have been about his mother's age and who quickly grew tired of my fumbling questions that were not resulting in any sale.

On the streets in the center of the city, the migrants who still had some money to buy diapers or Corn Flakes stood out from everyone else who was also buying diapers and Corn Flakes. The Central Americans did not stand out because of their color, like the Haitians or the Americans on the streets of Tijuana: the bracelet was as necessary to identify them as the yellow stars were on Jews' clothing, whom nobody could distinguish physically from their German compatriots.

While Donald Trump carried out his presidential campaign and spoke of the great wall that he would build along the border with Mexico, millions of us were watching the third or fourth season of *Game of Thrones*. We saw a great wall, five hundred thousand kilometers long, two hundred meters tall, and seventy meters wide, built to protect an empire from the uncivilized hordes. The wall's guards, the star among them being Jon Snow, defended against the savages' attacks with catapults and cascades of scalding oil. For me, the recent scenes of helicopters warding off the migrants' attack on the border wall with rubber bullets and teargas matched up very well indeed with these images impressed in our collective unconscious. Especially with the dramatic post-production carried out by the media for people's television screens. The close-up on the children's faces (who were actually crying because their mothers were forcing them to keep walking or were refusing to buy them chocolate), embellished with the dry ice effect of the gas, served to amplify the indignation of those who were convinced this was a barbaric invasion just as much as that of those who condemned the abuse of force against defenseless families. I was there, I ran with them, I reached the gates, I retreated once confronted with teargas, and I didn't see any more violence than I am accustomed to seeing during the protests I have taken part in over the course of my life. The proximity of the border and the presence of the helicopters certainly gave it a distinct tone, more acute, but this was mainly symbolic and not due to the events themselves. When I saw the edited images that night on television it became clear to me that fuel was being poured onto a conflict of unknown proportions, one of the first battles of the great war of the rich against the poor, the former quartered in their luxury facilities, sucking up all the planet's resources, and the latter deprived of even water to drink.

---

The line of people dividing the street in two entranced me with its slow movements and unchanging repetition. I watched it for hours, which then turned into days. If I had known from the beginning what I was looking for, I would have perhaps reacted faster, like the reporters from the news chains who knew the terrain, and exactly what they were interested in finding. In an hour or two they finished their reportage and left with the job done to rest at their hotel, or to continue their investigation somewhere else. I, however, was stranded outside a baseball field, on a street cordoned off by police with an almost permanent line of people waiting for food, without any report to submit to anyone and with questions that were far too vague. What were they thinking, these thousands of people who came such a long way to slam into a wall, with nothing more than a few blankets on their backs? Was there a common trait I could correctly label them with, lumping them all together with the same needs and possible solutions? Could I conclude by saying anything definitive at all about the migrants who made up the caravans?

I was so engrossed in contemplating the line that it took me a while to notice the guy who had sat down next to me on the sidewalk to eat. He had indigenous features and was one of the nicest looking people I had seen in the camp. He revealed that he came from a place so beautiful it was like paradise, and I immediately believed him.

"Is it a jungle?" I asked.

"Yes, it's so green. There are so many trees," he replied, his eyes shining.

While we spoke, he ate without utensils (because there weren't any left) his plate of soupy beans with rice. He used his index and middle fingers more skillfully than someone from Japan trapping the last grain of rice between their chopsticks. I had never seen anyone eat such wet food with their hands so elegantly. I was astonished, especially because in my family of European migrants, we are savages at the table: we instinctively attack our food as though we might be thrown back into a concentration camp at any moment.

Pedro told me how he'd arrived in the early hours of the morning in a freight truck with a group of thirty people; they got out as they were entering the city and walked from there. He confirmed with a big smile that he was one of the boys who slept until midday on the sidewalk, in the middle of all the commotion. He gave me two distinct reasons why he'd left the paradisiacal place where he was from. The first was that he had promised himself he would see another country before he died. He was twenty-three years old. The second was to prove to his family, especially his siblings, that living somewhere else was possible, that they need not be forever chained to one plot of land. What he said about the coffee plantation he lived on I already knew: the plummeting price of beans, the ever-increasing price of pesticides and fertilizer, the mildew plague destroying part of the harvest, the modified seeds they needed to buy, in short: the sum total of harm that crushes those who continue to cultivate their small parcels of land in a globalized world that rewards only mass production.

One meter away from us, on a blanket spread out over a part of the street, four young men around twenty years old were lying down between bags of clothes. Their voices were getting louder, so we began to hear fragments of their conversation.

"I felt like a fucking idiot," one was saying. "I looked over the edge of the wall to the other side and there was an American cop right there, we were staring at each other and the asshole took a photo of me with his phone. Now I'm on their records, the sons of bitches."

Pedro told me that he had traveled independently, that he'd only joined the caravan once on Mexican territory, that before then he had never heard of any caravans. He left paradise with his cousin (his insistence on referring to his place of birth this way made me begin to suspect, and this turned out to be true, that the region actually bore this name). He said that they went all the way to Mexico on their own. He lost his relative in a chase, when the immigration police caught up with them. As he ran off and hid in some bushes, Pedro managed to glimpse his cousin practically handing himself in to those who were chasing them; he didn't even try.

"He was so tired, he couldn't keep going."

"And where do you think he is now?" I asked him.

The group of young men shuffled closer together to make space for one more, while the one who had been captured in a photo taken by the American patrol officer kept telling the story of his wall adventure.

"Another guy jumped over the other side and they caught him almost before he had hit the ground, so I thought I better turn around," he was saying.

"He's probably already back in Honduras, at home," Pedro said after a while. "Although maybe he's nearly caught up with us here, he was so excited about getting to the United States. He was desperate to make it, I wouldn't be surprised to bump into him here."

"Couldn't you call home and ask?"

"I can't get through. I think they cut off the line. Hopefully it will get fixed, and then I'll call."

He didn't seem at all worried. Or perhaps the concepts of police torture, blackmail, extortion, and murder carried out by organized crime networks in Mexico did not form a part of his consciousness, or he did not allow them to penetrate his reality because he needed all of his strength to continue on his own journey.

"No fucking way, last night they didn't let me get back, a couple of police up there stopped me, where that hotel is that charges fifty pesos for two hours. It wasn't until I showed them my bracelet that they let me go," the boy who had just joined them was saying.

In Mexico, it has always been difficult to guess what the cops might do, who they'll decide to harass on any given night, if it will be the undocumented immigrants wearing a bracelet or the locals without one.

"Do you think they have hot water in that hotel?" one of them asked.

"Who knows."

"If I don't get through I'm going to work here in Tijuana," Pedro told me.

"What kind of work would you like?"

"Anything going."

Although I had only spoken to around five people apart from the brief exchanges of opinion about the interviews (or chats with people sent by the church who after nightfall would hand out candles and make us sing), I knew that the question-and-answer dynamic was always the same. All they wanted to know about me was if I was a reporter or if I worked for an NGO (I always said no to avoid being placed in either category) and if I was from the United States or from Tijuana, to which I replied I was from Mexico City. That was all. One young guy who came up to me to tell me about how they had just killed his brother in Honduras just walked off as soon as he realized I was nobody, that I would be of no immediate help to him. Another abandoned me after I was unable to answer his question about an organized group of deportees in Tijuana who could confirm the whereabouts of her daughter in the United States. But the majority of the members of the caravan were happy to answer a thousand questions and, after probing a little further, to tell their whole story.

An involuntary asymmetry was established between those who asked and those who answered, because it was the latter who had no papers, who had to justify themselves and be likeable. On the other hand, those of us who asked the questions were stood on territory where the simple fact of our nationality gave us immense power, to the point where the exchange would soon deteriorate into a kind of interrogation. In what was perhaps paltry compensation, we served as a reflective surface for their words, a mirror in which they could see themselves. When a migrant answers questions, they are once again narrating themselves, reinventing themselves with the help of other eyes. Even when they are lies in the process of becoming the truth.

With his Styrofoam plate in one hand, without any trace of food anywhere except for the shine on his lips that betrayed the Navy chef's heavy-handedness with the oil, Pedro's gaze settled on what was in front of him. Just then the boy with the bandages around his head and nose arrived and sat with his friends, the ones lying next to us; he arrived with two others, whom he referred to as his representatives and who settled in between the bags of clothes.

"I already told them to get rid of any reporters, I'm not doing any more interviews, they're pushing it. They've even got me smoking, *papá*."

"You're a star now," I said, involving myself in the conversation from where I was sitting. "Aren't you afraid they'll identify you? That they'll put you down as a violent person and not let you in?"

"I'm getting in whatever it takes and with my whole family, who knows what they'll do, *papá*, but I'm getting in."

"You're with your family?"

"My family are these people sitting here in front of you," he said, gesturing toward all the guys on the blanket. "And there used to be more of us, but some of us didn't come back."

"Where are they?"

"Who knows. Maybe already on the other side."

It is not fortuitous that migrants arrive on foot, or that they walk for long stretches under the sun. The lines of people that walk along the freeways in caravans are telling us something. First of all, that their bodies march for thousands of kilometers in order to take their petition for asylum all the way to the wall. It is infinitely longer than the four kilometers those of us who live in Mexico City march to ask for justice, from the Angel to the Zócalo; more than from Central Park to Washington Square in New York, more than from Paris to

Versailles, the route taken by a hoard of the starving in October of 1789. The latter contingent, formed principally by women in rags, walked twenty-two kilometers in the rain until they reached the palace gates. Their objective was for the king of France to witness their desperation, the same desperation felt by the entire city, and get him to help them. In Versailles, however, the court went on with their parties and their galas. Rumor has it that it was at this time that Marie Antoinette uttered her famous words: "If they have no bread, let them eat cake." Yet historians claim that the exasperated mob brought about the return of the king and his family soon after to the old palace in Paris, the Louvre, so as to see to the hunger of their people.

The multitude that walks from the slums of Honduras to the gates of the United States reminds me of those women who tried out being revolutionaries for a night and managed to get the king's attention. It was not yesterday that migrants began leaving their impoverished countries and crossing the barrier that separated them from a life of dollars. But walking in large groups in the light of day, exposing their wounds, that is new. Versailles, where the party and galas continued, is now the United States. "Look at us, you abusive *gringos*," they seem to be saying. "We won't hide like criminals anymore, alongside the unspeakable dangers of the shadows, paying huge sums of money to the illegal network that controls all the ways in and out of the United States. Look at us, there are thousands of us."

The Central American caravans that appeared on the scene in 2018 (or that at least grew sufficiently large that year to get the world's attention) have turned into a deafening protest. The first of these caravans arrived in Tijuana in April, comprising one thousand two hundred people; the second, in November, numbered more than six thousand; the third and fourth are walking in 2019, unrelentingly, merged into one single flow of dissent against an economic order that permits the movement of money and natural resources up north, but not of people.[1]

During one of the first negotiations in Tijuana with representatives of the United States' authorities, which started at the beginning of December 2018, a group of migrants requested fifty thousand dollars a head to retrace their steps back to their land of the poor. One Honduran, around forty years old, laughed into a television camera. "We said fifty thousand dollars just for the sake of saying something, it's impossible to know how much the U.S. owes us. They steal our resources, so part of what they have is ours. They must share it. That is what we are asking for. Have you heard of Noam Chomsky? He explains it very well." The cameraman admitted he had not heard of this man.

Although in all likelihood the majority of these Central Americans began their exodus with no ideological stance at all, their only objective being to reach the United States and join the work market, the caravans become more political with every kilometer they cover, and over time this tendency will only intensify.

Many kinds of walls have been erected, but the most visible ones have never been the most effective. José Revueltas wrote a book entitled *Walls of Water* to describe the time he spent in the penal colony on the Islas Marías, 112 kilometers from the Mexican coast, a distance that made escape almost impossible. Similarly, in their towns and slums, the world's poor live behind walls of air, as invisible as they are difficult to traverse in order to escape. Thousands of kilometers separate them from a place where, legend has it, you can earn a decent life through honest work, and where your safety is guaranteed. The journey through these kilometers of air that confine them to their place of birth and exploitation is dangerous. They would be doing the world's most powerful people a huge favor if they would just stay in their assigned areas, work for scraps, and not attempt to escape. Those who penetrate these walls of air, then the intervening borders, and finally face the tallest barriers and technology built to stop only them, the poorest and most desperate people of all, are the ultimate rebels of our times; they are the necessary force for the ignition of revolutions. But perhaps there will be no revolution, as we are yet to find out if the members of this caravan will be, in the end, just cannon fodder in a war already lost by those who have nothing to those who have it all.

# A WALL TO DIVIDE THE DESERT

NAIEF YEHYA

TRANSLATED BY ELLEN JONES

What is a wall, if not the calcification or metallization of inequality and lack of public safety? A wall is a crude device for controlling space, restricting movement, and delimiting territory. When employed as political tools, walls serve to deny access to people, animals, and goods. That being said, even the highest, hardest, most impenetrable walls end up being eroded and worn down by time. It's clear that, in walls, human culture has found a crucial means of protection, a monument to the preservation of the differences between what lies on one side and what lies on the other. For the paranoid among us, walls are a simple, attractive symbol. They can be extremely efficient, but they are also puzzles to be solved. Ten meters, thirty meters, a hundred meters high? Cement, iron, wood, wire? Extending two meters, four meters underground? Their every dimension presents an obstacle that invites ingenuity in anyone wishing to overcome it. The technological race between those building the walls and those who need to scale them is never ending.

June 16, 2015, which might otherwise have been a completely irrelevant date, was a glorious day in the annals of unintended comedy. It will most likely be remembered, however, as the day when U.S. politics took a dangerously xenophobic turn that precipitated a period of confrontations and catastrophes in its relations with the rest of the world, and especially with its neighbor across the border to the south. That day, a bizarre public announcement took place in the excessively gold lobby of Trump Tower on Fifth Avenue in Manhattan. The real estate magnate, reality TV star, and five-times-bankrupt businessman Donald Trump descended the escalator accompanied by his third wife, Melania, Neil Young's famously liberal song "Rockin' in the Free World" playing (without the musician's permission) in the background, and, having been introduced by his much-beloved daughter, Ivanka, announced his pre-candidature for the presidency. His words, full of grandiloquent promises, grudges, complaints, and contempt, were a kind of hysterical babbling. He presented ludicrous ideas, with little consistency and even less syntactical coherence, that were very hard to take seriously. He attacked politicians, lobbyists, and the then president, Barack Obama, but his real target was Mexican people. His ignorant and provocative representation of Mexicans as a threat was packed with ambiguities that, as the campaign progressed, would give rise to a kind of crusade against our country.

Trump began his attack thus:

> When do we beat Mexico at the border? They're laughing at us, at our stupidity. And now they are beating us economically. They are not our friend, believe me. But they're killing us economically.

The notion of Mexico "beating" its powerful northern neighbor at the border and "killing them economically" is incomprehensible to anyone with a basic understanding of the politics, trade, and tangible reality of a rich nation's relationship with a poor one, but also for anyone with a modicum of common sense. What kind of war or competition is taking place on Trump's imaginary border? From this bizarre perspective, Mexico is imagined as a scheming, opportunistic adversary, capable of taking on the world's primary superpower and bringing it down through sheer business acumen. It is a primitive understanding of a complex binational relationship from a poorly informed businessman with proto-fascist ideology and a victim complex, who persists in his belief that the United States' labor, commercial, criminal, and social problems are the responsibility of Mexico's government and its immigrant-invaders.

The words that most resonated from his speech and that were repeated ad nauseam were as follows:

> When Mexico sends its people, they're not sending their best. They're not sending you. They're not sending you. They're sending people that have lots of problems, and they're bringing those problems with us. They're bringing drugs. They're bringing crime. They're rapists. And some, I assume, are good people.

These strident words, deserving of Aryan Nations or the Ku Klux Klan, caused much surprise and were headline news both in the United States and around the world. Not long afterward, Trump reiterated his strange, worrying accusation: "They're sending us the wrong people." With this incoherent babble, he did not seem to be referring to the economic immigration of Mexicans, as he would do later, but rather to the alleged "sending" of people by "Mexico," as if immigrants were state-sponsored infiltrators charged with selling drugs, committing crimes, and raping and corrupting the natives; as if they were evil agents of a narco-state or gangs of provocateurs serving a sinister regime. He also asserted that these were Mexicans with "lots of problems," coming to wreak havoc at the heart of the nation. Strange—the idea of a malicious invasion seems somewhat at odds with the idea of invaders with problems. But nevertheless, this absurd, insane discourse began to take shape, replete with lies, insults, errors, and inaccuracies, and eventually became the touchstone of Trump's alternative vision of reality.

His malleable words became ideological plasticine, codified signs that each person would choose to understand however suited them best. They led to the promise to build a huge, beautiful wall (can any wall be considered beautiful?) on the border between the United

States and Mexico, and eventually to the deportation of eleven million undocumented workers and the withholding or imposition of enormous taxes on shipments that for Mexico are crucial. The accusation against Mexicans was taken up by some unemployed and underemployed Americans as a war cry against the cheap, undocumented labor they imagined was the reason they were out of work. It hasn't been very hard to prove that most of these jobs, in the United States and in other developed countries, were lost because of industrial automation and the use of robots. What is more, the manufacture of very low-cost products in China and other Southeast Asian countries has had a far greater impact on U.S. production plants than the employment of undocumented Mexicans.

Trump confused two very different things in that speech. He was condemning, on the one hand, the Mexican state (whose trade with the United States totaled $583 billion in 2015, making it the United States' third most important trading partner) and, on the other hand, the undocumented Mexicans who live and work in the United States (some of them for decades) and who are in many ways indispensable to its economy—in farming, construction, factory work, and the service industry. It's clear that the director of Trump University needed desperately to point the finger at someone convenient, someone who represented a threat, some vulnerable enemy whom he and his followers could insult and attack, and who was little able to mount a defense. Mexicans, alongside Central Americans, became the ideal scapegoats for Trump's campaign. One tweet at a time, Trump launched incendiary attacks that were received by his followers with fanatical fervor. The level of violence against Mexicans began to increase in the run up to the election, reaching a peak on August 3, 2019, with the Walmart massacre in El Paso, Texas, by an individual who wanted so badly to protect his country from immigrants that he murdered twenty-two people and left twenty-four seriously injured.

During Trump's campaign rallies the two most popular cries

were "Lock her up!," referring to Hillary and her alleged crimes, and "Build the wall!" The promise he made, in his tangled, chaotic grammar, was:

> I would build a great wall, and nobody builds walls better than me, believe me, and I'll build them very inexpensively. I will build a great, great wall on our southern border, and I'll have Mexico pay for that wall.

From that moment on, in every public event, Trump asked his supporters: "And who's gonna pay for the wall?" and the crowd would respond enthusiastically in unison: "Mexico!" For months, this interchange, with its sordidly Pink Floydian overtones, fed the crowd's resentment and desire for revenge against Mexico. Many initially believed Trump was talking about a symbolic wall, but when questioned he would always respond by redoubling the threat and swearing he referred to a physical wall, ten, fifteen, twenty meters high, depending on his mood. It's clear that Trump's "beautiful wall" is more than just an insane plan to erect a concrete or metal barrier more than 3,201 kilometers long, spanning a landscape that ranges from urban areas to rugged mountains, deserts, and rivers. It also symbolizes a rejection of otherness—the otherness represented by the United States' expanding Spanish-speaking population; it's a retrograde, nostalgic fantasy of isolation that betrays a medieval understanding of security. The wall is, furthermore, a screen on which desires, fantasies, and horrors are projected.

Like any demagogue, Trump knew that in the absence of ideas or policy proposals the best thing to do was to promise the impossible and ignite people's hate and rage against a common enemy, whether real or imagined. Nothing unites the masses more than an appeal to their victimhood and the humiliations they have suffered—the proverbial Two Minutes Hate from George Orwell's *1984*. The rejection of illegal immigration was an easily digestible cause not just for conservatives but also for the far right. Hate unifies, and this cause undoubtedly provided a key injection of energy into the proletarian bases, both rural (many of whom paradoxically rely on the cheap labor of illegal workers) and urban, who needed someone they could hold responsible for their problems.

Trump's belligerent rhetoric did not stop when he won the presidency. Five days after taking office, on January 25, 2016, the president signed an executive order to build the wall, at the same time that Luis Videgaray, the then Mexican secretary of foreign affairs, and Ildefonso Guajardo, the secretary of economic affairs, were in the White House preparing for a visit from the then Mexican president, Enrique Peña Nieto. The impossibility of negotiating and the fact that Trump was still bragging about how Mexico would pay for the wall meant the inevitable cancellation of that White House visit. It also led to a phone call between the two heads of state in which Trump is rumored to have said that if Mexico could not impose order and stop the cartels, the United States would send troops in to do it for them—a possibility that once again became a cause for anxiety after the dreadful assassinations of members of the LeBaron family in November 2019, which served as an excuse for Trump to once again "offer" the U.S. army's support in the fight against the cartels. When Mexico refused to pay for the wall, Trump said he would impose a massive tariff on Mexican products or else find other ways to make them pay. He wanted his wall so badly that he asked Congress to approve a budget to be covered by U.S. taxpayers themselves, so that he could guarantee construction would begin as soon as possible. He'd figure out a way to make Mexico pay for it later.

By giving free rein to racism, Trump's Mexico-phobic campaign is already bearing fruit in the form of increased toxicity. The idea of punishing Mexico "for taking advantage of the United States" is actually counterproductive because to a large extent the wall Trump is so desperate for already exists, in the form of Mexico's brutal federal anti-immigrant policing program, supported by the brand-new

National Guard, which oversees the detention of many thousands of Central Americans traversing Mexico in the hope of crossing the U.S. border. This is how a great many victims of violence and terror, fleeing their countries and seeking asylum, end up in the hands of the Mexican authorities, where they have little chance of being treated humanely and much less of being granted asylum. The wall is nothing but an antiquated civic symbol, a geometrical shape trying to keep people out without addressing the problems that brought them there in the first place. It's a way of closing our eyes, a two-dimensional hiding place that exposes rather than conceals—it exhibits us, turns us into shadows fearful of the outside world.

The irony, of course, is that the North American Free Trade Agreement was devised as a way of eliminating borders and facilitating the transit of people and goods between the countries of North America. Today, the borders have been corporatized and militarized, as much through the presence of the Border Patrol, Immigration and Customs Enforcement (ICE), soldiers, and heavily armed civil militias (Arizona Minuteman Project–style), as through Predator B drones, spy towers built by the Israeli company Elbit Systems, and VADER radars. In addition, Trump's government has called on police departments across the country to cooperate with anti-immigration efforts and eliminate the concept of sanctuary cities.

A border, on the one hand, is above all a social construction, an imaginary line that has real-world consequences. A wall, on the other hand, is clearly a solid object that makes manifest the idea of the border. A wall cutting through the desert sounds insane, almost surreal: dividing one wild, hostile terrain into two, parting the sands so that no one can cross them, creating an enormous prison in the middle of nowhere. From Jericho to the Israeli West Bank by way of Berlin and Hadrian, walls have long been imagined as a means of detaining hordes of barbarians, of creating a sense of safety. But they cannot protect themselves from the passage of time and are eventually doomed to collapse. They are nothing more than vertical, two-dimensional shapes—yet they are our only response to problems so complex they haven't a hope in hell of being fixed by stacking one stone on top of another.

# Acknowledgments

First and foremost, we are deeply grateful for the motivation that each of the contributors to this book showed to our invitation. The humanitarian and insightful words that fill these pages constitute a gleam of hope to the political and social crisis at the border.

We owe special thanks to Samantha Schnee for taking the lead role in translating this book, and to the rest of an exceptional group of translators, Ellen Catherine Jones, Jessie Mendez Sayer, Victor Meadowcroft, Lisa Dillman, and Sophie Hughes, whose hard work gave us this book in English.

We would also like to thank our agent, Jennifer Lyons at Jennifer Lyons Literary Agency, LLC, for all the time and hard work put into getting this project off the ground. This book is a reality thanks to her encouragement and support from the very beginning.

Finally, we would like to express our appreciation to Ben Woodward for his invaluable insights and support in getting this project off the ground and to all the team at The New Press for their enthusiasm and respectful comments and corrections throughout the editing and review stage.

# Editor Biographies

**Carmen Boullosa** is a Mexican novelist, poet, and playwright. She is the author of nineteen novels (including *The Book of Anna*, translated by Samantha Schnee), two books of essays (including, coauthored with Mike Wallace, *Narcohistory: How Mexico and the USA Jointly Created the "Mexican Drug War"*), seventeen collections of poetry (including *Hatchet*, translated by Lawrence Schimmel), and ten plays (seven staged, *Cocinar hombres* and *Trece señoritas*—set design by Magali Lara—and *Vacío*, with Jesusa Rodríguez, directed by Julio Castillo). Since the seventies, Carmen Boullosa has created and printed artist's books, frequently in collaboration with Magali Lara and other Mexican artists. She is the recipient of the prizes Casa de América de Poesía Americana in Madrid, Xavier Villaurrutia in Mexico, Anna Seghers and LiBeratur in Germany, and Novela Café Gijón and Rosalía de Castro in Spain. She has won five NY-EMMYs for the show *Nueva York*—at CUNY-TV and has been a Guggenheim and a Cullman Center Fellow. The NYPL acquired her papers and artist books. She has been visiting professor at Georgetown, Columbia, NYU, and Blaise Pascal at Clermont Ferrand; was a faculty member at City College CUNY; and is now at Macaulay Honors College.

**Alberto Quintero** is an editor from Mexico and a PhD candidate in Modern Thought and Literature at Stanford University. He is the editor in chief of Literalia, a digital publishing and translation platform connecting Mexican authors with readers across the world. From 2014 to 2016, he was a member of the Fulbright Foreign Student Program at The New School, and he is currently an EDGE Fellow at Stanford University.

# Contributor Biographies

Born in Ayutla Mixe, Oaxaca, **Yásnaya Elena Aguilar Gil** is an Ayuujk linguist, writer, translator, and human-rights activist. She has a master's degree in linguistics from UNAM. Her work focuses on the study of disappearing native languages in Mexico. She is a member of the Colegio Mixe, a research group seeking to promote cross-disciplinary research into the Mixe language group. She has written for a variety of media in Mexico, including *Letras Libres*, *Nexos*, and *Revista de la Universidad de México.*

**Jhonni Carr** holds a PhD in Hispanic linguistics from the University of California, Los Angeles. Specializing in Hispanic sociolinguistics, she investigates the power dynamics of displayed languages in the public space of Southern California and Mexico. In her work, she uses interdisciplinary methods to explore these areas' signage (i.e., linguistic landscape) and residents' attitudes toward the presence and absence of different languages. Originally from San Diego, she teaches in the Department of Spanish & Portuguese at the University of California, Berkeley.

**René Delgado** is a journalist and political analyst. He was editor in chief of the Mexico City newspaper *Reforma*, which he helped found in 1993. He retired as editor in chief in 2017 and continues to contribute a weekly column, "Sobreaviso," as well as the show *Entredichos* on the paper's website. He has authored four books: *La oposición: debate por la nación* (*The Opposition: Dispute for the Nation*, Grijalbo); *Ovando y Gil:*

*crimen en víspera de elecciones* (*Ovando and Gil: Crime the Day Before Elections*, Ediciones de Cultura Popular); and the novels *El Rescate* (*The Rescue*, Grijalbo) and *Autopsia de un Recuerdo* (*Autopsy of a Memory*, Grijalbo).

Born in Actopan, Mexico, **Yuri Herrera** is a writer and a professor of Spanish and Portuguese at Tulane University in New Orleans. Herrera studied politics in Mexico, creative writing in El Paso, and received a PhD in literature at Berkeley. He has written three short novels, all of which have been translated into English: *Kingdom Cons*, *Transmigration of Bodies*, and *Signs Preceding the End of the World*, which was included in many best-of-year lists, including *The Guardian*'s Best Fiction and won the 2016 Best Translated Book Award. His latest books are *A Silent Fury: The El Bordo Mine Fire* and the short story collection *Diez planetas*.

Born in Santiago, Chile, and raised in Mexico City, **Claudio Lomnitz** is the Campbell Family Professor of Anthropology at Columbia University. He's the author of several books, all set in Mexico, including *Death and the Idea of Mexico* and *The Return of Comrade Ricardo Flores Magón*. In addition to his academic publications, Lomnitz is a regular contributor to the Mexican media. He writes a bi-weekly column for the newspaper *La Jornada* and a monthly column for *Nexos*. In 2010, he was awarded Mexico's National Drama Award for his play *El verdadero Bulnes*, which he wrote with his brother, Alberto Lomnitz. Their most recent play is the musical *La Gran Familia*, which opened the 2018 Festival Internacional Cervantino, in Guanajuato, Mexico, with Mexico's National Theater Company. Claudio Lomnitz's most recent book, *Our America*, is a reflection on exile and transculturation that moves between Eastern European and South American history, by way of the story of his grandparents, and will appear in the spring of 2021, with Other Press.

**Valeria Luiselli** was born in Mexico City and grew up in South Korea, South Africa, and India. She is the author of the award-winning novels *Faces in the Crowd*, *The Story of My Teeth*, the essay collections *Sidewalks*, and *Tell Me How It Ends: An Essay in Forty Questions*—all published by Coffee House Press. *Tell Me How It Ends* was described by the *Texas Observer* as "the first must-read book of the Trump era" and was a finalist for the National Book Critics Circle Award for Criticism. Her most recent novel, *Lost Children Archive* (Knopf), was longlisted for the Booker Prize and the Women's Prize for Fiction. Luiselli is a finalist for the Carnegie Medal and the recipient of a MacArthur Fellowship.

Born in Mexico, **Román Luján** has lived in the United States for fifteen years. He has published several books of poetry in Spanish, including *Deshuesadero*, *Drâstel*, and *Sánafabich*. Coeditor of two anthologies of Mexican poetry, he has translated the work of several English-language poets into Spanish, including Juliana Spahr, Leslie Scalapino, and Donato Mancini. Translations of his poetry have appeared in *Jacket2*, *Aufgabe*, *The Lillian*, and *Matter*. He teaches Spanish at the University of California, Berkeley.

**Alejandro Madrazo Lajous** obtained an LLB from ITAM in Mexico City and both an LLM and a JSD from Yale Law School. He is a tenured professor of law at the Center for Research and Teaching in Economics (CIDE) in Aguascalientes, Mexico, where he created and headed the interdisciplinary Drug Policy Program before going to Yale as a Schell Center Visiting Fellow. He is a member of the National System of Researchers in

Mexico and a trustee of the Board of the International Society for the Study of Drug Policy (ISSDP). He has published work on the history of legal thought, constitutional law, sexual and reproductive rights, and tobacco control. He is the author of *Revelación y Creación. Los fundamentos teológicos de la dogmática jurídica.*

**Jean Meyer** is a Franco-Mexican historian born in Nice, France, in 1942. He received his PhD in Paris for his work titled *La Cristiada* (*The Cristero War*), which has been repeatedly republished since the year 2000. He is a teacher and researcher who, after graduating from the Colegio de México, the Sorbonne, the University of Perpignan, France, and the Colegio de Michoacán in Zamora, Mexico, has worked since 1993 at the Mexican Center for Research and Teaching in Economics (CIDE). As well as continuing to study Mexican history, he has begun to research the history of Russia/the USSR, antisemitism (especially among Christians), and the history of priestly celibacy in the Roman Catholic Church. He is the author of *Rusia y sus Imperios, 1895–2007* (*Russia and Its Empires, 1895–2007*), *Yo el francés* (*I, the Frenchman*), and *La estrella y la cruz* (*The Star and the Cross*), among other books. He writes every Sunday for the Mexican newspaper *El Universal.* He is fond of the international history magazine *Istor*, published by the history department at CIDE.

Born in Villa María, Córdoba, Argentina, **Paula Mónaco Felipe** is a Mexico City–based journalist. She is the author of the book *Ayotzinapa, horas eternas* (Ediciones B) and co-author of the book *Palabras como golpes, como balas* (Rayuela). She has worked for *La Jornada*, the TeleSUR network, and *El Telégrafo* in Ecuador, and she has written for the *New York Times*, *Revista Gatopardo*, *Newsweek en español*, and *Periodistas de a*

*Pie*, among other media outlets. She helped produce *Los días de Ayotzinapa*, a Netflix docuseries that disputes the Mexican government's account of how and why forty-three students from Ayotzinapa Rural Teachers' College vanished in Iguala in 2014, and she helped in the investigation of the movie *Vivos* (Ai Wei Wei). She also participated in *Después de la guerra*, a documentary series on TeleSUR about current political and social conflicts in Mexico.

Born in Mexico City, **Emiliano Monge** is a writer and a political scientist. Monge is the author of the novels *Morirse de memoria, El cielo árido,* which won the XXVIII Jaen Novel Prize and the Otros Ámbitos Prize; *Las tierras arrasadas*, which won the Elena Poniatowska Ibero-American Novel Prize; and *No contar todo,* which won the Bellas Artes Prize for published work. He is also the author of the books of short stories *Arrastrar esa sombra*, which was shortlisted for the Antonin Artaud Prize, and *La superficie más honda,* as well as the children's book *Los insectos invisibles.* His short stories have been included in many anthologies. In 2011, he was recognized by the Guadalajara International Book Fair as one of the twenty-five most important writers in Latin America, and in 2017 was selected as one of the thirty-nine best Latin American writers under age thirty-nine by the Hay Festival in Bogotá. He is a regular contributor to Mexican and international media, and he writes a column for the newspaper *El País.*

**Porfirio Muñoz Ledo** is a Mexican politician and diplomat with many years of public service behind him. He served as the Mexican Embassy's Cultural Adviser in France, Deputy Minister of the Presidency of the Republic, Minister of Public Education, among other roles. He was Mexico's representative in the United Nations. He was named the Mexican Ambassador of the European Union and Permanent Observer in the European Council. He was the founder and president of the Revolutionary Democratic Party (PRD) in Mexico. The MORENA party selected him as a parliamentary candidate for the 64th Congress, where he has taken on the role of President of the Board of Directors. He is the author of several books including *La ruptura que viene* (*The Approaching Rupture*), *La vía radical para refundar la República* (*The Radical Road to Re-establishing the Republic*), and *Memoria de la palabra* (*Memory of the Word*). *Sentencias Políticas* (*Political Sentences*) was published recently. He is a weekly contributor to *El Universal* as well as to a dozen other local newspapers.

Born in Mexico City, **Guadalupe Nettel** is a writer and the director of Revista de la Universidad de México. Nettel has a PhD in linguistics from the École des Hautes Études en Sciences Sociales in Paris, and has published both fiction and non-fiction. She is the author of *El huésped*, which won the Anna Seghers Prize; *El cuerpo en que nací*; and *Después del invierno*, for which she won the Premio Herralde in 2014. Her collection of short stories *El matrimonio de los peces rojos* won the Premio Internacional de Narrativa Breve Ribera del Duero. Nettel is a regular contributor to both Spanish- and French-language magazines, including *El País*, the *New York Times en español*, *Letras Libres*, and *L'inconvénient*. In 2008, she was voted one of the thirty-nine most important Latin American writers under the age of thirty-nine at the Bogotá Hay Festival. Her work has been translated into eighteen languages.

Born in Florida, Uruguay, **Juan Carlos Pereda Failache** is a Uruguayan-Mexican philosopher and a professor emeritus at the Instituto de Investigaciones Filosóficas of the National Autonomous University of Mexico. Pereda is the author of more than ten books, and he is the winner of the Ensayo Siglo XXI Prize for his *Los aprendizajes del exilio.*

**Cisteil X. Pérez Hernández** is an entomologist working on biodiversity, scientific collections, and species conservation. Currently, she is doing postdoctoral research at the Institute of Ecosystems and Sustainability Research, in the National Autonomous University of Mexico. She has published eleven papers in scientific journals, co-authored one book, and written eight book chapters. Also, she has participated in twenty-three national and international symposia and congresses. She is also a member of the Mexican National Research System, level I. Occasionally, she does science communication, mainly as a member of *Cúmulo de Tesla*, an arts and science collective.

**Ana Puente Flores** majored in political science at the City College of New York. She was a Skadden Arps Legal Honors Program Fellow and a Beyond Identity scholar-activist. For almost five years she has been involved in the migrant justice movement, with a gender focus. As Institutional Development and Research Director at the Politics of Sexual Violence Initiative (PSVI), she researched femicide in Mexico City and collaborated in research for papers such as Emissaries of Empowerment, and The Female Fighter Series. With the PSVI she helped establish an academic program called Beyond Identity: A Gendered Platform for Scholar-Activists. Ana is the creator of a self-published zine called *Ñanda Mañachi* (*Lend Me the Road*) where she explores being a witness to family detention. In the summer of 2018—during the beginning of the family separation policy—she was a legal intern at the Dilley Pro Bono Project. During her internship, she prepared detained families who are seeking asylum for their credible-fear interviews. She is also the co-creator and facilitator of a writing workshop, developed in conjunction with Valeria Luiselli, for teens in migrant detention. Currently she works at Kids In Need Of Defense, where she serves the youngest population of child detainees in the New York as a paralegal.

Born in Mar del Plata, Argentina, **Leonardo Tarifeño** is a writer, literary critic, and journalist. He is the author of *No vuelvas*, a journalistic chronicle about the deportation of Mexican immigrants from the United States. Tarifeño was the editor of the book section of *Rolling Stone* and *La Nación* in Argentina, a journalist for *Gatopardo* in Colombia, a literary critic for *Letras Libres* in Mexico, and an editor of *El Ángel,* the cultural supplement of the newspaper *Reforma* in Mexico.

Born in Mexico City, **Eduardo Vázquez Martín** is a cultural promoter, poet, editor, and journalist. He is the director of the cultural center Antiguo Colegio de San Ildefonso in Mexico City. With many years serving as a cultural promoter, he has held various positions, including Mexico City's Director for Cultural Development, National Coordinator of Communication at Instituto Nacional de Antropología e Historia (INAH, National Institute of Anthropology and History), director of the Museo de Historia Natural y Cultura Ambiental (MHNCA, Museum of Natural History and Environmental Culture) in Mexico City, among others. He was a founder and the deputy manager of the cultural magazine *Milenio,* and he has contributed to other important publications including *Vuelta* and *Nexos*, as well as to cultural supplements of major newspapers including *La Jornada* and *Reforma*. He is the author of several books, including *Navíos de piedra*, *Comer sirena*, *Entre las sábanas*, *Minuta*, *Naturaleza y hechos,* and *Lluvias y secas*.

Born in Mexico City, **Juan Villoro** is a journalist and the author of novels, short stories, and essays, and he has received the Herralde Prize for his novel *El testigo*. He has been visiting professor at Princeton and Yale, and is currently teaching at Stanford. Some of his works can be found in English: the novel *The Reef*, the short story collection *The Guilty*, and collected articles on soccer, *God Is Round*.

Born in Mexico, **Jorge Volpi** is a novelist and essayist. As a writer he has engaged the genres of novella and essay. He is the author of several novels, including *In Search of Klingsor*, winner of the Biblioteca Breve Prize and the Deux Océans-Grinzane Cavour Prize; and the essays *Mentiras contagiosas*, which won the 2008 Mazatlán Award, and *El insomnio de Bolívar*, awarded the 2009 Debate-Casa de América Prize. He has received grants from the John S. Guggenheim Foundation and is presently a member of National System of Creators in Mexico. He has been a professor at Emory University, Cornell University, Universidad de las Americas Puebla, University of Pau and Pays de l'Adour, the Catholic University of Chile, and Princeton University. He was made a Knight of the Order of Arts and Letters of France, and Knight of the Order of Isabella the Catholic of Spain. He is a contributing writer for *Reforma* and *El País*. His books have been translated into twenty-five languages. He was the director of the International Cervantino Festival in Guanajuato, Mexico.

Born in Mexico, **Yael Weiss** is a writer, editor, and translator. She studied literature at the Sorbonne and has received a Certificate in Advanced Studies of French Literature from the Paris Nanterre University. She created Archivo Abierto, an app for the Fondo de Cultura Económica, the oldest and most important publishing house in Mexico, which brings together the FCE's archives, including the first editions, correspondence, audio recordings, and photographs of great writers. She's the author of *Cahier de violence* and the editor of *Constelación de poetas francófonas de cinco continentes.* Weiss has been a part of the Program Jóvenes Creadores del Fondo Nacional para la Cultura y las Artes, FONCA (2009–2010), and she is currently an editor at *Revista de la Universidad de México.*

Born in Mexico, **Naief Yehya** is an industrial engineer, journalist, writer, film, and cultural critic based in Brooklyn. He is the author of the novels *Obras sanitarias, Camino a casa, La verdad de la vida en Marte*, and *Las cenizas y las cosas;* the short stories collections *Historias de mujeres malas* and *Rebanadas;* and the essays *El cuerpo transformado, Guerra y propaganda, Pornografía: obsesión sexual y tecnológica, Pornocultura: el espectro de la violencia sexualizada en los medios*, and his recently published *Drone Visions: A Brief Cyberpunk History of Killing Machines.* He has contributed to the Mexican newspaper *La Jornada* and the cultural magazine *Letras libres*, among others. Yehya's work deals mainly with the impact of technology, mass media, propaganda, and pornography in culture and society.

# Translator Biographies

**Lisa Dillman** lives in Decatur, Georgia, and teaches in the Department of Spanish and Portuguese at Emory University in Atlanta. She has translated some twenty-five novels, including *Such Small Hands, August, October,* and *A Luminous Republic* by Andrés Barba; *Signs Preceding the End of the World* (winner of the 2016 Best Translated Book Award), *Kingdom Cons,* and *The Transmigration of Bodies* (shortlisted for the 2018 Dublin Literary Award) by Yuri Herrera, *The Heart Tastes Bitter, A Million Drops,* and *Above the Rain* by Víctor del Árbol. She is currently working on a novel by Alejandra Costamagna.

**Sophie Hughes** has translated novels by Latin American and Spanish authors such as Laia Jufresa, Rodrigo Hasbún, Enrique Vila-Matas, and José Revueltas. Her translation of Alia Trabucco Zerán's *The Remainder* was shortlisted for the 2019 Man Booker International Prize, and in 2020 she was twice longlisted for the same prize, with Fernanda Melchor's *Hurricane Season* and her co-translation, with Margaret Jull Costa, of Enrique Vila-Matas's *Mac and His Problem.* Sophie is the co-editor of the anthology *Europa28: Writing by Women on the Future of Europe* in association with Wom@rts and Hay Festival.

**Ellen Jones** is a researcher, editor, and literary translator based in Mexico City. She has a PhD from Queen Mary University of London and is Reviews Editor at *Hispanic Research Journal.* She writes regularly about multilingualism and contemporary Latin American literature, including for publications like *The*

*Guardian*, the *Times Literary Supplement*, and the *Irish Times*. Her translation from Spanish of Rodrigo Fuentes's short story collection *Trout, Belly Up* (Charco Press) was shortlisted for the Translators Association First Translation Prize. Her translation of Bruno Lloret's novel *Nancy* is published by Giramondo Publishing and forthcoming from Two Lines Press.

**Victor Meadowcroft** is a translator from Portuguese and Spanish, and a graduate of the MA in Literary Translation program at the University of East Anglia. With Margaret Jull Costa, he has produced co-translations of stories by Agustina Bessa-Luís, a pillar of twentieth-century Portuguese literature, which appeared in the anthology *Take Six: Six Portuguese Women Writers*. His translations of works by María Fernanda Ampuero, Itamar Vieira Junior, and Murilo Rubião have appeared in the literary journals *Latin American Literature Today* and *Mānoa: A Pacific Journal of International Writing*. He is currently working on co-translations of two novels by Evelio Rosero with Anne McLean.

**Jessie Mendez Sayer** is a literary translator and former literary scout based in Mexico City. She studied history and Spanish at the University of Edinburgh. She has translated work by authors such as Guillermo Arriaga, Alonso Cueto, and Alberto Barrera-Tyszka.

**Samantha Schnee**'s translation of Carmen Boullosa's *The Book of Anna* was published by Coffee House Press in April. Her translation of Boullosa's *Texas: The Great Theft* was published by Deep Vellum in 2014 and was shortlisted for the PEN America Translation Prize. She is the founding editor of Words Without Borders and currently serves as secretary of the American Literary Translators Association. She chaired PEN America's

Heim Translation Grants jury from 2107 to 2020 and served on the jury of the EBRD Literature Prize in 2019. She is a trustee of English PEN, where she chaired the Writers in Translation committee, sitting on the selection panel for the PEN Translation grants from 2012 to 2017. She lives in Houston, Texas.

# Notes

## After the White Noise by Yuri Herrera

1. I refer here to Hayden White's *The Historical Text as Literary Artefact*, in which he maintains that historical and literary representations share literary tropes, regardless of their aims and modes of circulation. It's not a theory exempt from criticism, but the main idea is quite useful as a way of illustrating how certain nationalist narratives are created.

The 2016 Cervantes Institute Report, *El español: una lengua viva* (*Spanish: A Living Language*), to cite one of many possible examples, states that when considering only native speakers, the United States ranks fifth in number of Spanish speakers with 42.5 million, after Mexico, Colombia, Spain, and Argentina. But when the calculation takes limited-proficiency speakers into account, that figure rises to 57 million and puts the United States in second place, trailing only Mexico.

2. By the year 2060, according to national census calculations, the number of Spanish speakers will reach 119 million, meaning that one in three U.S. residents will speak Spanish.

## Please Don't Feed the Gringos by Claudio Lomnitz

1. Jane H. Hill, "Intertextuality as Source and Evidence for Indirect Indexical Meanings," *Journal of Linguistic Anthropology* 15, no. 1 (June 2005): 113–24.

## Language Solidarity: How to Create a Force Field with Words by Jhonni Carr and Román Luján

1. T. Snyder, *On Tyranny: Twenty Lessons from the Twentieth Century* (New York: Tim Duggan Books, 2017).

2. A. Hassan, "Hate-Crime Violence Hits 16-year High, F.B.I. Reports," *New York Times*, November 12, 2019, retrieved from https://www.nytimes.com/2019/11/12/us/hate-crimes-fbi-report.html.

3. "Here's Donald Trump's Presidential Announcement Speech," *Time*, June 16, 2015, retrieved from http://time.com/3923128/donald-trump-announcement-speech.

4. "Here's Donald Trump's Presidential Announcement Speech."

5. D. Fernández Vítores, *El español: una lengua viva. Informe 2019* (Instituto Cervantes, 2019), retrieved from https://www.cervantes.es/imagenes/File/espanol_lengua_viva_2019.pdf.

6. B. Spolsky, "Language Policy," in J. Cohen, K.T. McAlister, K. Rolstad, and J. MacSwan (eds.), *Proceedings of the 4th International Symposium on Bilingualism* (Somerville, MA: Cascadilla Press, 2005), 2152–64.

7. Inner ICE or Border Patrol agent.

8. Antena, *How to Build Language Justice* (Houston, TX: Antena Books/Libros Antena, 2014), retrieved from http://antenaantena.org/wp-content/uploads/2012/06/langjust.pdf.

9. J.H. Hill, "Covert Racist Discourse: Metaphors, Mocking, and the Racialization of Historically Spanish-Speaking Populations in the United States," in *The Everyday Language of White Racism* (New York: Wiley-Blackwell, 2008), 119–57.

10. O. García and L. Wei, *Translanguaging: Language, Bilingualism and Education* (London: Palgrave Macmillan, 2014), retrieved from https://doi.org/10.1057/9781137385765.

## Rape and the Idea of Mexico by Alejandro Madrazo Lajous

1. This chapter is the second piece in a broader project I am currently pursuing. My aim is to write a book on the genealogy and architecture of Mexico's constitutional imagination. Part of this chapter points to that broader project, and I try to be explicit when that is the case so as not to confuse the reader. But the chapter is also, I believe, a contribution in itself, so I want to offer it as a stand-alone piece here, specifically contributing to a dialogue about the current situation of our continental neighborhood and its walls, especially the imagined ones.

I owe the opportunity to carry out the research to the generosity of the Orville H. Schell, Jr. Center for International Human Rights, where I spent a year as a senior fellow at Yale Law from 2017 to 2018. My deepest gratitude goes to everyone who made that possible. I would also like to thank Owen Fiss, Paul Kahn, and Claudio Lomnitz for their encouragement to continue to write on this matter. Furthermore, I want to thank three distinct groups of people who read and commented on this piece. First, to the participants of the SELA Seminar in Buenos Aires, during the summer of 2019, where I first presented a version of this paper and received both encouragement and valuable critique from participants. Second, to my feminist friends and admired colleagues who read some version of this piece and offered encouragement and critique, but, more importantly, bibliography and reflection: Sarah Aguilar, Paula Arroio, Rebeca Calzada, Dahlia de la Cerda, Laura García, Catalina Pérez Correa, Gisella Pérez de Acha, and Estefanía Vela. Finally, my colleagues and students at the CIDE Región Centro Faculty Seminar, who offered both affectionate and ruthless critique and even more bibliography, especially my two commentators (one formal, one informal), Javier Treviño and Andrew Paxman. To all of you, I say thank you, and I ask for patience, as much of your advice is not yet reflected here, but it will undoubtedly weigh more as I continue to explore the genealogy of Mexico's constitutional imagination through the lens of the U.S. invasion of 1846–1848. Finally, I want to thank my research assistants, Gerardo Contreras and Estefanía Álvarez, for their patience and hard work, and the editors of this volume for opening the doors of a contemporary and much-needed dialogue to my speculations about our shared history.

2. Sinisa Malesevic, *Nation-States and Nationalisms: Organization, Ideology and Solidarity* (Cambridge: Polity Press, 2013), 282.

3. On the importance of territory in Mexican political imagination, see my article, "A Sovereign People: How Revolution Undermines the Rule of Law in Mexico," *Boston University International Law Journal* 37, no. 1 (Spring 2019).

4. Claudio Lomnitz holds that the virgin of Guadalupe, the Constitution of 1857, and, finally, Death have sequentially been the three national totems for Mexico. See Claudio Lomnitz, *Death and the Idea of Mexico* (Brooklyn, NY: Zone Books, 2005), 41.

5. Lomnitz, *Death*, 21.

6. A moderately realistic look at Mexico's past would show, however, that our past is anything but lineal or unified: the land that Mexico now inhabits is fractured by mountains and ravines, and by parochial languages, deities, customs, clothing, etc. that have been developed by the peoples that have populated the various areas over time. See, for instance, Enrique Florescano, *Etnia, Estado y Nación* (Miami, FL: Aguilar, 1997).

7. Octavio Paz, *El Laberinto de la Soledad* (New York: Penguin Books, 1997); see chapter IV, "Los Hijos de la Malinche."

8. Paz, *El Laberinto*, 103.

9. Lomnitz, *Death*, 20.

10. Sinisa Malesevic, "The Chimera of National Identity," *Nations and Nationalism* 17, no. 2 (2011): 282.

11. Malesevic, "Chimera," 272.

12. Rape, of course, plays different functions in war. See Janet Halley, "Rape in Berlin: Reconsidering the Criminalisation of Rape in the International Law of Armed Conflict," *Melbourne Journal of International Law* 9, no. 1 (2008), 78–124.

13. Joan W. Scott, "Gender: A Useful Category of Historical Analysis," *American Historical Review* 91, no. 5 (December 1986): 1067 and 1069.

14. The name the Spaniards used to refer to Malintzin or, later, Malinche.

15. Malintzin was given to Cortés and his men as a slave, a gift to symbolize an alliance with a coastal polity early on in the exploration of the American mainland by Spanish forces, so one can hardly say that she "gave herself" voluntarily without biting one's tongue. It is also imprecise to portray her as being abandoned as soon as she was no longer useful, first because she seems never to have ceased to be useful and second because Cortés sustained a considerably enduring and committed relationship with her, especially considering the itinerant life he led, particularly *after* the conquest of Tenochtitlán. For a more realistic and informed version of Malintzin's life, see Camilla

Townsend, *Malintzin's Choices. An Indian Woman in the Conquest of Mexico* (Albuquerque: University of New Mexico Press, 2006).

16. See Madrazo, "A Sovereign People."

17. Peter Guardino, *The Dead March: A History of the Mexican-American War* (Cambridge, MA: Harvard University Press, 2017), 4.

18. "Ese es el modelo—más mítico que real—que rige las representaciones que el pueblo mexicano se ha hecho de los poderosos: caciques, señores feudales, hacendados, políticos, generales, capitanes de la industria. Todos ellos son 'machos,' 'chingones,'" Paz, *El Laberinto*, 106.

19. I will not develop this idea here, for it warrants much attention in itself. However, I feel it is an important disclaimer I needed to make in order to explain my interest in the matter.

20. Paz, *El Laberinto*, 93–94. This identification was so strong in relation to the United States during (and, I would say, after) the invasion that Mexicans believed that the underdogs within the United States—Indians and slaves—might rebel against the U.S. government during the war. See Guardino, *Dead March*, 219.

21. Janet Halley, "Rape in Berlin," 105.

22. Over the past thirty years, with deepening economic integration and thriving Mexican migrant communities in the United States, the threatening character of the United States had seemingly subsided in the minds of many Mexicans. The rapidity and effectiveness with which Trump has resuscitated the impression of—and resistance to—a bullying Uncle Sam south of the border speaks to the endurance of the American as a threatening bully in the Mexican collective imagination.

23. We need to consistently remember that the Conquest, although led politically and diplomatically by Spaniards, was also led by—and mostly staffed by—Tlaxcalans, Cempoalans, Huexotzincas, Texcocans, and many other Mesoamerican polities in a broad coalition that defeated the Aztecs and their lingering allies.

24. For a sociological analysis of who these men were, what they did, what shaped their experiences and political ideals, and the importance of their legacy to the establishment of Mexico, see Richard N. Sinkin, *The Mexican Reform, 1855–1876* (Austin: University of Texas, 1979).

25. Sinkin, *Mexican Reform*, 23.

26. Quoted in Sinkin, *Mexican Reform*, 152. Emphasis mine.

27. Catharine MacKinnon, *Are Women Human? And Other International Dialogues* (Cambridge, MA: Belknap Press, 2006), 170.

28. Mexico gained independence from Spain after a decade-long conflict in 1821. The American Invasion of Mexico began in 1846, scarcely twenty-five years later.

29. Guardino, *The Dead March*, 344.

30. See Tena Ramírez, *Leyes Fundamentales de México 1808–2005*. (México: Editorial Porrúa, 1964).

31. Brian Connaughton, *Entre la voz de Dios y el llamado de la patria: religión, identidad y ciudadanía en México, siglo XIX* (Mexico: Fondode Cultura Económica, 2011), at 32. This providentialism had roots in the milleniarist ideas of early evangelization under the Franciscan order immediately after the Conquest (see Lomnitz, *Death*, chapter 1). See also Guardino, "In the Name," at 353.

32. Guardino, "In the Name," 361.

33. Guardino, *The Dead March*, 358.

34. Guardino, *The Dead March*, 212–13.

35. Guardino, "In the Name," 363. The Church actively engaged in financing and rallying resources—human and other—for the war effort. However, it also encouraged and financed a revolt against government at a crucial point in the war and insisted on the notion that government should be instrumental to spiritual salvation. On page 359 Guardino sums it up: "One of the many ironies that surround the war is that the Mexican Catholic Church became known afterward, not for its contribution to the defense of Mexico, but instead for encouraging armed resistance against the government to protect Church property," at 359.

36. It is important to further explain this emphasis: it is easy—and correct in many ways—to focus on the later French Invasion (1862–1867) as the real undoing of the Church's political hegemony, as it emerged in a deeply discredited form after having backed the losing side of *that* war. But I cannot get around the fact that religious intolerance—arguably the one constitutional consensus during the first half of the nineteenth century—saw its nadir *before* the French Invasion, in what was the first constitutional project to be approved *after* the U.S. Invasion, the liberal Constitution of 1857. The absence of religious intolerance—which *is* different from the consecration of religious tolerance, I must admit—in a Mexican Constitution I believe must be seen as a key turning point in the construction of our political imagination. It is, after all, the formal abandonment of religion as the epicenter of identity. That took place *after* the U.S. Invasion and *before* the French Invasion, as soon as the liberal leadership took power and before it deployed its agenda of institutional reform in the *Leyes de Reforma*. We could say that it is all part of a long-running process: the experience of the U.S. Invasion provoked a shift away from Catholicism as the epicenter of national identity (which had already been proposed unsuccessfully under the presidency of Vicente Guerrero at the end of the 1820s and the administration headed by Vice President Gómez Farías during the early 1830s), the Reform movement signaled a renunciation of that epicenter, and the French Invasion confirmed that turn. But I believe, for the reasons I expose in this chapter, that the turning point came during the U.S. Invasion.

I want to thank my colleagues Andrew Paxman and Mike Bess for making it clear that I needed to underline this point. I understand that I may be giving undue weight to a clause in a constitutional text, but I cannot help being a constitutional lawyer trying to understand constitutional imagination.

37. Sinkin, *Mexican Reform*, 24.

38. Sinkin, *Mexican Reform*, 26.

39. Paul Kahn, *Sacred Violence* (Ann Arbor: University of Michigan Press, 2008), 150.

40. Guardino, "In the Name," 344.

41. Guardino, "In the Name," 347.

42. Guardino, *The Dead March*, 118.

43. Guardino, *The Dead March*, 177.

44. Guardino, *The Dead March*, 111.

45. Guardino, *The Dead March*, 26.

46. This conception of Mexican as a (mixed) race, which was wholly alien to Mexicans at the time, would become pivotal. Claudio Lomnitz pinpoints the emergence of a "racialization of Mexicans" precisely at the time of the U.S. Invasion of Mexico and the subsequent integration of Mexicans remaining in annexed territory into a racialized U.S. society as a "race" uniform within itself yet distinct from other races—neither black nor white—distinctions that were central to the United States. Claudio Lomnitz, "Los orígenes de nuestra supuesta homogeneidad. Breve arqueología de la unidad nacional en México," *Prismas, revista de historia intelectual*, 14, pp. 17–36, 26.

47. Guardino, *The Dead March*, 25; Guardino, "In the Name," 348.

48. Guardino, *The Dead March*, 218–19.

49. Guardino, *The Dead March*, 297.

50. Guardino, *The Dead March*, 297.

51. Guardino, "In the Name," 354.

52. Guardino, *The Dead March*, 215.

53. Guardino, *The Dead March*, 142–43, 281, and 232–33, respectively.

54. Hampton Sides, *Blood and Thunder* (New York: Doubleday, 2006), 168.

55. Sides, *Blood and Thunder*, 167.

56. MacKinnon, *Are Women Human?*, 171.

57. MacKinnon, *Are Women Human?*, 158–59.

58. MacKinnon, *Are Women Human?*, 222–23.

59. It is important to note that General Winfield Scott, who led the army that invaded central Mexico, was particularly emphatic in reining in abuses that would enrage the civilian population. Accordingly, his troops were far more respectful than those under General Zachary Taylor's command in the north of Mexico. See Guardino, "In the Name," 357. Yet it was Taylor's army that started the war and that had the dubious privilege of giving first impressions to the Mexican population, so the abuses carried out in the north,

although they may have been less frequent as the war shifted to central Mexico, probably loomed larger in the imagination of Mexican civilians.

60. Guardino, *The Dead March*, 109.

61. Guardino, *The Dead March*, 110.

62. MacKinnon, *Are Women Human?*, 211.

63. Paul Kahn, *Sacred Violence*, 164.

64. MacKinnon, *Are Women Human?*, 227.

65. Guardino, *The Dead March*, 163.

66. Guardino, *The Dead March*, 280.

67. Guardino, *The Dead March*, 300.

68. See Sinkin, *Mexican Reform*, 24.

69. For a magnificent attempt at reconstructing the Mexico City uprising against U.S. troops, see Luis Fernando Granados Salinas, *Sueñan las piedras. Alzamiento ocurrido en la ciudad de México*, 14, 15 y 16 de septiembre de 1847 (México: Ediciones Era, 2005).

70. See Guardino, *The Dead March*, 323–24: "Various Democrats advocated the complete absorption of Mexico into the United States or the establishment of a protectorate. Why should American expansionism not take full advantage of a defeated and racially inferior foe? Others were a bit less ambitious, lobbying for the acquisition of some territories that are now in northern Mexico. . . . Some believed that the superior American race would eventually bring Mexicans up to its level, while others assumed that Mexico would always be governed by an American elite, essentially as a colonial possession."

71. Kahn, *Sacred Violence*, 165.

72. Kahn, *Sacred Violence*, 105–6.

73. Kahn, *Sacred Violence*, 161.

74. The process of memorialization was highly politicized, with the (professional) army and the National Guard (composed of armed citizenry) cajoling for the position of martyrs undergoing self-sacrifice to save honor in the midst of defeat. The process is fascinating and crucial in understanding how the war was incorporated into collective memory for succeeding generations, but demands more space than what we have here. For an overview of that process, in comparative perspective to memorialization of the war in the United States, see Michael Scott Van Wagenen, *Remembering the Forgotten War: The Enduring Legacies of the U.S./Mexican War* (Amherst: University of Massachusetts Press, 2012).

75. Guardino, *The Dead March*, 179.

76. This does not mean that the Catholic Church vanished from the political scene at all. Well into the twentieth century, it was still a force to be reckoned with, and it was not until after the French Invasion that the liberal regime began really reining it in. But I hold that it was during the U.S. Invasion that, for the first time, its authority was substantively undermined in the collective imagination of the nascent polity. The blueprint for the Church-as-betrayer,

which would become decisive for liberal narratives during the French Intervention, lies here.

77. Guardino, *The Dead March*, 174.

78. MacKinnon, *Are Women Human?*, 232.

79. MacKinnon, *Are Women Human?*, 229–30.

80. MacKinnon, *Are Women Human?*, 215.

81. Sinkin, *Mexican Reform*, 148.

82. Guardino, *The Dead March*, 301.

83. This is not just rhetorical or metaphorical. Up until 2005, Mexican courts did not recognize that, legally, women could be raped by their husbands. Sexual intercourse forced upon a woman by her spouse was deemed an "undue exercise of a right"—which is a lesser crime—not rape. The reasoning behind the holding was that husband and wife had mutual rights to sexual intercourse with one another; therefore, if the sexual act was forced upon one of them by the other, the legal reproach could only extend to the violent *manner* in which sexual access was obtained, not to the sexual access itself: sexual access was a right. See Suprema Corte de Justicia de la Nación, *tesis de jurisprudencia* 1a./J. 10/94 stemming from the *contradicción de tesis* 5/92. The criterion was overturned in 2005 under request to modify the precedent Varios 9/2005-PS.

84. Guardino, *The Dead March*, 214.

85. On denial, see Stanley Cohen, *States of Denial: Knowing About Atrocities and Suffering* (Cambridge, UK: Polity Press, 2001). I want to thank Javier Treviño for pointing me in this direction, which I have yet to unpack fully.

86. Halley, "Rape in Berlin," 103–4.

87. Halley, "Rape in Berlin," 103–4.

88. Halley, "Rape in Berlin," 99–100.

89. Halley, "Rape in Berlin," 108.

90. Halley, "Rape in Berlin," 106. See also 105.

91. David J. Weber, *The Mexican Frontier, 1821–1846* (Albuquerque: UNM Press, 1982), 41. Separatist attempts included the creation of a República del Río Grande (encompassing Nuevo León, Coahuila—which still claimed Texas—and Tamaulipas) from 1839 to 1840 (see Weber, *Mexican Frontier*, 266); and California and New Mexico had threatened to separate as a República Mexicana del Norte as late as 1845 (see Weber, 271).

Separatism was not an exclusive privilege for the north: the Yucatán Peninsula alternatively sought both independence and annexation to the United States, Central America had successfully seceded soon after independence, and Chiapas had seceded during the early imperial experience under Iturbide and then come back into the fold of the nascent republic after his demise.

92. See Weber, *Mexican Frontier*, 122, 125, 157, and 159.

93. Sides, *Blood and Thunder*, chapter 19.

94. Weber, *The Mexican Frontier.*

95. See Weber, *The Mexican Frontier.*

96. Of course, the United States is just as addicted to denial. Trump's proposal to build a wall epitomizes the discourse that allowed him to mobilize a nativist, racist electoral base and win the presidential election, yet his "Make America Great Again" baseball caps are made in Mexico. The United States increasingly criminalizes illegal immigrants, yet its economy depends on the existence of massive immigration, a workforce rendered cheap by denying full salaries and legal rights because it can be labeled "illegal."

## Aeschylus and the Migrants by Jean Meyer

1. Aeschylus, *Suppliant Women*, trans. by Ian Johnston (Nanaimo, BC: Vancouver Island University, 2013, reformatted 2019), lines 428–29; 470–72. Available online at http://johnstoniatexts.x10host.com/aeschylus/suppliantwomenhtml.html (accessed December 6, 2019).

2. Aeschylus, *Suppliant Women*, lines 708–9.

3. Aeschylus, *Suppliant Women*, line 147.

4. Aeschylus, *Suppliant Women*, line 1217.

## Make Art, Not Walls by National Commission for Human Rights, Mexico

1. "Murales, No Muros" ("Make Art, Not Walls") was a project led by the National Commission for Human Rights in Mexico in 2018. It aimed to redefine the meaning of the wall, so often seen as an obstacle to migration, and instead propose it as a space for migrants to express themselves artistically. The murals presented here are the result of work by Mexico's National Commission for Human Rights in collaboration with art collectives, migrants, and various social groups across Mexico who work on issues related to migration.

2. Forced internal displacement is when a person or group of people is obliged to flee their place of residence for another location within the same country due to a range of circumstances that might include generalized violence, an armed conflict, human-rights violations, or natural or man-made disasters.

## A Wall That Threatens Biodiversity by Cisteil X. Pérez Hernández

1. Robert Peters, William J. Ripple, Christopher Wolf, Matthew Moskwik, Gerardo Carreón-Arroyo, Gerardo Ceballos, Ana Córdova, Rodolfo Dirzo, Paul R. Ehrlich, Aaron D. Flesch, Rurik List, Thomas E. Lovejoy, Reed F.

Noss, Jesús Pacheco, José K. Sarukhán, Michael E. Soulé, Edward O. Wilson, Jennifer R.B. Miller et al., "Nature Divided, Scientists United: U.S.–Mexico Border Wall Threatens Biodiversity and Binational Conservation," *BioScience* 68, no. 10 (October 2018): 740–43, https://doi.org/10.1093/biosci/biy063.

2. News on the Big Bend Natural Area of Binational Interest: http://www.wwf.org.mx/noticias/noticias_desierto_chihuahuense.cfm?uNewsID=207964.

3. NatureServe, NatureServe Explorer: An online encyclopedia of life [web application]. Version 7.1. NatureServe, Arlington, Virginia, 2019. Available at http://explorer.natureserve.org/servlet/NatureServe?searchName=EchinocereU.S.+chisoensis.

4. R. Hatfield, S. Jepsen, R. Thorp, L. Richardson, and S. Colla, *BombU.S. crotchii*, The IUCN Red List of Threatened Species 2015: e.T44937582A46440211. Available at http://dx.doi.org/10.2305/IUCN.UK.2015-2.RLTS.T44937582A46440211.en.

5. R. Hatfield, S. Colla, S. Jepsen, L. Richardson, R. Thorp, and S.F. Jordan, 2014. IUCN Assessments for North American *Bombus*. spp. Available at https://www.xerces.org/wp-content/uploads/2014/12/North-American-BombU.S.-Red-List-assessments-10-2014.pdf.

6. Semarnat/Conanp, 2009. Recovery Play for the Sonoran Pronghorn (*Antilocapra americana*), México, Secretaría de Medio Ambiente y Recursos Naturales/Comisión Nacional de Áreas Naturales Protegidas. Available at https://www.biodiversidad.gob.mx/especies/especies_priori/fichas/pdf/pace_berrendo.pdf.

7. U.S. Fish and Wildlife Service, 2015. Draft recovery plan for the Sonoran pronghorn (*Antilocapra americana sonoriensis*). 2nd revision. U.S. Fish and Wildlife Service, Southwest Region, Albuquerque, New Mexico. Available at https://www.fws.gov/southwest/es/Documents/SpeciesDocs/SonoranPronghorn/SonoranPronghorn_DraftRecoveryPlan_Final_December2014.pdf.

8. MODIFICACIÓN del Anexo Normativo III, Lista de especies en riesgo de la Norma Oficial Mexicana NOM-059-SEMARNAT-2010, Protección ambiental-Especies nativas de México de flora y fauna silvestres-Categorías de riesgo y especificaciones para su inclusión, exclusión o cambio-Lista de especies en riesgo, publicada el 30 de diciembre de 2010. Disponible en http://dof.gob.mx/nota_detalle.php?codigo=5578808&fecha=14/11/2019.

9. G. Ceballos, *Mammals of Mexico* (Baltimore, MD: Johns Hopkins University Press, 2014), 957.

10. L. López-Hoffman, R.G. Varady, K.W. Flessa, P. Balvanera, "Ecosystem Services Across Borders: A Framework for Transboundary Conservation Policy," *Frontiers in Ecology and the Environment* 8 (2014): 84–91.

## Walls of Air by Yael Weiss

1. It has been over a year since this article was written. Among other developments within the delicate landscape of migration, measures—demanded by the president of the United States—were implemented with the intention of destroying the caravans' collective order from the moment they reach the border between Mexico and Guatemala, which now looms as the new extended border of the United States with the northern triangle of Central America. On January 24, 2020, Mexican armed forces pursued the members of the first caravan of the year, which had crossed the Suchiate River, and arrested 800 people. It was an aggressive move, designed to discourage future caravans and force migrants to search for more dangerous and clandestine options.

# Publishing in the Public Interest

Thank you for reading this book published by The New Press. The New Press is a nonprofit, public interest publisher. New Press books and authors play a crucial role in sparking conversations about the key political and social issues of our day.

We hope you enjoyed this book and that you will stay in touch with The New Press. Here are a few ways to stay up to date with our books, events, and the issues we cover:

- Sign up at www.thenewpress.com/subscribe to receive updates on New Press authors and issues and to be notified about local events
- Like us on Facebook: www.facebook.com/newpressbooks
- Follow us on Twitter: www.twitter.com/thenewpress
- Follow us on Instagram: www.instagram.com/thenewpress

Please consider buying New Press books for yourself; for friends and family; or to donate to schools, libraries, community centers, prison libraries, and other organizations involved with the issues our authors write about.

The New Press is a 501(c)(3) nonprofit organization. You can also support our work with a tax-deductible gift by visiting www.thenewpress.com/donate.